The Interrupted Moment

The Interrupted Moment

A VIEW OF
VIRGINIA WOOLF'S NOVELS

Lucio P. Ruotolo

Stanford University Press
Stanford, California

Stanford University Press
Stanford, California
© 1986 by the Board of Trustees of the
Leland Stanford Junior University
Printed in the United States of America
Original printing 1986
Last figure below indicates year of this printing:
97   96   95   94   93   92   91   90   89   88

CIP data appear at the end of the book

For Jonathan Kistler

Acknowledgments

It is with great pleasure that I dedicate this book to Jonathan Kistler, the teacher who introduced me to the work of Virginia Woolf. I am one of many Colgate University undergraduates who benefited from his capacity to bring a literary text to life. I mention also Colgate's Earl Daniels, whose letter to the *Saturday Review of Literature* in 1931 anticipated and described the brilliance of *The Waves* in the face of more than a few unappreciative American reviews.

I am indebted above all to my friend and colleague J. J. Wilson, who has contributed so much to the perpetuation of Woolf studies in this country. Her conviction and energy led to the creation of both the Virginia Woolf Society and the *Virginia Woolf Miscellany*. She has been a continual source of inspiration and support.

I would like to convey special thanks to Wilfred Stone, Susan Squier, and Nina Auerbach, who read the first version of my book in its entirety. Their valuable suggestions con-

Acknowledgments

tributed so much to its completion. I am no less grateful to George Dekker, Herbert Lindenberger, and Jay Fliegelman for their valuable comments on portions of the manuscript, and to Linda Jo Bartholomew for her perceptive editing.

I have been particularly fortunate at Stanford to have come to know many talented graduate students working on Virginia Woolf. In addition to Susan Squier, I would like to convey special thanks to four in particular who, over the course of the last decade and a half, have helped create a stimulating environment for the study of Virginia Woolf: first Ellen Hawkes, more recently Patricia Klindienst Joplin, Carol Lashof, and Victor Luftig. My book owes a great deal to their influence. Let me also thank Gary Spear for his fine Shakespearean eye in identifying one of Woolf's literary allusions. The list of Stanford undergraduates whose insightful readings have contributed to my understanding of her novels is too long to mention. Let me thank all of them.

I began work on this book while living at Monk's House, where I had the good fortune to meet and benefit from the generosity of many East Sussex neighbors, most notably Quentin and Anne Olivier Bell, Angelica Garnett, and Trekkie Parsons. I thank Nigel Nicolson for his continued help on Woolf matters. Among other English friends to whom I am grateful are Richard Morphet and the late Pamela Diamand for their insights on Bloomsbury. Let me also acknowledge my gratitude to Dr. Lola L. Szladits, Curator of the New York Public Library's Berg Collection, and Bet Inglis of the University of Sussex Library for their patience and help over the years.

I thank the Department of English and Stanford University for helping meet the expense of preparing my manuscript for publication. The chapter "The Unguarded Moment: *Mrs. Dalloway*" appeared originally, in somewhat different form, in Ralph Freedman's collection of essays, *Virginia Woolf: Revaluation and Continuity* (Berkeley, Calif., 1980).

Acknowledgments

Finally, it is with love and unmatched gratitude that I turn to thank my wife, Marcia, for enduring the interruptions the evolution of my book has exerted on her daily life. Her contributions, as she knows, range far beyond psychological support.

L.P.R.

Stanford, California
February 1986

Contents

*Just as his body has become an "interrupted" thing
in his own eyes, so is the world,
nature, society perceived by him as "interrupted."*

MIKHAIL BAKHTIN

*A frequent observation of me in my most unguarded moments
taught him in no long time
to place an unreserved confidence in my innocence.*

WILLIAM GODWIN

The Interrupted Moment

Chapter One

INTRODUCTION

For interruptions there will always be.
VIRGINIA WOOLF

On a morning toward the end of 1940, Virginia Woolf records finishing the first draft of *Between the Acts* and how at "this moment" her thoughts have shifted to consider her next book: "Anon, it will be called." The explanation for the inspiration, she adds somewhat enigmatically, "should refer to Louie's interruption, holding a glass jar, in whose thin milk was a pat of butter." Characteristically, Woolf works this intrusion into her own preceding speculations: "I am a little triumphant about the book. I think its an interesting attempt in a new method. I think its more quintessential than the others. More milk skimmed off. A richer pat."[1]

Throughout the novelist's life and fiction, interruptions arouse inventive impulses. At times the event is more dramatic than her cook's domestic intrusion. The storm that strikes the *Euphrosyne* in *The Voyage Out*, for example, upsets and reforms narrative relationships. Most frequently these disruptions occur subtly, as when Ralph Denham appears at tea

I

toward the opening of *Night and Day*. The deployment of such disorienting moments in the eight novels under consideration* constitutes, in the view of this study, an important aspect of Woolf's experimental intention.[2]

A choreography for Woolf's fiction inevitably develops from the rhythm of broken sequence. Those characters who join the dance create a new and constantly shifting pattern, sustained and nourished, I would argue, by a succession of interruptions. To be open to life in Woolf's fictional world is to remain open to an aesthetic of disjunction situated at the heart of human interplay. Those who allow the often-random intrusion of others to reshape their lives emerge at times heroically. Those who voice distaste for interruption fall back, invariably it seems, into self-supporting insularity. Septimus Smith, a victim of shell shock in *Mrs. Dalloway*, complains that his wife Rezia "was always interrupting." Struggling to maintain the continuity of his inward world, with one important exception he resists her intervention. The confident Mr. Bankes in *To the Lighthouse* prefers dining alone to enduring the discomfort of "interruptions" at Mrs. Ramsay's dinner table. Mrs. Ramsay, in turn, derives most pleasure from those moments when, free of other people, she can simply "be herself, by herself." Alone, free of attachments, she employs her imagination to transcend "the fret, the hurry, the stir" of a persistently impinging world.

However much Woolf relishes such cloistered moments of solitude, they tempt her most memorable heroines to ignore political as well as aesthetic realities. To withdraw from an abrasive external world presumes for women in particular an excessive reliance on the protection of men, what Woolf, in describing her own inheritance, terms "a legacy of depen-

---

*I take seriously Woolf's designation of *Orlando* as "A Biography" and so do not include it for discussion here. Along with *Flush*, *Roger Fry*, and Woolf's shorter biographical essays, it deserves and will continue to receive fuller treatment under a different experimental rubric.

dence."³ Sheltered by ruling patriarchs throughout history, women understandably have looked toward men to support such moments of leisure. The fluctuations Woolf discerns in modern life make this need for governance and direction increasingly more attractive. Lucy Swithin, who resists her brother's masterly overtures in *Between the Acts* and responds intuitively to the village pageant, is nonetheless moved like Mrs. Ramsay to accept a final order of values, to reduce life's unnerving multiplicity to harmonious singularity. It follows that the favorite time for each is evening, "when nothing interrupted."

In a most relevant essay Woolf compares the experience of modern times with the impact of being ill. What characterizes each, in her view, is an "unending procession of changes" inevitably undermining "the doings of the mind." Urging her reader to relinquish for the moment the time-honored safeguards of Western thought and literature, she advocates, however playfully, "a new hierarchy of the passions." In illness, with reason unmoored, "undiscovered countries" emerge mysteriously from the "wastes and deserts of the soul" to interrupt all semblance of order and stability. Her invitation to explore the ensuing "anarchy and newness" is not made casually.⁴ Aware of the risks—unguarded moments occasion blows from a world at best impervious to human needs—Woolf understandably regards such voyages with some misgiving.

In the autobiographical essay "A Sketch of the Past," Woolf recalls her childish presumption that the "sudden shocks" she received from the external world were "simply a blow from an enemy hidden behind the cotton wool of daily life." Each such recollection involved an interruption of her own expectations. In one disorienting instance the memory of seven brothers and sisters competing for their mother's attention evokes a familiar lament: "Can I remember ever being alone with her for more than a few minutes? Someone was always interrupting."⁵ As an adult Woolf recognizes the value of these early blows: "They are now always welcome; after the first surprise, I always feel instantly that they are particularly valuable. And I go on to suppose that the shock receiving capacity is what makes me a writer."[6]

Under the impact of interruption she will grow increasingly less confident in the authority of others to supply centrality for her life. Thrown back on her own resources, Woolf, in company with the characters of her fiction, comes to entertain a world demanding incessant readjustment, a world, as she describes her own childhood, in which "nothing remained stable long."[7]

Woolf's first published story, "The Mark on the Wall" (1917), reflects the ambivalence with which interruption moves the writer, in this case her narrator, toward an unmediated world of "movement and change." Seated in front of the fireplace, her eyes fixed on burning coals, she finds her imagination rather sluggishly contriving an old fancy: a flag; a castle; a cavalcade of red knights riding up a black rock. Then, unexpectedly, "for the first time," an object emerges into sight. "Rather to my relief the sight of the mark interrupted the fancy, for it is an old fancy, an automatic fancy, made as a child perhaps."[8] Inspired by this fresh intrusion, her thoughts spring into the future. Newly animated, her mind expands to include a world where nothing is predetermined or constricted, where each perception seems grounded in a continually shifting landscape. The result is both a story and the compensating authorial desire for regained equilibrium.

Artistically, the barrage of objects that follows sweeps the viewer along with frightening rapidity—"if one wants to compare life to anything, one must liken it to being blown through the Tube at fifty miles an hour"—evoking the customary need for mediating distance: "I want to think quietly, calmly, spaciously, never to be interrupted, never to have to rise from my chair, to slip easily from one thing to another, without any

4

sense of hostility, or obstacle. I want to sink deeper and deeper, away from the surface, with its hard separate facts. To steady myself, let me catch hold of the first idea that passes... Shakespeare."⁹

The realization of a distinctively external dimension of time and space motivates her in two forms of evasion: psychologically, to retreat like Septimus in madness back into herself; intellectually, to fix on an incontestably honored literary model. Avoiding contradiction with its inevitable friction would appear to induce a peace of mind Woolf prizes. *A Room of One's Own* illustrates how even the smallest sense of grievance distorts a woman's art: "at war with her lot," Charlotte Brontë could not "write calmly."¹⁰

The fact that women, subject "to all kinds of casual interruptions," were forced to live more discontinuous lives, particularly if they aspired to some form of artistic achievement, proves an unexpected advantage. Ironically, *A Room of One's Own* links women's historical deprivation of separate space—"kept in one room, and to one occupation"—with the fictional Mary Carmichael's capacity to tamper with traditional literary sequence. Reading Mary's prose, Woolf half complains in a tone that recalls the narrator of "The Mark," "was like being out at sea in an open boat."

Woolf initially expresses "certain grievances against" Mary for interrupting her own rhetorical expectations. Plunged into this baffling fluidity where the basis for all preference seems obscured, she is transformed in her consciousness of literature and of life: "For whenever I was about to feel the usual things in the usual places, about love, about death, the annoying creature twitched me away, as if the important point were just a little further on. And thus she made it impossible for me to roll out my sonorous phrases about 'elemental feelings,' the 'common stuff of humanity,' 'depths of the human heart,' and all those other phrases which support us in our belief."¹¹ Freed

simultaneously from "the expected order" and from her "grievance," she recognizes and censures the inertia that has made
her "lazy minded and conventional into the bargain."

Tolerance for interruption is all but synonymous in Woolf
with the quality of comprehension itself. The presumption describes her relationship to literary texts as well as to the world
at large. The very talent of good reading means indulging a
world not necessarily one's own. "If you open your mind as
widely as possible, then signs and hints of almost impercep-
tible fineness, from the twist and turn of the first sentences,
will bring you into the presence of a human being unlike any
other." She compares the act of reading to the act of seeing,
and enjoins her reader to turn and break away: "Is there not
an open window on the right hand of the bookcase? How de-
lightful to stop reading and look out! How stimulating the
scene is, in its unconsciousness, its irrelevance, its perpetual
movement." [12]

Where every reader or writer entertains similar inclinations
as a necessary break from concentrated effort, Woolf allows
these disruptive pauses to affect the basis of her thinking.
Stepping outside the given, she looks for inspiration in that
genderless no-man's-land between the acts of human intervention. The defining intention of her narrative strategy is to
loosen the hold we are disposed to establish both on the world
and, as readers, on the text before us. [13] If this seems a choice
for indeterminacy, the alternative signifies a reductive neglect
of an inscrutably larger external world. It is the very hierarchical attitude of mind, what Mikhail Bakhtin terms "the
valorized-hierarchical category of the past," that Woolf too
finds inapplicable to modern life. [14] Her critique of education,
most evident in *Three Guineas*, assaults the representatives of
culture who, privileged to classify phenomena, dispense truth
from the height of an unquestioned authority. One notes in
this regard her invitation to the university lecturer to step

down from his podium to discourse more genuinely from the floor. Woolf's medium, like Bakhtin's, remains dialogical.

In the diary entry immediately preceding her cook's interruption, Woolf characterizes four distinguished contemporaries writing their books as "little boys making sand castles. This refers to H. Read; Tom Eliot; Santayana; Wells. Each is weathertight & gives shelter to the occupant."[15] By contrast, she continues, "I am the sea which demolishes these castles." While Herbert Read's criticism of Roger Fry motivates this attack, it is the pontificating tone of his recently published autobiography that moves her for the second time in several months to employ the phrase "tower dwellers." However much she may admire the authors praised in Read's new book, his propensity to wall certain writers in and "others out" suggests an architecture of closure. Woolf encourages the overseers of the world—novelists and professors as well as political leaders—to step down into the tumult of a "classless and towerless society," and she affirms an alternate "common ground."[16]

The Interrupted Moment sets forth my claim that Woolf's evolving aesthetics encompass both existentialist and anarchist presumptions. In this light, it is ironic to find her diary critique of hierarchy motivated by the autobiography of a writer whose predilection for both anarchism and existentialism was well known. Herbert Read's offending criticism of Fry expresses, moreover, that same distaste for closure Woolf's diary turns back on him. Claiming "Fry's deepest instinct was not adventurous," Read complains specifically of Fry's preference for "the protectiveness of the Ivory Tower."

Woolf's own culturally derived disposition to create "weathertight" castles, art forms that stand above refutation, moves her to collaborate in undercutting her own design. Only when existing structures lose centrality and become, in her idiom, porous and transparent, does nature in some mysterious way inspire experimental ventures. For Woolf the incau-

7

tious freedom to pursue such options grows proportionately with her willingness to confront disorder. In his autobiography the anarchist Read marks the line from Nietzsche—"one must have chaos within one to give birth to a dancing star"—as an early source of his philosophical inspiration.[17] Woolf's diary image of herself as the demolishing sea reflects something of this impulse to begin through an act of radical disengagement from an education that has stressed, in her mind, competitive rather than cooperative values. In each case the goal is not chaos but mutuality, the effort to reconstitute social intercourse on more communal grounds.

Not all structures stand condemned through her sand-castle simile, but only an architecture she conceives to be misapplied to the aesthetics of the novel. Had Woolf read Bakhtin she would no doubt have added his strictures on the outdated poetics of an epic past to the Russian criteria she praised so highly. He echoes her language in a phrase he employs frequently in his essay "Epic and Novel" to describe the "language of tradition." It appears in a particularly relevant passage of *The Dialogic Imagination*: "Precisely because it is walled off from all subsequent times, the epic past is absolute and complete. It is as closed as a circle; inside it everything is finished, already over. There is no place in the epic world for any openendedness, indecision, indeterminacy. There are no loopholes in it through which we glimpse the future."[18]

Windows in Woolf's novels form an important medium through which interruption is manifest. Their function, metaphorically at least, remains suspect if not irrelevant to the tower dweller. Once formulated, his or her overarching vision requires little if any emendation, indeed depends, in a manner of speaking, on the exclusion of an ever-fluctuating external world. Avoiding the haphazard multiplicity of life, tower dwellers, Woolf points out with self-incriminating honesty, fall prey to a familiar desire to retain what D. H. Lawrence aptly termed "the old stable ego":[19] "They have been great egotists. That too was forced upon them by their circumstances. When everything is rocking round one, the only person who remains comparatively stable is oneself. When all faces are changing and obscured, the only face one can see clearly is one's own. So they wrote about themselves."[20]

Woolf's recollection of her mother and nursery, "the most important of all my memories," conveys a sense of undisturbed protectiveness, but the corresponding image of a window emerging in the midst of enclosure supplants this first memory. She remembers "lying half asleep, half awake" in her nursery at St. Ives, and the ecstasy of the subsequent moment as associated in some way with the widening dissolution of self: "It is of hearing the blind draw its little acorn across the floor as the wind blew the blind out. It is of lying and hearing this splash and seeing this light, and feeling, it is almost impossible that I should be here."[21]

She is tempted to express the moment in terms of a large canvas abounding with color, the light showing through, the edges blurred as in a Rothko painting.[22] Instead she pursues and renders a different ambience. At the center of every picture, "very definite; very upright," stands her mother, filling so authoritatively that dimensionless space of childhood. Unlike the world at large, this center requires no alteration. For Woolf, "living so completely in her atmosphere," everything external seems at best irrelevant. "She was the whole thing."[23]

Two conflicting images emerge from Woolf's earliest recollections of childhood, one of the wind and sea beyond the protective walls of her nursery, the other of her mother Julia Stephen, a model for that wholeness and perfection she desires to attain. Through Woolf's autobiographical recounting, the healthy sense of protectiveness associated with her mother expands into a pervasive metaphysical principle of order and centrality. Controlling, as it were, the confusion of the world, her mother comes easily to personify those classical decorums that have allowed Western culture to survive each threat of vagrancy.

In terms of art, such intentions include, as Bakhtin understood, an outdated expectation of artistic fulfillment. From Aristotle and Horace to Boileau, the Russian critic found a poetics "permeated with a deep sense of the wholeness of literature," a wholeness that he considered anathema to all notions of the novel; "it is characteristic of the novel that it never enters into this whole, it does not participate in any harmony of the genres."[24]

One cannot overemphasize the degree to which the appeal of this tradition tempts Woolf to fall back on exemplary artistic strategies of her own patriarchal heritage. "The great writer," she reminds herself in "Robinson Crusoe," who triumphs over the external world, "brings order from chaos; he plants his tree there, and his man here; he makes the figure of his deity remote or present as he wills. In masterpieces—books, that is, where the vision is clear and order has been achieved—he inflicts his own perspective upon us."[25]

Even though a Hardy or a Proust is commended for wrenching old supports from readers, for imposing a different sense of structure—"our vanity is injured because our order is upset"—Woolf is inclined at such times to become artistically less adventuresome. Although her aesthetic of the novel invites comparison with Bakhtin's, it is easy to understand why so many of her best-known passages are often employed to support an opposing aesthetic of wholeness. In the very passage where she affirms the shock-receiving capacity, we find her adopting a defensively omniscient view of her art: "I make it real by putting it into words. It is only by putting it into words that I make it whole; this wholeness means that it has lost its power to hurt me."[26] Art at such moments too easily becomes a method of avoiding nature's admonition to confront unending change.

Woolf's letters and diaries reveal how fully a compulsive

need for authority affected and constricted her closest relationships. Her sister Vanessa, her husband Leonard, and, perhaps more than either, her close friend Vita Sackville-West
assume the role of protective guardians. Aware of her own
fears about life, she describes Vita as lavishing on her "the maternal protection which, for some reason, is what I have always most wished from everyone."[27] Recalling Mrs.
Ramsay's presiding influence on Lily Briscoe, Vita's strong presence,
"like a lampost, straight, glowing,"* interposes an old way of
seeing and doing. The fault, of course, is not Vita's. Virginia
seems aware of the need to move on her own behalf without
the constancy of a defining center, be it Julia or Vita, Vanessa
or Leonard.

To move outside the boundaries of a familiar world occasions for all Woolf's heroines anxieties that tempt them back
into postures of dependence. Clarissa Dalloway, shaken by an
"awful fear" of experience—"one's parents giving it into one's
hands, this life to be lived to the end"—finds reassurance in
the recurring presence of her husband "reading the *Times*" at
breakfast. Fearful that "nothing persists," Rhoda stumbles in
The Waves because she finds no one to lead her. Tied to an old
script, fearful of the very space her play has created, Miss La
Trobe in *Between the Acts* feels enslaved by her audience.

From my perspective, Woolf's novels form the arena of her
own struggle to resist that wholesome proportion the doctors
of her fiction, among others, are quick to prescribe—witness
her strenuous effort to resist seduction by Mrs. Ramsay's "party
round a table." The promise of wholeness, designed to oppose
"fluidity out there," invites what has already been described as
an architecture of closure.

The mediating artist, rising above "the spasmodic, the obscure, the fragmentary, the failure," is inclined from this privi-

---

The Diary of Virginia Woolf (New York, 1980), 3: 204. These words
echo Julia Stephen's last words to Virginia: "Hold yourself straight, my little
Goat." Woolf, *Moments of Being* (New York, 1976), p. 84.

leged ground to become a soldier "in the army of the upright," descending imperially "to civilize, to share, to cultivate the desert, educate the native." However sensible this course of action may at times seem to her, Woolf clearly urges non-compliance: "We become deserters. They march to battle. We float with sticks on the stream; helter-skelter with the dead leaves on the lawn, irresponsible and disinterested and able, perhaps for the first time for years, to look round, to look up— to look for example at the sky."[28]

Avoiding the unexpected, choosing the security of pre-scribed actions, her characters repeatedly decline such invita-tions to disengage. Under the influence of Mrs. Ramsay, Lily Briscoe is tempted to contemplate and reproduce an object of art complete in itself. Bernard, despite his delight in the con-fusion of the moment, at the end of *The Waves* comes to regard people and experience outside his own well-framed narratives as the enemy. If Woolf makes their respective incantations so appealing, indeed invites us to share a world immune from in-terruption and change, it is because she would have us confront and hopefully resist our own largely educated predilections.

Innumerable readers and critics have been moved, and I suspect misled, by the poignancy with which Woolf's language arouses a comforting sense of artistic wholeness. However fulfilling scenes such as the Boeuf en Daube dinner in *To the Lighthouse* may be, they create a disposition for stasis Woolf compels us, as she must herself, unremittingly to question and oppose. "Like Clarissa Dalloway (and Terence Hewet), Mrs. Ramsay can create moments of unity that remain intact in the memory," as one of Woolf's best early critics puts it.[29] Yet to stress this virtue is surely misleading. Ideas that remain "in-tact" are ideas ill-disposed to change. We may recall in this light Leonard Woolf's response to the absolutism of totalitarian ideology in *Quack, Quack!*: "A true belief is little more than a stepping stone to something else; it keeps the mind fluid, vola-tile; it sets it riding off on new adventures."[30]

Introduction

Even though Virginia Woolf longed to find some sustaining pattern above or behind the jumble of human experience, she suspected transcendental truth as she suspected the hierarchical claims of Whitaker's Table of Precedency: "The Archbishop of Canterbury is followed by the Lord High Chancellor; the Lord High Chancellor is followed by the Archbishop of York. Everybody follows somebody, such is the philosophy of Whitaker; and the great thing is to know who follows whom."[31]

Far less fixed and absolute, her characters' deepest convictions appear, much like their author's, consistently open to influence and change. To read her well, we must try similarly to suspend some derived expectations. Even the best of her commentators have not always found this easy to accomplish. Applying the very values of hierarchy she repudiates, more than a few critics view her first heroine as a woman who has failed to take heed of proper models: neither aunt nor fiancé can save Rachel Vinrace from a chaos of her own making. Since her fiancé's poetics follow Proust's, it seems reasonable to presume "that Rachel's attitude is wrong and Terence's right."[32] The "few perfect moments" that redeem The Voyage Out (such critics, it seems, long for perfection) occur as Rachel, in accord with society's intentions as they apply to a young unmarried woman lucky enough to be chosen by an honorable and attractive young man, submits to social decorum. Rachel's existential doubts about marriage are often read from this perspective as symptomatic of Virginia Stephen's own unhealthy state of mind while composing the novel.

The promise of leadership reappearing in Woolf's work represents a fulfillment that proves, more often than not, destructive of life and art. The advice, first of Helen and Terence, subsequently of Jacob, Mrs. Ramsay and Bernard-become-Percival, fosters, I suggest, closure and bad faith. However beloved and magnanimous these figures may be to their author as well as to her readers, they all, dutifully conventional, share a common disinclination to experiment.[33] Jacob may well be "an exemplar of all the other young men whose promise the war destroyed,"[34] and for this reason we regret his untimely death, but for Woolf such promise merely perpetuates reactionary values.

In the 1970's Mitchell Leaska and Carolyn Heilbrun questioned the assumption that Mrs. Ramsay represented an ideal sort of woman.[35] Most subsequent criticism evidently remains unconvinced. Restating earlier assumptions that the novel's chief purpose was "to capture and render stable and permanent the essence of Mrs. Ramsay," critics continue to affirm its celebration of marital love while applauding Mrs. Ramsay's role at the center of the family, "the foundation of social life" in the words of one commentator.[36] It follows that the problem lies with those like Lily (and before her, Rachel) whose will to experiment threatens unanimity. Unable to respond to Mr. Ramsay's plea for sympathy—"it is to her immense discredit sexually"—Lily is marked as the deficient one. To regard Lily as the heroine of *To the Lighthouse,* rather than as "the child who communicates [Mrs. Ramsay's] light to the world," may offend readers who find pleasure in Mrs. Ramsay's gifts.[37]

The merging of Bernard with Percival in *The Waves* conveys an acceptance of that same wholeness Mrs. Ramsay would pass on to those who follow, a legacy Lily emphatically declines by refusing Mr. Ramsay accord. The present study submits that *The Waves,* far from simply an honoring of Thoby Stephen or an impulse to revive a legacy of romance,[38] commemorates art's tenuous struggle to resist the appeal of closure. Most critics see Bernard at the conclusion of this novel as the ideal artist, intent on creating unity, struggling "to conquer chaos and give form to the vision."[39] Such analyses presume, perhaps too confidently, that Bernard is Woolf's spokesman. The story Bernard shapes and sets down before the stranger in the restaurant is, much like Mrs. Ramsay's dish, "a complete thing," a coherent object of art, insusceptible to change. Woolf suggests in *A Room of One's Own* that such a work, requiring no collaboration, is "doomed to death. It ceases to be fertilised."[40] In this context the transcendence one critic identifies with the traditional leap of poets—the final ride suggests a "leap at immortality"[41]—may appear, antithetically, a return to patriarchal omniscience.

At the end of *The Years* Eleanor Pargiter, close to eighty years old, returning to the family circle, hollows her hands as if "to enclose the present moment," perhaps for one last time. Rather than a return to pattern,[42] such a contraction, I argue, involves for Woolf a rejection of human potentiality.

It is in Woolf's last novel, *Between the Acts* (1941), that the consolation both of wholeness and of governance receives its most compelling critique. The survival of the human species, much less art, appears contingent on society's willingness to question, like the audience of Miss La Trobe's play, what it takes mostly for granted. The future after the defeat of fascism envisioned in the *Times* is prophetically insufficient. Its prediction of everyone in a new flat filled with the latest appliances builds to an ironic "all liberated; made whole."

As *Three Guineas* suggests, Woolf has in mind different alternatives that must inevitably offend a culture nourished on virtues of acquisition. We the readers, in company with Colonel Mayhew, seated impatiently as the action of the play flags, resist the invitation to do nothing, an advice that sounds particularly naïve and suicidal at times when military preparedness seems the only course for survival.*

Those who seek models of wholeness in the novel point to the figures of Lucy Swithin and Mrs. Manresa for unifying

---

*Phyllis Rose points out that this was an especially desperate period for Woolf, a time when her personal need for order must have been most strident. *Woman of Letters: A Life of Virginia Woolf* (New York, 1978), p. 231.

paradigms, to the former for the spirit, to the latter for the body. But surely it is Isa and Miss La Trobe, in similar states of disarray, who prompt our deepest admiration. *Between the Acts* postulates a series of temptations for the author and her readers, from the consolation of art to the nostalgia for rural England, only to leave us all without a center, equally dispersed, equally open to the impact of interruption.

The uncertainty with which Woolf ends her first novel will become a conscious strategy through which to disrupt more traditional modes of narration and thereby allow the advent of something radically new. With the center vacant, the text itself becomes the medium of revelation, though of a nature different from that of pointedly religious epics. Where an informing vision emerges for Dante Alighieri through the figure of Beatrice or structurally through the number nine, for Woolf the idea of the holy resides quite literally in those "chasms" the narrator of *Jacob's Room* points to within "the continuity of our ways." Whether such intrusions signify the "loopholes" Bakhtin describes or the rejuvenating pause through which a mysterious sense of shared experience inspires renewal, they mark in Woolf's fiction moments of profound possibility. However brief the human life span—Woolf describes it in her first novel as that "short season between two silences"—the most mundane particularities of existence continue to startle and arouse her heroines, once, that is, they have resisted the enticements of patriarchal generosity.

The ensuing chapters presume that the important issues for Woolf as a creative writer develop in complexity with each of her novels. By structuring my book chronologically I would emphasize the quality of this thematic development. Central to all her thinking is the revelation of interruption, heralding change, and the growing expectation that society is on the verge of radical transformation.

One begins, I have also suggested, by being chaotic. My chapter on *The Voyage Out* records Woolf's first fictional attempt to cultivate the art of doing nothing. Chapter Three shows that *Night and Day*, if the most traditional of her novels, saw her break with literary conventions and her reception of those upheavals that describe the new Georgian age. Katharine and Ralph can be said to mature in proportion to their capacity to indulge interruption. Chapter Four, on *Jacob's Room*, discusses interruption in terms of the fragmenting of the narrator's voice.

The expansion and confusion of narrative boundaries informs Woolf's attack on patriarchal hierarchy. The chapters on *Mrs. Dalloway* and *To the Lighthouse* focus on the virtues of anonymity. Though of thoroughly different backgrounds and persuasions, Clarissa Dalloway and Lily Briscoe both create art forms whose vitality does not depend on continued omniscient intervention. Each steps back from the center to allow her creation to take on a discernibly eccentric life of its own. Woolf's last three novels develop this theme. *The Waves*, dispensing entirely with an omniscient narrator, confronts the impact of a world in which the very concept of centrality collapses. The absence of Percival, like the sudden departure of Mrs. Ramsay in "Time Passes," introduces a world without authenticating rulers. The subversion of omniscience moves her finally with *The Years* and *Between the Acts* to envision an egalitarian society without constricting hierarchies or patriarchal leaders, where each new interruption emerges, however anarchically, with a promise of renewal.

Woolf's novels, like the work of many great writers, remain complex and diverse in their range of interests and themes. They lend themselves to a wide variety of critical approaches. Thematic interpretations such as mine inevitably risk appearing reductive, a tendency Woolf was quick to associate with lectures and in one notable instance with a professor of English literature.

Let me acknowledge at the outset some "desire to convert,"[43] which Woolf no doubt would accurately identify as a limitation of my profession. I can only hope the readings that follow elicit what she did presume to be the proper end of lectures and criticism, namely, "human intercourse." At the heart of such dialogic presumptions is the expectation of what Woolf terms, in *A Room of One's Own*, an unending "marriage of opposites."

Chapter Two

BEING CHAOTIC
The Voyage Out

Nietzsche looked toward an inward chaos for inspiration. Rachel Vinrace, heroine of *The Voyage Out,* is motivated by the chaotic impact of things external to herself. Since Virginia Woolf's earliest impressions of that larger world involved the sea and sky, one is prepared to find the opening six chapters of her first book set on board a steamship.

An ocean setting allows her to give vent to feelings of radical disengagement she experienced in the spring of 1905 on a trip to Spain. "I feel," she writes to Violet Dickinson, "as though I had been cut adrift from the world altogether." Her own sea voyage was apparently not entirely satisfying. Bored as well as exhilarated, Virginia describes one instance when the ship had lost power: "We had to stop and drift with sails for about 7 hours, which was very dull." [1] Rachel, in the course of many revisions, emerges as a character far more receptive to such intervals of broken sequence. Reshaping perhaps her own experience, Woolf learns the art of indulging such pauses. With the novel's completion they become the means through which Rachel interrupts society's manipulative intentions.

Sea voyages are by their nature parenthetical. Between the acts of departure and arrival, accustomed roles and routines seem often implausible if not unreal. It is, moreover, a time when passengers may freely acknowledge a preference for doing nothing at all. Woolf's own attitude toward such in-activity, however, was at best equivocal. Throughout her life, the thought of existing without work or the distraction of play aroused her anxiety. "The only way I keep afloat is by work-ing," she writes in her 1929 diary. "Directly I stop working I feel that I am sinking down, down."[2] At the same time she was painfully aware that her artistic vision required such a de-scent into inactivity. An earlier entry compares her sense of being in the world to standing on "a little strip of pavement over an abyss."[3] A sense of giddiness as she looks down tempts her to stay upon the surface, where things remain reassuringly firm and substantial, and where disruptive speculations about life and its meaning seldom arise.

From the start of *The Voyage Out*, Rachel Vinrace is in-clined to see the most familiar of occurrences in an unusual light. Questioning the daily routines of her two aunts, "she could not explain to herself why suddenly as her aunt spoke the whole system in which they lived had appeared before her eyes as something quite unfamiliar and inexplicable, and them-selves as chairs or umbrellas dropped about here and there without any reason" (36).[4]

Somewhat later Woolf's heroine is similarly struck by "the utter absurdity" of a woman walking forward to hand her a letter, and by the strangeness of the thought "that things should exist at all." In this moment of existential doubt Rachel finds herself "overcome by the unspeakable queerness of the fact that she should be sitting in an arm-chair, in the morn-ing, in the middle of the world" (125). All aspects of that meaning she has derived, perhaps too easily, from society slip away as she finds herself literally and metaphorically at sea. She is an outsider by virtue of her eccentric view of things; her function in the novel at such times is to subvert the well-intentioned people who would guide and instruct her in the ways of the world.

Reversing the usual format of the *Bildungsroman*, Woolf offers a heroine who will not grow into the world as it is constituted. If Rachel learns anything in the course of a short lifetime, it is the art of disengagement. Certain aspects of this resistance emerge before her journey has really begun.

The quality that first distinguishes Rachel from those who surround her is described rather pointedly as "a fine natural indolence" (33). She seems the only person aboard the *Euphrosyne* who relishes the idea of doing nothing, of ignoring the shipboard routine. Inspired by the crew, the passengers find ways to work: Ridley Ambrose takes up his Greek; Mr. Pepper, whose habit on land is to cycle before breakfast, passes time on this morning by "cutting up roots with a penknife"; seated close by, Ambrose's wife Helen works no less industriously at her embroidery while reading G. E. Moore. Between stitches and thoughts of philosophy she finds herself wondering what her niece is doing. The text supplies the answer: "At that moment Rachel was sitting in her room doing absolutely nothing" (33).

Mr. Vinrace has already lectured his daughter on the propriety of a workday schedule. As captain of the ship, he is too busy to keep track of her: "'I'm busy till one,' said her father, enforcing his words as he often did, when he spoke to his daughter, by a smart blow upon the shoulder. 'Until one,' he repeated. 'And you'll find yourself some employment, eh? Scales, French, a little German, eh?'" (28).

Where Helen Ambrose finds her young niece's passivity a symptom of insufficient education, Woolf would emphasize rather an early discomfort over prescribed social roles. Waiting to receive her aunt and uncle aboard ship, Rachel feels "unnaturally braced" by the polite decorums of "civilized people." Helen notes her unwillingness to take on the usual responsibilities at their first social function together—Rachel chooses to remain silent rather than help carry on the conversation—and makes subsequent plans to educate her. Like women before and presumably after, she must learn the strategy of "promoting men's talk without listening to it" (17). She must be led into the circle of that world they share in common; she must be brought into the action. Rachel's stillness, it seems, offends something deeper than social decorum in Helen. Even the listlessness of her body—"she might have done something with her hands" (17)—makes Helen uncomfortable.

The source of her irritation is more than the realization that for the next four weeks she will have no one with whom to share a more sophisticated discourse. Not until St. John Hirst appears on solid land will this possibility occur. Helen seems rather to censure an absence of definition that makes the young girl as amorphous and chaotic as the sea or air: "When you said something to her it would make no more lasting impression than the stroke of a stick upon water. There was nothing to take hold of in girls—nothing hard, permanent, satisfactory" (20).

Resisting definition, Rachel would preserve space outside a society at best unreceptive to her own intuition of life and movement. The choice to remain outside the narrative of history, however, constitutes finally for Woolf a no-less-restrictive mode of being. Helen's concern that her young niece will remain captive of her own subjective moods and impulses reflects in part Woolf's own reservations about the inward voyage. Hers remains a voyage outward.[5]

Despite Helen's responsiveness to the external world, she appears ironically insensitive to those sociological forces that motivate Rachel's discontent. Presuming that such disaffection arises solely from a youthful intolerance for everything outside her own experience, Helen misses the thrust of Rachel's critique, just as Vanessa may have disregarded her sister's early polemics. One such instance occurs in discussing Rachel's passion for the piano:

> "I heard from Aunt Bessie not long ago," Helen stated. "She is afraid that you will spoil your arms if you insist upon so much practising."
> "The muscles of the forearm—and then one won't marry?"
> "She didn't put it quite like that," replied Mrs. Ambrose.
> "Oh, no—of course she wouldn't," said Rachel with a sigh. (20)

Ignoring the substance of Rachel's point, Helen seems aware only of an insufficiency of language, of her "tendency to use the wrong words" (20). Whether Woolf considers this a consequence or a denial of Helen's Bloomsbury credentials is less clear. It is only fair to assume, however, that Helen's sophistication extends much as the narrator's does to a critique of the culture that has formed her niece. She knows that, like most girls of her time and class, Rachel has been educated by a variety of kindly patriarchs who "would as soon have forced her to go through one piece of drudgery thoroughly as they would have told her that her hands were dirty" (33–34). Music is one of the few occupations she has been allowed to pursue freely. Given small opportunity, Rachel has made the most of playing the piano as well as of being disorganized.

Woolf, nurtured as she was in the inquiring ambience of Bloomsbury, remains sympathetic to all those who seek to extend the boundaries of human knowledge. Yet she seems more eager in *The Voyage Out* to explore an eccentricity of mind and spirit she no doubt recognizes in her own psychological makeup. The distance Rachel would preserve from those who love her, as well as from those who would direct her, reflects Woolf's effort to preserve growing room for her own creative aspirations. Where sister and husband may understandably have viewed her flirtation with nothingness as an implicit threat to life and health, she came increasingly to believe that in order to begin, the artist must loosen her hold on everyday reality. "One must begin," as she puts it in her 1924 diary, "by being chaotic."[6]

Woolf appreciated the stability Vanessa and Leonard contributed to her survival both as a person and as an artist, a stability that she associated more than once with the mind's capacity to create order. The overwhelming panic she describes when faced with unmediated experience was caused, she explains in her autobiographical sketch, from a feeling of inadequacy: "The sense of horror held me powerless" until "I found a reason; and was thus able to deal with the sensation. I was not powerless. I was conscious."[7] Against such statements, however, we should place those evocations of visions that arise in the absence of human volition. Like her young protagonist, Woolf was caught between the Bloomsbury inclination to explicate the nature of phenomenological experience and the inclination, derived perhaps from her reading of the Romantic poets, to let it be.

Helen, seated on deck as their steamer moves out to sea, stitches her "great design of a tropical river running through a tropical forest" (33) with the assurance of an artist who has organized every detail. In control of her art, she knows where the spotted deer will eventually browse, what they will eat, where the bananas, oranges, and pomegranates will lie, and from what direction the attacking natives will appear. Since Helen's embroidery anticipates the narrative—the Amazon will prove a critical feature in Rachel's short life—we may presume that the artist's omniscience here extends beyond the design of her composition. Death as well as life resides in this dark forest. Rachel's doom seems assured once she allows its unmediated rhythms to invade her being.

Nurse Lugton's Golden Thimble, a children's story Woolf wrote for her own niece some years later, suggests a relevant gloss on the image of the artist-weaver.[8] Nurse Lugton falls asleep while sewing her tapestry. When her thimble and needle are still, the figures she has formed come to life; the antelope nods to the zebra, the giraffe nibbles on a tree leaf. Roaming over the lap of their creator, the wild beasts exist free of her control. Only when she awakens are they frozen once more into those unchanging postures destined to hang from Mrs. Gingham's drawing-room windows for a lifetime, if not for an eternity. The dynamics of art, Woolf suggests, begin for children at least in that interval of darkness when the creator rests.

Woolf knew that art is the outcome of human effort. She knew as well that the vision on which the artist depends comes often mysteriously from sources that resist exposure, from a depth greater than human thought and language can hope to fully enclose. In the modern context all living things—not least, in her mind, words themselves—resist the encircling sovereignty of what Bakhtin terms, we recall, the epic past.

For earlier ages circularity expressed the apotheosis of life and motion implicit in the very structure of the cosmos. In Woolf's fiction the figure of circularity is employed almost always to represent a culture turning back incestuously upon itself, a state of being impervious to renewal. The point is illustrated most poignantly in *Three Guineas,* where the author compares involvement in the social system to caterpillars circling head to tail around a tree.[9] In *The Voyage Out,* London, static and circular, appears from the deck of the departing *Euphrosyne* like "a circumscribed mound . . . a crouched and cowardly figure, a sedentary miser" (18).

As the Ambroses stand by the Embankment at the opening of the novel, they seem by temperament unprepared for a voyage, much less an adventure. Stopping near Waterloo Bridge, where people often pause to look at the river, Helen fixes her attention on one thing: "It is always worth while to look down and see what is happening. But this lady looked neither up nor down; the only thing she had seen, since she stood there, was a circular iridescent patch slowly floating past with a straw in the middle of it" (10).

Literally and figuratively immobilized by the prospect of

leaving her children and journeying into a new environment, Helen resists from the first the temptation to venture out of circularity. As for her husband, he will soon be indoors "encircled by books." Seated alone in his cabin, later in his study in Santa Marina—"like an idol in an empty church" (170)— he seeks wholeness in solitude. Only Rachel's illness and death ultimately interrupt his design.

Before the *Euphrosyne* reaches South America Woolf introduces two new characters, Mr. and Mrs. Dalloway, who join the ship in Lisbon. Their aristocratic manner disrupts the rapport the other passengers have already established. All agree that "the interruption was upsetting" (41). It is a very different, class-bound world the newcomers introduce, a world that views Bloomsbury directness as a breach of good taste. At dinner Richard Dalloway speculates on how difficult it is to keep the conversation rolling with people of a lower class. The group seems on the verge of reconciling social differences when a turn in the weather upsets the new harmony: "No politeness could ignore it" (70). As they return to their cabins to retrieve some small semblance of equilibrium, their thoughts and feelings scatter and disperse like the sea. "Their sensations were the sensations of potatoes in a sack on a galloping horse. The world outside was merely a violent grey tumult" (71).

The new conditions serve the purpose of suspending the characters' former roles. "For two days they had a perfect rest from their old emotions" (71). In the midst of this interim the basis of all relationships seems to change. Even Helen, who has found Clarissa Dalloway's snobbery so unappealing, inexplicably feels "a kind of liking" for her. Then, as the storm ends and the world regains its familiar contours, they abruptly revert to their former roles: "They were no longer atoms flying in the void, but people riding a triumphant ship on the back of the sea. Wind and space were banished; the world floated like an apple in a tub, and the mind of men, which had been unmoored also, once more attached itself to the old beliefs"

(72). As the ship gets under way again, a sense of enclosure seems to envelop everyone on board save Rachel.

On the first day of the voyage, Rachel and Helen find themselves walking on deck. The wind is blowing hard and Mrs. Ambrose, already assuming a maternal role, worries that her companion will be cold. Rachel's excitement, however, proves infectious: "'It blows—it blows!' gasped Rachel, the words rammed down her throat. Struggling by her side, Helen was suddenly overcome by the spirit of movement" (18). But the chaotic moment is short-lived.

In Rachel's case this new state of movement and change evokes a sense of contrast with the static world of uninterrupted ritual. On shore as on shipboard, people go about their daily business systematically incurious toward everything outside their purview. Only the *Euphrosyne*, the presiding Grace, merging with Woolf's protagonist, seems to move like wind and sea with a power and intention of her own:

She was more lonely than the caravan crossing the desert; she was infinitely more mysterious, moving by her own power and sustained by her own resources. The sea might give her death or some unexampled joy, and none would know of it. She was a bride going forth to her husband, a virgin unknown of men; in her vigour and purity she might be likened to all beautiful things, worshipped and felt as a symbol. (32)

It is not the forecast of death or the foreshadowing of Rachel as Milton's Sabrina that elicits such identifications at this point in the narrative, but the exuberant expectations of independence and movement. The reader recalls in this respect the young boys beside the Thames "launching wads of paper for a cruise" (10), eager as Helen is not for change and new adventure.

Helen criticizes Rachel's passivity and finds her inclination to "change her view of life about every other day" (163) even more troublesome; only a proper education, she feels, can rectify such tendencies. Ironically, precisely this shifting quality of mind anticipates the inflection of Woolf's narrative voice. Like Rachel later in the novel, moving "in and out of peoples' minds, seeking she knew not what" (259), Woolf's narrators become with *Jacob's Room* increasingly chaotic.

Woolf's image of the passengers' state of mind following the storm reflects an early indictment of what, fairly or not, she assumes to be the formulating principles of traditional Western culture. "Old beliefs" call for the militant subjugation of all that is mysterious and ill-defined in life. First and foremost is the threat of the void, manifest by the intrusive reality of "wind and space."

Rachel's first encounter with male sexuality, however modest, proves to be more disruptive than the storm. Richard Dalloway, stepping out of his cabin for the first time in days, collides with her on deck. The wind is still up and, "too much blown about to speak," they retreat to Rachel's cabin, where she has evidently been reading, among other books, *Wuthering Heights*. For a few minutes they speak of her reading; but when the ship suddenly lurches, he takes her in his arms and kisses her passionately. It is not the kiss so much as the experience of something radically other—"She felt the hardness of his body and the roughness of his cheek" (76)—that interrupts and qualifies what in the past has remained an essentially verbal recognition of men. In conversation no such confrontation was possible. Words, however potent, do not in fact touch us. This is not to say that a speaker cannot intimidate or dominate another, but rather that words predicate distance. Mrs. Brown, accosted by Mr. Smith in Woolf's essay, maintains some small privacy in the face of his verbal assault.[10]

While Dalloway's kiss transforms his language into something "terrifying," it is not so much the words—"You tempt me"—as the irreducible quality of his touch that unsettles Rachel. For someone of her age and background, love, like politics, has remained almost exclusively a literary experience. The sense of discovery opens almost at once a widening breadth of choice. If, as she considers after leaving the cabin, "something wonderful had happened," it is not so much the discovery of human sexuality that describes the impact as a realization that the external world "seemed to hold infinite possibilities she had never guessed at" (76).

In Woolf's first novel as in her last, mysterious things happen at those moments when the normal routines of everyday life are upset, sometimes by social behavior, more often by nonhuman forces. Just as the sea subsumes and reforms the contours of the shore, so the night can be said to renew the day. Such intrusions occur largely when reason sleeps, in Woolf's idiom "with the police off duty."[11] It is not the rejuvenating power of sleep that leads her to celebrate night, however, but rather its capacity to confuse our customary manner of seeing. Where darkness in the case of Lucy Swithin and Mrs. Ramsay obscures interruption, the absence of light for most of Woolf's heroines occasions contradiction. In fact and metaphor it is a shadowy continent toward which the *Euphrosyne* journeys, one designed to unsettle expectations.

In the heart of a primeval darkness, Woolf places a familiar world of British tourists, safely harbored in the Santa Marina Hotel.[12] If she describes them with a realist's eye for detail, she keeps us aware of an encroaching forest world that, like Nurse Lugton's tapestry, comes to life in the absence of human intervention. So at an early point in the hotel narrative, we confront that hour of night when everyone sleeps, "between the extinction of Hewet's candle" and the rising a few hours later of the first servant boy. Only the novelist remains to authenticate such empty time between the acts of social intercourse. "Looking out of the windows," she tells us, "there was only darkness to be seen"; but from this darkness emerge different species of being: "Until all people should awake again the houseless animals were abroad, the tigers and the stags, and the elephants coming down in the darkness to drink at pools. The wind at night blowing over the hills and woods was purer and fresher than the wind by day, and the earth, robbed of detail, more mysterious than the earth coloured and divided by roads and fields" (111).

By contrast, the activities of the tourists appear particularly moribund. Their day begins punctually with the sounding of a breakfast gong. Once the procedure of eating is over, "the ladies as usual circled vaguely, picking up papers and putting them down again, about the hall" (111). The overriding concern is to find something with which to occupy themselves. "And what are you going to do today?" is the recurring refrain. The routine of being tourists supplies a number of answers. Since the community is almost exclusively British, other rituals bind them together, supplying a sustaining rhythm. There are, moreover, things to be seen and recorded in a foreign country. The tourist's eye, like the lens of a camera, preserves and authenticates the tropical landscape. One feels somehow more solid once experience has been so codified, its novelty translated into the traditional idiom of a common history.

The intellectual St. John Hirst—"One of the three, or is it five, most distinguished men in England" (144)—is no less susceptible than the guests he brilliantly derides to reducing the external world to photographic singularity. When, on their return from the fateful excursion up the Amazon, he is excited by a herd of wild deer breaking into an opening in the forest, he can only exclaim: "What an ass I was not to bring my Kodak!" (279). As with Helen, the only woman he really admires, Hirst's enemy remains those experiences he cannot substantiate and identify, which is to say circumscribe. Not surprisingly, Hirst, following Rachel's death, experiences "a strange sense of quiet and relief" among the very hotel community he has ridiculed throughout the novel. They share a world in common.

During an early discussion with the friend who is to become

Rachel's fiancé, Hirst describes the human predicament in terms of man's inability to move outside his own limited experience:

> "Take this hotel. You could draw circles round the whole lot of them, and they'd never stray outside. . . ."
> "Are we all alone in our circle?" asked Hewet.
> "Quite alone," said Hirst. "You try to get out, but you can't. You only make a mess of things by trying." (107)

The words motivate his final retreat. Ceasing to think about his grief-stricken friend, Hewet after Rachel's death sits "motionless" in his chair, soothed by the conventional chatter the guests supply.*

At the center of *The Voyage Out*, the waltz emerges as the apotheosis of that wholeness Rachel may hope to derive from the world of men, namely the eventuality of matrimony.† Similarly, the engagement between the young guests Susan and Arthur, who have met at the hotel, is marked no less appropriately by "the triumphant swing of the waltz" (152). But Rachel, like her author, confesses a distaste for dancing. And one may assume from Mrs. Thornbury's remarks at the party that Rachel is the exception. "I have brought out five daughters," the matron informs the gathering, "and they all loved dancing!" (158). Caught up in the general excitement, however, Rachel finds herself charmed by the circular harmony of this occasion.

Unable to enter the crowded room, Helen and Rachel

---

* Most critics regard this conclusion as a fulfilling resolution. Jean Guiguet describes it as "the closing harmony." *Virginia Woolf and Her Works* (New York, 1965), p. 200.

† In his film *2001*, Stanley Kubrick dramatically conveys the rhythm that catapulted man from the Stone Age into space. A shining metallic satellite, revolving in orbit around the earth, moves appropriately to the circular beat of a Strauss waltz. Science and art combine to signify the dynamic of civilized culture.

stand immobilized in the doorway as the couples swirl by on the dance floor. The sense of stasis and exclusion—"They could not move"—is all but unbearable. " 'We are suffering the tortures of the damned,' said Helen. 'This is my idea of hell,' said Rachel" (152). Just as Susan escapes "the long solitude of an old maid's life" (140) through Arthur's intervention, so the two women are spared further suffering by the timely appearance of men. Ironically, St. John Hirst, who has no taste for dancing or for music, takes Rachel "resolutely by the elbow" and follows Hewet's lead with Helen: "We must follow suit" (153). His eccentric and angular movements defeat his good intentions, however. It remains for Hewet, presiding in the manner of Euphrosyne over such festivities, to introduce Rachel, first on the dance floor and then through his own proposal of marriage, to the wholeness of life and time.

Once chosen, the two women seem content like the others to circle round the room forever. Those who remain on the sidelines seem no less inspired by the ambience of circularity. Even Mr. Pepper celebrates this form of wholeness as he turns to praise "round dances, country dances, morris dances and quadrilles, all of which are entirely superior to the bastard waltz" (151).

On the dance floor reality seems compressed within each set of music. The five-minute interludes are stoically endured. The very setting of the hall seems constructed to minimize interruption. Windows are closed and well curtained, as much to keep out irrelevant sights and sounds as to eliminate drafts. For one night at least reality is centered on one thing. Only Hirst, irreverently maintaining his tutorial role and chastising Rachel for her lack of reading—"D'you mean to tell me you've reached the age of twenty-four without reading Gibbon?" (154)—creates a breach in the ceremony. In this interval before Hewet asks her to dance, Rachel is moved by the truth (however sexist) of Hirst's remarks—she in fact knows so little—to push open a window and step outdoors. She is the first to venture out of the party, the first to confront the liberating darkness.

Her action anticipates a number of scenes throughout Woolf's fiction in which various characters, major and otherwise, are drawn to windows in the midst of festivity. Here the event constitutes more than a romantic impulse for solitude. While Hewet soon makes his appearance through that same bay window, Rachel is no feminine counterpart of the Byronic hero who indulges grievance in expectation of the woman who will follow him. What breaks through to Rachel as she stands alone in the garden is the startling impact of trees in themselves, emerging like Wordsworth's "huge peak" in Book One of *The Prelude,* to engage her perception: "The forms of great black trees rose massively in front of her. She stood still, looking at them, shivering slightly with anger and excitement. She heard the trampling and swinging of the dancers behind her, and the rhythmic sway of the waltz music. 'There are trees,' she said aloud" (155).

Invigorated both by the pause and by the interruption of her grievance, Rachel rejoins the dance with a certain independence of spirit. When, later in the evening, the musicians decide rather suddenly to go home, this freedom emerges more visibly in the guise of innovation. That the musicians could be tired and bored after fulfilling their contract strikes the guests as preposterous. Anticipating Bernard's lack of concern for his waiter at the close of *The Waves,* their self-centered intentions exclude more than the world of nature outside the ballroom. As she peruses the sheets of music left behind, Rachel, who had pleaded no less adamantly for them to continue, finds herself suddenly disenchanted. The illustrated covers convey images of romantic death that qualify the pleasure she has just felt with Hewet:

> She remembered that the general effect of the music to which they had danced so gaily was one of passionate regret for dead love

and the innocent years of youth; dreadful sorrows had always separated the dancers from their past happiness.

"No wonder they get sick of playing stuff like this," she remarked,
reading a bar or two; "they're really hymn tunes, played very fast,
with bits out of Wagner and Beethoven." (165)

Rachel's answer is first to occupy the void created by the
musicians' absence and play the piano, and then, once her own
small repertoire is exhausted, to urge the dancers toward a new
design. Choosing to play a Mozart sonata, she calls on each of
them to "invent the steps" (166). The experiment proves an
immediate success. Moved by her suggestion, the dancers become boldly innovative. Helen seizes Miss Allan and trips
around the room "like a child skipping through a meadow,"
and Hirst, as if in answer to Rachel's instruction—"This is the
dance for people who don't know how to dance"—leaps from
one foot to the other in happy and chaotic abandon. The general effect is to inspire all of the dancers to improvise steps
derived from their own experience. Mr. Pepper's movements
reflect his talent for figure skating, Mrs. Thornbury's the country dances of her childhood in Dorset, and the Elliots' gallop
their fondness for horses. "Some people were heard to criticise
the performance as a romp; to others it was the most enjoyable
part of the evening" (166).

When Hewet shouts for "the great round dance," it is not a
return to the triumphant waltz that marks the end of the evening. Instead, the remaining party form "a gigantic circle,"
hold hands, and dance around to "D'you ken John Peel?"
Their increased velocity sends the whole circle into disarray,
the dancers "flying across the room in all directions, to land
upon the floor or the chairs or in each other's arms as seemed
most convenient" (166–67). Aroused by this chaotic movement, Rachel, like her aunt in the wind on board ship, is intoxicated by the tumultuous feeling of "letting go."

The experience remains with her the following morning.
Walking through the countryside, she feels the preceding

night "encroaching upon the day," inspiring her to reenact its unsettling impact. Recalling faces and voices, she begins "saying things over again or saying things differently, or inventing things that might have been said" (173). The merging of time past and present in her mind expands as it intensifies the moment; the sense of "opportunity for doing exactly as she liked, sprung more wonderfully vivid even than the night before" (173–74). As on the terrace at the dance, what emerges through these reflections is the force of Rachel's independence. So, when her own imaginative reconstruction is rudely interrupted by a no-less-immediate world, Rachel adapts to the change creatively: "The interruption of a tree, which although it did not grow across her path, stopped her as effectively as if the branches had struck her in the face. It was an ordinary tree, but to her it appeared so strange that it might have been the only tree in the world" (174).

The distinguishing quality of Rachel's freedom involves her capacity to allow other things and people room to emerge in her perception free of manipulation. She does not require experience as a support for her own largely ill-formed intentions. From Woolf's perspective such naïveté remains essential if Rachel and her species are to survive. She drops the volumes of Balzac and Gibbon she has been carrying, and seats herself on the ground with Wordsworthian irreverence. Playing with the surrounding foliage, laying flowers and stalks side by side, caressing them as if they had become childhood companions, she is imbued with the sense that these objects individually "had their own life and disposition" (174).

In this state of mind, ignoring, as it were, Wordsworthian imperatives, she does not quit her books but turns to read them. As she does, Gibbon's prose takes on new life: "Never had any words been so vivid and so beautiful." Like the single tree, "they seemed to drive roads back to the very beginning of the world" (175).

Rachel is in fact excited by the sense of multiplicity such

intrusions evoke. In each case it is the realization of many options before her that motivates the impractical thought that even an unmarried lady in 1908 might have more in store for her than her society anticipates. She becomes despondent when her mind, under the necessity of exploring the persistent question of "love and marriage," is no longer free to play with more than one idea. As *The Voyage Out* moves toward its tragic conclusion, the question of whether such options really exist for a woman remains perplexingly unclear. The choice to enter history would appear to preclude any posture short of that disciplined tenacity Helen and Hirst prescribe. Rachel understands early in the novel that to marry Hewet and enter their world, she must become "a soldier prepared for battle" (176), a choice Woolf seems determined to spare her first heroine.

Rachel resists more than one invitation to take a more aggressive role in life. Charging that women's chief problem is their failure to act politically, Evelyn Murgatroid demands of Rachel: "What do you *do?*" (248). Her punning reply—"I play"—feeds Evelyn's need to reach and to convert her: "Look here, you must join. . . . I'm certain that if people like ourselves were to take things in hand instead of leaving it to policemen and magistrates, we could put a stop to—prostitution . . . in six months" (248).

Taking a hand in things means adopting the tactics of those in power; women can effect social change once they learn in the manner of men to fight for it. Supremely self-confident, Evelyn has neither the time nor the inclination "to listen to other people's thoughts" (249). She is given to talk without pausing. Her concern for women, moreover, appears superficial. In the presence of Mr. Perrott, her dreams of domination extend to other continents: "They were great captains sent to colonize the world" (264). Here with Rachel she pursues a more modest if less successful campaign.

Like Helen, Evelyn finds Rachel's "vagueness" disarming.

36

There seems nothing substantial in her makeup, nothing susceptible to proselytizing. The failure to reach her—"She
searched up into her face as if she were trying to read what
kind of character was concealed behind"—compels an action
both sexual and masculine in appearance: "She put her hand
on Rachel's knee" (249). Watching her guest on the bed looking at photographs, Evelyn "could not help seeing that Rachel
was not thinking about her" (251). Egotistically, as if all separate worlds depended on the sanction of her consciousness to
exist, she must ask in amazement, "What was she thinking
about, then?" Failing again to elicit a response, Evelyn turns
finally to regard items of clothing: "her shoes, her stockings,
the combs in her hair, all the details of her dress in short, as
though by seizing every detail she might get closer to the life
within" (251). The verb "to seize," like Adam's first assault on
Eve in *Paradise Lost,* signals a no-less-acquisitive intention.

Somewhat later in the narrative, Hewet will experience the
discomfort of Rachel's independence. Her aloofness, understood as the ability "to cut herself adrift from him," causes
similarly acquisitive feelings: "There's something I can't get
hold of in you" (302). Rachel's inclination to resist such overtures reflects Woolf's earliest reservations about the form of
submission that all such intimacy appears to require.

Woolf was inclined to view love as the religion of egotism,
a passion based, as she will suggest in *Mrs. Dalloway,* on the
efficacy of conversion.[13] Such, at any rate, is what being in
love tends to become in a patriarchal society. The origins of
love, like the origins of life, would seem to promise something
quite different: a revelation of new life. The river trip Rachel
and Hewet take into the expanse of the Amazon jungle becomes in Woolf's mind a metaphor for all romantic expectations, a journey outside the boundaries of objective space and
time. As such, it constitutes an intrusion.

First on the river and then in the forest, it is the loss of
definition that reshapes the travelers' lives. As the boat con-

tinues to churn its way up the Amazon, life and movement seem more and more to be aspects of this chaotic new world. The jungle, pulsing with strange rhythms of its own, serves further to isolate the six British travelers from one another. Language as well as ritual subsides. Seated "in an irregular semi-circle," they soon lapse into those "long spaces of silence" that seem to surround each passing event and sound. Rachel and Hewet are most vulnerable to the moment: "they were waiting together, and being drawn on together, without being able to offer any resistance" (267).

When the tourists disembark for a short time, remaining on the bank of the river, each reverts almost at once to his or her defining role. Helen reads and begins another conversation with Hirst; Mrs. Flushing sets up her easel; Mr. Flushing searches for a suitable view for his wife's painting. The activity serves further to isolate Rachel and Hewet, who are "left standing by themselves without occupation" (269). However unpremeditated, the withdrawal of the others seems intended to fulfill a larger plan. Hewet takes the cue: "Terence saw that the time had come as it was fated to come, but although he realised this he was completely calm and master of himself" (269). Urging Helen to accompany them, he retains the sense of decorum. Her refusal and ineffectual reply—"What will you gain by walking?"—opens the door to the very eventuality Helen fears. Rachel "was in love, and she pitied her profoundly" (263). It is not for Helen Ambrose to intervene.

Mr. Flushing, who has proclaimed himself leader of this expedition, gives them one hour to be alone. In this space of time they seem destined both by tradition and by inclination to make their connection—that is, once Hewet takes the lead.

The text explores the quality of their attraction for each other during their walk through the forest. While marriage remains implicit, it is never mentioned. That analysis comes later. The tropical surrounding, with its dense creepers and swordlike leaves, inviting psychological analogue, seems a projection of their own yet-unstated feelings. This unfamiliar world constrains thought as well as talk. Without definition they move like walkers "at the bottom of the sea," where an engulfing quiet immobilizes mind and body. Here it is Hewet, throwing a fruit skyward, who resists the silence.

Asking Rachel if this profound stillness frightens her, with his first words he invites renewed dependence. Rachel replies that she likes it, before another pause, like the silence, falls on them. Seizing on the word of preference, Hewet applies it to himself—"You like being with me?"—while Rachel, her sense of identity all but dissolved, replies without self-designation, "Yes, with you." With each recurring pause the rhythm of a selfless world affects Hewet as well: "we" replaces "I" in his speech.

"We are happy together." He did not seem to be speaking, or she to be hearing.

"Very happy," she answered.

They continued to walk for some time in silence. Their steps unconsciously quickened.

"We love each other," Terence said.

"We love each other," she repeated. (271)

Their voices, breaking the hush, combine at this moment "in tones of strange unfamiliar sound which formed no words," impelling them first to walk faster, then to fall down in each other's arms. On the ground they are aware of sights and sounds from the surrounding jungle, "making a bridge across their silence." Ironically, what mars the moment is the loss of connection with the external world, the realization that in their present state of intimacy they have no place to go. The sense of impasse strikes Rachel most forcibly: "'Terrible—terrible,' she murmured after another pause," as the churning sound of the river, "senseless and cruel," duplicates her feeling of unrelenting enclosure.[14] Recalling his orders to be back within the hour, Hewet, who has been crying, regains command of himself while Rachel, no less dutifully, takes on the role of follower, "stopping where he stopped, turning where he turned" (272). At the decisive moment, however, it is Rachel rather than her fiancé who initiates the action. Frozen instinctively by the sight of the others on the riverbank, "They could not go on. They stood hand in hand for a minute or two in silence. They could not bear to face other people. 'But we must go on,' Rachel insisted at last" (272–73).

Throughout the novel Rachel charges Helen and Hirst with lacking the passion and volition to keep things going. When her two guardians agree that a trip upriver will not show them anything new, Rachel replies pointedly: "You don't help; you put an end to things" (262). In contrast to a social imperative, espoused by Helen no less than Richard Dalloway to "keep the ball rolling," Rachel's openness moves her continually to acts of renewal. In the forest, as in Evelyn's hotel room, Rachel resists all forms of closure. That the couple's reentry proves ultimately ineffectual is no fault of Rachel's. It is rather her author who appears at this time to have reservations about the future. On the eve of her own marriage, we can imagine her speculating, like Ursula in *Women in Love*, whether such commitment may prove the end rather than the beginning of experience.[15]

Rachel and Hewet's prospective marriage anticipates a series of sacrifices Woolf seems less willing to honor than her young heroine. In their first scene together after returning from the river, Rachel, now formally engaged, plays a piano sonata while Hewet returns to his novel called "Silence, or the Things People Don't Say." P. K. Joplin exposes in full the irony of this title.[16] No less ironic on this occasion are Hewet's interruptions, designed as they are to narrow rather than widen Rachel's existential options. Such are not the interruptions Woolf celebrates. Although he claims to enjoy her total absorption in Beethoven—"There she was swaying enthusiastically over her music, quite forgetful of him,—but he liked that quality in her" (291)—we find him intruding with a series of argumentative notes intended however playfully to make her stop. Once successful, his motivation becomes clear to her:

"I can't play a note because of you in the room interrupting me every other second."

"You don't seem to realise that that's what I've been aiming at for the last half-hour," he remarked. "I've no objection to nice, simple tunes—indeed, I find them very helpful to literary composition." (292)

Soon Hewet makes it plain that what Rachel should be doing is replying to congratulatory letters from their friends: "I ought to be writing my book, and you ought to be answering these" (295). She dutifully submits to the tiresome routine of producing conventional phrases, an "art of narrative" (299) designed in Hewet's mind to make her less the child and more the adult. Adopting a fatherly attitude, he is prepared to become her guardian as well as her lover; the two merge, it seems, in his idea of matrimony.

The diffusiveness of Rachel's being that first attracted Hewet now threatens to engulf him as fully as the forest. Confronting her assumption "that human beings were as various as the beasts at the zoo," he tries to contain her within more familiar proportions. According to Hewet, "There was an order, a pattern which made life reasonable. . . . Once linked together by one such tie she would find them not separate and formidable, but practically indistinguishable, and she would come to love them when she found that they were like herself" (299). The argument that civilized life is at its core "reasonable" masks neither the singularity of his thesis nor the suspicion that it remains flagrantly self-supporting.*

* It must be acknowledged here that a majority of critics see Terence in far more positive terms. I have already cited James Hafley in Chapter 1. More recently, Michael Rosenthal describes Terence as one who "penetrates to the stark truth at the heart of all Woolf's novels. . . . In Terence's company, Rachel begins to emerge from the layers of timidity and conventional

Hewet's fears concerning his future wife reflect reservations over what he no less than Hirst sees as the nature of women: "You've no respect for facts, Rachel; you're essentially feminine" (295). Such statements do not offend her. In love with Hewet, she finds herself reacting uncritically to the sound as much as to the meaning of the words, a fact that her prospective husband finds alternately attractive and frustrating.

Like Evelyn, and as he did in the forest, Hewet probes the detail of her face in an effort to decipher what she is and what she may become once they are married and living in London. A sense of urgency and threat underlying his playfulness is felt more than once: "'What I like about your face is that it makes one wonder what the devil you're thinking about—it makes me want to do that—' He clenched his fist and shook it so near her that she started back, 'because now you look as if you'd blow my brains out. There are moments,' he continued, 'when, if we stood on a rock together, you'd throw me into the sea'" (297–98).

Inspired by the rich variety of life, Rachel wants "many more things than the love of one human being—the sea, the sky" (302). This again anticipates *Women in Love*,[17] but here it is the man who seeks to anchor himself to one place: "She seemed to be able to cut herself adrift from him, and to pass away to unknown places where she had no need of him. The thought roused his jealousy. 'I sometimes think you're not in love with me and never will be,' he said. . . . 'There's something I can't get hold of in you. You don't want me as I want you—You're always wanting something else'" (302).

To preserve their relationship, Rachel submits. At the very

---

belief which had previously restricted her." *Virginia Woolf* (New York, 1979), p. 57. Maria DiBattista concludes her book by conflating Terence with his author: "The novelist who began her career desiring to write a novel about silence, about things people don't say, approaches the end of her career." *Virginia Woolf's Major Novels: The Fables of Anon* (New Haven, Conn., 1980), p. 235.

moment her aloofness threatens Hewet most, she leaps from his imaginary "rock," enticed by the idea of being "flung into the sea": "He caught her in his arms as she passed him, and they fought for mastery, imagining a rock, and the sea heaving beneath them. At last she was thrown to the floor, where she lay gasping, and crying for mercy" (298).* When their game is over, no less dutifully taking up needle and thread to repair the tear in her dress, she appears ready for matrimony and, in her author's eyes, a premature death. That the two ideas merge reflects a pessimism Woolf's own successful marriage later served no doubt to qualify. In her first novel, however, as in her last, human sexuality intertwined with the politics of paternalism traps men and women alike.

Rachel's illness and subsequent death are more than paradigms of capitulation. Interrupting our optimistic as well as our artistic inclinations, Woolf's unmotivated ending seems intended to upset all expectations of "pattern." In company with Rachel's friends, we find each vestige of support slipping away. Helen's obsessive protectiveness and Hirst's intellectual obsession with abstract ideas may be viewed in this context as strategies of retreat from a chaos that will not finally lend itself to their forms of mediation. Each avoids ambiguity as each avoids the forest. However pragmatic, such rigor proves unsatisfying.

Like Thomas Mann's Offenbach, Hirst feels compelled to experience something new. Old before his time, he has taken a holiday in what he expects to be an exotic arena. While life in the Santa Marina Hotel does not turn out to be particularly new, he looks forward to their expedition up the Amazon, "for, once away from the hotel, surely wonderful things would happen" (278). But like Helen, who will not allow herself to become "the victim of unclassified emotions," he is finally in-

---

* Since no man can marry a mermaid, Rachel's subsequent statement— "I'm a mermaid! I can swim . . . so the game's up" (298)—suggests another way of eluding Hewet.

capable of experiencing the revelations he seeks. His regret that "nothing happened" on the river or in the forest is revealing. Unnerved by the forest, his mind resists each invitation to be unreasonable. "God's undoubtedly mad," he speculates. "What sane person could have conceived a wilderness like this, and peopled it with apes and alligators? I should go mad if I lived here" (275). Instead, he translates this madness into a comic and obscene "poem on God."

Similarly, Helen rejects all experience foreign to her logos. Her morbid fears, aroused by the native village, abate once the riverboat is steaming "back towards civilisation" (286). Her duty toward Rachel and Hewet serves to distract her from thoughts of life's uncertainty: "She kept her eyes anxiously fixed upon the lovers, as if by doing so she could protect them from their fate" (286). If it is too late, she can still blame the couple "for having ventured too far and exposed themselves" (286), for having involved themselves in the deadly processes of an existence untempered by "European influence." Rachel's illness, if not her death, serves to extend Helen's role. Through Rachel's crisis she evades her own.

Presuming that the crisis is the just and inevitable consequence of transgression, Hewet, too, questions the wisdom of all such voyages out. The unreasonable choice by the Ambroses to live outside the hotel, like the precipitous river expedition itself, exposes them to a host of foreign threats. He at least has found a connection. In tracing his own loss of stability to the moment he carelessly and thoughtlessly allowed himself to be moved by loving Rachel, he makes further connections. He thinks of "Arthur and Susan, or Evelyn and Perrott venturing out unwittingly, and by their happiness laying themselves open to suffering such as this. How did they dare to love each other, he wondered; how had he himself dared to live as he had lived, rapidly and carelessly, passing from one thing to another, loving Rachel as he had loved her?" (345).

As days lengthen into weeks and the power of Rachel's ill-

ness overwhelms each effort to contain it—"Would everything go down before it?" (346)—the apprehension that there
is nothing to be done makes daily life all but intolerable, particularly for the men. Acknowledging that "he had never been
so bored since he was shut up in the nursery alone as a child"
(335), Hewet suffers as much from his own confinement as
through Rachel's. The "strain and boredom" of doing nothing
affects Hirst as well: "If only, he thought to himself, as he lay
in the darkness, something would happen—if only this strain
would come to an end. He did not mind what happened, so
long as the succession of these hard and dreary days was broken;
he did not mind if she died" (349).

Standing by himself on the terrace as Rachel had, Hewet
cannot face the darkness, much less remain alone. The night,
in collusion with Rachel's illness, seems to conspire against
wholeness, his own well-being. Longing "for some one to talk
to," he forces himself to move indoors, only to find the drawing room empty. "Hirst was asleep, and Ridley was asleep;
there was no sound in Rachel's room" (343). The appearance
of Nurse McInnis fails to restore self-confidence. With Rachel
absent, there is no one to lead him out of the forest: "Never
again would he feel secure; he would never believe in the stability of life, or forget what depths of pain lie beneath small
happiness and feelings of content and safety" (345).

The desire for a wholeness free of blemish marks Hewet's
persistently romantic expectations: "There had always been
something imperfect in their happiness. . . . It had been fragmentary and incomplete" (345). Seeking through him to ex-
pose the religiosity of her age's sexual pretensions, Woolf
illustrates how fully man's fulfillment requires woman's un-
conditional dependence. Such need remains in her mind synonymous with love.

When, some minutes before her death, Rachel comes out
of her delirium to see and recognize him, Hewet responds with
a plea she is too weak to answer: "'It's been wretched without

you,' he said. She still looked at him and smiled, but soon a slight look of fatigue or perplexity came into her eyes and she shut them again. 'But when we're together we're perfectly happy,' he said. He continued to hold her hand" (353).

Only through dying does she sustain the illusion he requires. No longer free to question—Rachel's final "perplexity" dissolves once her eyes close for the last time—she affords in death a foundation for Hewet's peace of mind that she could not give him so long as she lived. With her last breath, Hewet affirms an unchanging future: "She had ceased to breathe. So much the better—this was death. It was nothing; it was to cease to breathe. It was happiness, it was perfect happiness. They had now what they had always wanted to have, the union which had been impossible while they lived" (353).

With her presence enclosed and retained, like the image on a photograph, his mind can begin "to work naturally again," which is to say circularly: "It seemed to him that their complete union and happiness filled the room with rings." Outside the window, the sight of "a halo round the moon" inspires new confidence that pattern does in fact persist: "We shall have rain to-morrow" (354). When other people intrude, however, and he is forced from the room, Hewet can only scream and struggle in necrophilic rage to repossess this perfect moment.

Chapter Three

BREAKING WITH CONVENTION
Night and Day

At issue in *Night and Day* is whether words can survive a society that employs them almost exclusively to verify its own
emotions.[1] The question that fascinated Woolf in life as in art
is basically epistemological: if the object of thought and passion remains independent of one's observations, how, short of
an acquisitive act, can one come to reach it?

In a much-quoted passage from her diary, she describes the
awesome experience of a fin breaking the surface of the water
and how it moves her somehow to begin a new novel.[2] Woolf
acknowledges that by writing she does not in fact penetrate
such events, but she tends to employ figures of speech that
emphasize some aspect of the vision contained: a fish is netted,
an experience englobed. However unobtrusively, language
must supply for her the enclosing form through which its vision is rendered legible to others. This leads her to question
whether human understanding thereby inevitably reduces the
reality of each external circumstance to its own presupposi-

tions. Is art inescapably an imperialistic adventure calling, like Mrs. Flushing in the presence of thunder and lightning, for acts of conversion?

The Voyage Out ends with the exuberant Mrs. Flushing returning from the roof of the hotel with a command for verification: "'Splendid! Splendid!' she muttered to herself. Then she turned back into the hall and exclaimed in a peremptory voice, 'Come outside and see, Wilfred; it's wonderful.'"³ The expectation that her husband share this aesthetic experience seems generous and good. It is the proselytizing sound of her voice, however, that Woolf clearly emphasizes, an imperative tone designed to preclude dissenting opinions—in the context of this study, to exclude interruption.

Woolf remains at times mysteriously confident of the power of words to resist being used arbitrarily, in pursuit of exclusively predetermined conclusions. Such acts involve, she will suggest in "Craftsmanship," a sacrilege on their very nature: "They [words] hate being useful; they hate making money; they hate being lectured about in public. In short, they hate anything that stamps them with one meaning or confines them to one attitude, for it is their nature to change."⁴ Pinned down like butterflies in a collection, "they fold their wings and die." *Night and Day* turns from the death of a heroine to explore what for a writer remains no less critical, the demise of language. Her second novel, like her last, confronts the question of why words fail. In the spirit of D. H. Lawrence and those American writers she praises for daring to take liberties with the English language, she would have us recoil from words gone dead.⁵

At first reading *Night and Day* does not appear, I think, to be the sort of book in which such questions come to life. One less than sympathetic reviewer termed it "the dullest novel in the language," while a number of friendly critics considered the book to be undistinguished. E. M. Forster called it "an exercise in Classical realism," and Katherine Mansfield charged the novel with evading the central issues of postwar twentieth-century society.[6] More recently, Quentin Bell has persuasively argued that Woolf, recovering from a serious breakdown, intended it to be "a fairly pedestrian affair, . . . something which would not bring her too close to the abyss from which she had so recently emerged."[7] If in fact less successful than her other novels, and however "recuperative" it may have proved, *Night and Day* reveals sociological intentions that will continue to shape the thrust of her fiction. Its overriding purpose is to confront and resist the deadly proportion of outdated literary and social conventions.

When Lytton Strachey praised Woolf's use of dialogue, she responded with enthusiasm that this was one of her central aims in writing *Night and Day.* "I can't help thinking it's the problem, if one is to write novels at all," she wrote, concluding on the subject of genre with a telling aside: "which is a moot point."[8] The presumption might be that in choosing to highlight what people say to one another she evades the abyss, the reality of what remains unsaid and unmediated.

Discussing aspects of Jane Austen's art in terms that would appear to question her own earlier motives, Woolf speculates after reading *Persuasion* about the sort of novels its author might have written had she lived on. She discerns signs that Austen was on the verge of discovering a larger and more mysterious world: "She would have trusted less . . . to dialogue and more to reflection to give us a knowledge of her characters. . . . She would have devised a method, clear and composed as ever, but deeper and more suggestive, for conveying not only what people say, but what they leave unsaid; not only what they are, but what life is. She would have stood farther away from her characters, and seen them more as a group, less as individuals."[9]

If these words appear to confirm at least one of Mansfield's criticisms—"It is impossible to refrain from comparing *Night and Day* with the novels of Miss Austen," she wrote in her

review—the treatment of relationships in Woolf's novel invites some rather different literary comparisons. Again, *Women
in Love*, with its shifting deployment of allegiances, comes to
mind. Woolf, like Lawrence, expands our notion of sexual
roles at the same time that she conveys the limitations of
her characters' matrimonial expectations. Above all, it is the
abruptness of these narrative shifts that informs an important
aspect of their modernism. In Woolf such transitions emerge,
as I have argued, chiefly through the form of interruption.

At an important stage of *Night and Day*, a reservation arises
in Katharine Hilbery's mind, interrupting the course of events
that seems to be carrying her toward an inevitable marriage
with William Rodney. When pressed to explain her feelings,
she confesses that her misgivings, extending beyond the choice
of a spouse, encompass the very basis of love and marriage. No
less than Lawrence, Woolf celebrates language's capacity to
make feeling manifest. Even Rodney, in the midst of trying to
dissuade Katharine, senses with apprehension the change that
has come to characterize her deeper feelings once she has pronounced them. "Beneath her steady, exemplary surface ran a
vein of passion which seemed to him now perverse, now completely irrational." Contributing to his initial shock, we learn
that this depth of feeling "never took the normal channel of
glorification of him and his doings" (246).[10]

Where Katharine's analysis results in alienation—she no
longer thinks "like any other woman who is about to be married" (245) of house, husband, and sons—Rodney bluntly acknowledges the operative social structures that have formed
his consciousness of things. He even admits similar doubts: "I
assure you, Katharine, I've been through it all myself. At one
time I was always asking myself absurd questions which came
to nothing either. What you want, if I may say so, is some
occupation to take you out of yourself when this morbid mood
comes on" (245). The therapy he goes on to advocate as the
means of preserving one's sanity from the intrusion of disrup-

tive thoughts and passions is writing poetry. The comic element with which Woolf invests this theme is but one of many signs that she is developing new strategies.[11]

Katharine has not evaded poetry for want of a room of her own; it is rather that her taste is for the detached impersonality of mathematics and astronomy. Time at home, however, is spent largely in assisting her mother on the biography of a famous relative, the poet Richard Alardyce, and in helping with such domestic rituals as pouring tea. As the novel opens and Katharine presides over these rituals "for the six hundredth time, perhaps, without bringing into play any of her unoccupied faculties," she enjoys remaining aloofly silent; "she was evidently mistress of a situation which was familiar enough to her, and inclined to let it take its way" (9).

What emerges through the series of tea parties that fill Woolf's novels is that real talk seldom occurs, that people rarely say what they think, much less what they feel. The overriding intention seems rather to maintain some kind of verbal continuity, not an easy task in *Night and Day*, with new guests arriving sporadically in mid-sentence. Ralph Denham launches Woolf's plot by interrupting the "rounded structure" of Mr. Fortescue's words. The irony that Fortescue is an eminent novelist does not go unrecorded. Ralph's interruptions, in contrast with those of Terence Hewet, serve ultimately to widen the options of his fiancée.

Seated next to Katharine, Denham both interests and vexes her with his sustained silence following an initial discussion with Mr. Hilbery. Detecting "something hostile to her surroundings" in his resolute unwillingness to make small talk, she aggravates the situation by declining to employ "the usual feminine amenities." The combination of antagonism and attraction that characterizes their response to each other seems to anticipate the traditional love affair in the mold of *Pride and Prejudice*. Mrs. Hilbery rather unexpectedly extends the scenario by inviting her daughter to show their young guest the family relics. Through this "brilliant idea" she initiates what will become a widening breach in the continuity of matrimonial design, and the novel can be said to turn on her half-conscious impropriety. Her daughter, after all, is formally engaged to another man.

On Ralph's subsequent tour of the house, it is not so much what he says as what he does not say that continues to disconcert Katharine. His apparent lack of interest in her family history, evident whenever she pauses in her commentary, augments the tension. Aware of the difference in class that separates them, Ralph remains guardedly aloof. Where he could talk to her father more professionally on relatively equal terms, a growing sense of disparity complicates his relationship with Katharine. By not offering her the means of connecting him to the world she inhabits, he retains some vestige of independence. If the hint of sexual warfare does not excite Woolf, it nevertheless remains, as she perceives, a cornerstone of literary romance.

Ralph's breach of etiquette offends more than decorum. He seems to exist outside the boundaries of conventional behavior, and the inaccessibility of his mind occasions anxiety. When Katharine, like Hewet in *The Voyage Out*, feels impelled to grasp something tangible, she lists the details of his face, only to find each of her efforts collapsing into projections of her own derived expectations. With relief she falls back mechanically on prepared remarks about the family relics, thereby avoiding the spontaneity of a discussion that might lead her anywhere. Through this strategy she retains control.

The language of uninterrupted discourse in Woolf's novels tends to reinforce and incite "vanity, ostentation, self-assertion," and the compulsion to convert. Among the worst offenders is the college lecturer, whose format, she submits, is designed to eliminate reciprocity. On one occasion she speculates about more adventuresome forms of pedagogy: "Why not let them talk to you and listen to you, naturally and happily, on the floor? Why not create a new form of society founded on poverty and equality? Why not bring together people of all ages and both sexes and all shades of fame and obscurity so that they can talk, without mounting platforms or reading papers, or wearing expensive clothes or eating expensive food? . . . Why not abolish prigs and prophets? Why not invent human intercourse?"[12]

Ironically, it is such human intercourse that both Ralph and Katharine decline at the beginning of *Night and Day*. Antithetically, silence becomes the weapon through which Ralph hopes to move her: "He had the power to annoy his oblivious, supercilious hostess, if he could not impress her; though he would have preferred to impress her" (18). When he does speak, his words, inspired by the same impulse to triumph, take on a tone of finality that further impairs communication.

Katharine and Ralph next meet at Mary Datchett's party, where William Rodney is to lecture on "The Elizabethan Use of Metaphor." The expectation is for "a good solid paper, with plenty of quotations from the classics" (49). But the unfortunate Rodney, forced by his "impulsive stammering manner" to depart frequently from his prepared text or to misread it—at one point he turns over two pages at once—finds to his chagrin that "he had stirred his audience to a degree of animation quite remarkable in these gatherings" (53). As his talk ends, disastrously for him "in the middle of a sentence," it is the very loss of control that seems to engage his listeners: "Through his manner and his confusion of language there had emerged some passion of feeling which, as he spoke, formed in the majority of the audience a little picture or an idea which each now was eager to give expression to" (54). People reclining on mattresses are soon talking animatedly to those seated on chairs, all "in communication with each other." Rodney alone considers his performance a "ridiculous failure." Not until the end of the novel is he forced by circumstances to improvise once again. Frozen by decorum throughout his engagement to Katharine, he stammers his true feelings about Cassandra in a scene that recalls his state of mind at Mary's party, "like a speaker who has lost his notes" (497).

Like Rodney after the lecture, Ralph interprets his own performance at the Hilberys' as a failure to impress others, most notably Katharine, with his own superiority: "He was chafed by the memory of halting awkward sentences which had failed to give even the young woman with the sad, but inwardly ironical eyes a hint of his force" (23). Excited by Katharine's aloof independence, he daydreams that evening of making her "his new possession" in fantasy if not in fact. He finds himself reshaping her image to suit his "particular purpose," increasing her height and darkening her hair. "His most daring liberty was taken with her mind, which, for reasons of his own, he desired to be exalted and infallible" (24). Building to its hierarchical climax, the reverie ends as she descends from imperial eminence "to crown him with her approval" (25). Back home in Highgate, Ralph's sense of injured pride is reactivated by the morbid thought that even in his own family "he was a person of no importance" (26).

The unexpected appearance of Katharine at Mary's party supplies him with another chance. Choosing his words carefully, he approaches her after the lecture with a prepared question on a topic Mrs. Hilbery had introduced at tea. He is moved by the impulse to dominate, however, and his words find little room to grow: "Ralph could think of nothing further to say; but could one have stripped off his mask of flesh, one would have seen that his will-power was rigidly set upon a single object—that Miss Hilbery should obey him. He wished her to stay there until, by some measures not yet apparent to him, he had conquered her interest" (61). When he does speak again, his tone is painfully defensive as he mistakes Katharine's benign comment—"Nothing interesting ever happens to me"—to be directed at him: "I think you make a system of saying disagreeable things, Miss Hilbery. . . . I suppose

54

it's one of the characteristics of your class. They never talk seriously to their inferiors" (62).

Her remarks have not all been so casual. She discusses vocations with Mary, and her sense that she has accomplished
little in life brings on a revealing slip of the tongue: "'Don't
you see how many different things these people care about?
And I want to beat them down—I only mean,' she corrected
herself, 'that I want to assert myself, and it's difficult, if one
hasn't a profession'" (58). The merging here, however momentary, of self-assertion and subjugation suggests that women and
men are equally susceptible to the dynamics of their age.
While such comments lead Mary to term her new friend "an
egoist" (60), she too, in the course of the novel, gives way to
domineering impulses.

The mood of "gay tolerance and general friendliness" that
has made the party a successful affair proves less congenial
for Ralph and to some extent for Rodney. When the random
interruption of someone selling an opera ticket finally deprives Ralph of any opportunity to isolate Katharine, "the
completeness with which Katharine parted from him, without any attempt to finish her sentence" (63), offends something more than the propriety of language. As she leaves with
Rodney, Ralph finds himself driven to pursue them clandestinely through the dark streets of London. Like every romantic compulsion, the enterprise is purely self-indulgent.

Walking some distance behind them, Ralph cannot hear
Rodney intransigently defining his fiancée in terms of the
imperatives of marriage—"You're nothing at all without it;
you're only half alive" (66). Nor can he know that these words
serve once again to connect him with Katharine: "'I've been
told a great many unpleasant things about myself to-night,'
Katharine stated, without attending to him. 'Mr. Denham
seems to think it his mission to lecture me, though I hardly
know him'" (67).

Rodney defends Ralph as a man who "cares, naturally, for

the right sort of things" while asserting a sense of common cause—"We may lecture you till we're blue in the face." Thus it should not surprise us to find that Woolf soon pairs them. However different in tastes and social background Ralph and Rodney may be, we perceive how fully a common background shapes their behavior. Reading in Rodney's flat after meeting him on a street corner, Ralph feels his peace of mind restored by the enclosing serenity of Rodney's books, "orderly as regiments of soldiers" (73). Like an old philosophical discussion he has just renewed with Harry Sandys, the familiar passage he reads from Sir Thomas Browne revives memories of a collegiality free of disruptive intrusions, free of argumentative women.

Art offers the characters of *Night and Day* ample opportunity to withdraw from life's inconclusiveness. Standing before the Elgin Marbles, Mary finds herself swept into another world, "so secure did she feel with these silent shapes" (82). While Woolf appreciates the effect of such beautiful objects, she undercuts an aesthetic experience she feels to be sustained by protective impulses. Art's function is to vex as well as to celebrate. Mary allows the British Museum to shelter her from the burden of facing other people, most particularly Ralph, whom she thinks she loves. As she wanders aimlessly through the galleries in a state of detached enjoyment, daydreams of him dominate her mind. It is an engraving of Assyrian bulls that reveals the substance of her reveries: "She conjured up a scene of herself on a camel's back, in the desert, while Ralph commanded a whole tribe of natives. 'That is what you can do,' she went on, moving on to the next statue. 'You always make people do what you want'" (83). Involvement in Women's Suffrage does not affect the politics of her own sexuality.

A captive of no-less-debilitating compulsions, Katharine finds the prospect of marriage to Rodney attractive because it offers resolution if not independence. The thought of marrying him "appeared to loom through the mist like solid ground"

(124), something firm and reliable like the mathematical equations she prefers to imaginative literature. On a sexual level she responds to Rodney's strength with both maternal protectiveness and Lawrentian passion. She watches him heave open a rusty gate without apparent effort, and "the virility of this deed impressed her. . . . She felt a sudden concern for this power running to waste on her account, which, combined with a desire to keep possession of that strangely attractive masculine power, made her rouse herself from her torpor" (241–42). As in Woolf's first novel, no characters seem free from male imperatives. The same may be said of the author, in company with the readers she would reach.

What emerges most poignantly from Woolf's description of society's games is a growing apprehension in the minds of her players that to discard old answers is to remain empty-handed. Katharine's decision not to marry Rodney shocks him less than the realization that she does so with no concrete alternative in mind. Informed that "she did not want to marry any one" (242), Rodney continues with some desperation to find more rational explanations:

"You love some one else?" he cut her short.
"Absolutely no one."
"Henry?" he demanded. . . . "There is some one," he persisted.
(242)

At stake is the perpetuation of an accessibly predetermined future he shares with other men, namely, the expectation of fulfillment in marriage. Without such agreement Rodney loses his function. His admonition tempts Katharine to reconsider her duty to history if not to himself: "In a flash the conviction that not to care is the uttermost sin of all stamped itself upon her inmost thought; and she felt herself branded for ever. . . . Very well; she would submit, as her mother and her aunt and most women, perhaps, had submitted" (243).

In the absence of Katharine, Ralph turns to Mary to relieve

a similar sense of impending emptiness. Looking to her for pity and self-assurance, he anxiously creates a fantasy of the protective mother ministering to his every need:

> He would have liked to lay his head on her shoulder and sob, while she parted his hair with her fingers and soothed him and said: "There, there. Don't cry! Tell me why you're crying—"; and they would clasp each other tight, and her arms would hold him like his mother's. He felt that he was very lonely, and that he was afraid of the other people in the room. (228–29)

The intimacy Ralph craves from Mary is an extension of his need for protection "against the ghost of Katharine" (254), whose ungraspable reality continues to impede "the sensible life." When Mary will not help him by accepting his marriage proposal, Ralph angrily relegates her to that same "insanely jumbled muddle of a world" (253) whose sole function, it seems, is to defeat his intentions: "He had failed with Katharine, and now he had failed with Mary" (250). His grievance over being "trapped by the illogicality of human life" masks a deeper fear of nothingness, which is to say, of being left alone. As Mary is about to get up, "an instinctive desire to prevent her from leaving the room made Ralph . . . begin pacing up and down the nearly empty kitchen, checking his desire, each time he reached the door, to open it and step out into the garden" (253). With no prospective bride to sustain him, the frightening revelation that he must begin chaotically from nothing becomes, inadvertently, the basis of Ralph's own liberation: "He felt himself thrown back to the beginning of life again, where everything has yet to be won. . . . He was no longer certain that he would triumph" (254). He looks into the dying fire, and "it seemed to him that he had been defeated not so much by Mary as by life itself" (254). The most casual reader of Woolf anticipates that Ralph will benefit from such existential deprivation.

If Ralph's proposal is unsettling for Mary, so too is the appearance of Katharine at her flat later in the day. Mary is becoming absorbed again in an article she had been writing on democracy, after having spent tumultuous hours largely thinking about Ralph. She finds that her tolerance for interruption remains low: "'Why can't they leave me alone?' she thought bitterly, connecting Katharine and Ralph in a conspiracy to take from her even this hour of solitary study, even this poor little defence against the world" (268).

Mary, however, no less than Ralph, depends on Katharine to sustain a pattern of grievance. When Katharine, aware that she is unwelcome, prepares to leave, the impulse to detain her becomes irresistible: "Katharine was not to be allowed to go, to disappear into the free, happy world of irresponsible individuals." She must be informed of the right way "to feel" if not to think. Mary's opportunity to lead and to proselytize arises as her guest acknowledges her ignorance concerning the facts of social injustice to women: "She had Katharine at her mercy; she could, if she liked, discharge upon her head wagon-loads of revolting proof of the state of things ignored by the casual, the amateur, the looker-on, the cynical observer of life at a distance" (271).

Earlier that morning, the preset work routine of the Suffrage Office—Mary's employer, Mr. Clacton, termed it "the system" (256)—had helped restore her self-esteem. By the day's end she had been arguing with similar masculine ferocity—"helping the people of England," as her boss put it, "to think rightly" (257)—while becoming correspondingly "imperious and dominating" in her treatment of his associate, Mrs. Seal.

The fact that almost all the characters of *Night and Day* display such proselytizing proclivities is no doubt one reason Leonard Woolf termed its philosophy "melancholy." The charge prompted his wife to reply: "If one is to deal with people on a large scale & say what one thinks, how can one avoid melancholy? I don't admit to being hopeless though—only the spectacle is a profoundly strange one; & as the current answers don't do, one has to grope for a new one; & the process of discarding the old, when one is by no means certain what to put in their place, is a sad one."[13]

Her comments on "current answers" pertain both to matrimonial conventions—a central theme in four of her first five novels—and to the rhetoric of fiction. In each case the hope of something new requires readjustments. Like the Russian novelists she admired, Woolf invites her reader into an equally inconclusive world where nothing is final and "nothing is rightly held together." The important concept once again is "rightly": "Dashed to the crest of the waves, bumped and battered on the stones at the bottom, it is difficult for an English reader to feel at ease. The process to which he is accustomed in his own literature is reversed."[14]

The quality of this reversal frequently involves a suspension of sequence, as when Katharine, in the earliest instance, breaks off displaying the family relics to watch Ralph hold a small volume of Alardyce's poems in his hands: "She appeared to be considering many things. She had forgotten her duties" (18). For a few moments at least, they are moved to address one another. So too Rodney's inadvertent pauses brought the words of his lecture to life.

For either selfish or disinterested reasons—it is unclear which—Mary is on the verge of attacking Katharine, but finds herself pausing instead. A short, direct sentence highlights this unanticipated shift of intentions: "And yet she hesitated" (271). The act, or more aptly nonact, of hesitation occasions a change in the tone more than in the content of their words. It is as if Mary, relinquishing power, were allowing their respective feelings to emerge more freely and fluidly. While Katharine's ideas continue to evoke disagreement and even anger, the annoyance that had marked Mary's tone is gone. Soon the two women are groping to share unguarded thoughts with each other, exposing themselves without fear of change. What ensues is a sense of liberation for words as well as personality. "I find talking so difficult," Mary confesses more openly: "I should shut it up in my mind. Yes, that's what I'm afraid of. Going about with something in my mind all my life that never changes. I find it so difficult to change" (277).

Reciprocity, like change, involves a loss of stability and control. Mary understands that "her clear vision of the way to face life was rendered tremulous and uncertain, because another was witness of it" (277). From such doubt, however, there emerges a new basis for relationship. As Katharine stands thoughtfully by the fireplace, a still and solemn presence who a moment earlier had reminded Mary of Ralph, Mary allows "something unfamiliar" to break through her preconceptions. She is inspired once more to pause, and her thoughts emerge "without bitterness. She was surprised by her own quiet and confidence. She came back silently, and sat once more by Katharine's side. Mary had no wish to speak. In the silence she seemed to have lost her isolation" (278).

The mysterious way silence penetrates and authenticates the thrust of human speech is nowhere more evident in *Night and Day* than later that evening when Ralph discloses to Katharine the true state of his feelings for her. The scene occurs, predictably enough, near the river, a setting he chooses to avoid the interruptions that have marked each of their earlier interviews. The language through which he means to make Katharine "either justify her dominance or renounce it" is once again carefully choreographed: "He knew perfectly well what he wished to say, and had arranged not only the substance, but the order in which he was to say it" (296).

Walking by the river, however, he is distracted by details wholly irrelevant either to this scenario or to his image of Katharine. Her skirt blowing in the wind, the waving of feathers in her hat, move him continually off the point. Ironically, "the longer they walked thus alone, the more he was disturbed by the sense of her actual presence" (296). The silence, prolonged on his part by these distractions and on hers by Mary's disclosures, exerts at first a salutary influence: "'It's quieter by the river,' he said, and instantly he crossed over. 'I want to ask you merely this,' he began. But he paused so long that she could see his head against the sky; the slope of his thin cheek and his large, strong nose were clearly marked against it. While he paused, words that were quite different from those he intended to use presented themselves" (296–97).

The unpremeditated sentiments that next roll from his lips resound like a catalogue of romantic clichés: I dream of you; I think only of you; you are the most beautiful and truest thing in the world; life would be impossible without you. His unguarded feelings, openly expressed, echo the words of all rejected lovers from Shakespeare's Orlando to the young men Woolf heard more than once confess the suffering of unrequited love.* Ralph concludes his tormented adoration with what the reader of romantic fiction must construe to be a compelling non sequitur: "I am not telling you that I am in love with you. I am not in love with you." The statement is made with the same candor that has marked his preceding acknowledgments.

Katharine, who throughout this scene feels she is overhearing words meant for Mary, replies with less bewilderment than we might expect: "I didn't think that." What transpires in their dialogue is a discourse whose Bloomsbury inflection is unmistakable, undertaken with both passion and a sense of mutual concern:

> "I have not spoken a word to you that I do not mean," he added.
> "Tell me then what it is that you mean," she said at length.
> As if obeying a common instinct, they both stopped and, bending slightly over the balustrade of the river, looked into the flowing water. (298)

*Katharine is in fact no Rosalind, despite the repeated effort to describe her in these terms. Early in the novel Rodney suggests that she has no need to read Shakespeare since "she *is* Rosalind" (175), and later, Mrs. Hilbery, fantasizing about a future playhouse devoted to the Bard, speculates on her daughter's part: "You'd be Rosalind—but you've a dash of the old nurse in you" (306).

A "common instinct" to pause—it occurs twice in this scene—softens each inclination to proselytize and moves Katharine and Ralph to revise their opinions:

> "I thought that you criticised me—perhaps disliked me. I thought of you as a person who judges — "
> "No; I'm a person who feels," he said. (300)

As in the earlier scene between Mary and Katharine, the change in tone seems more important than the content of their language. Although Katharine listens to the detailed account of Ralph's family with such care "that she could have passed an examination in it, . . . she was no more listening to it than she was counting the paving-stones at her feet" (300). The pleasure she feels is not over the recognition of Ralph's true feelings, but over the realization that he has allowed her for the first time to be herself: "He certainly did not hinder any flight she might choose to make" (301). She is free to indulge the fancy of existing in two worlds—one walking with Ralph by the river, the other in her own dimension of algebraic signs and symbols. Yet "that her condition was due to him, or to anything that he had said, she had no consciousness at all" (301).

Despite Ralph's recurrently acquisitive needs, a pronounced change in behavior has occurred. In contrast to his former daydreams of Katharine, his mood now holds "none of the restlessness or feverish desire to add one delight to another" (301). More important, his sense of pleasure, rooted in the present, makes him receptive to a number of realities beyond his control. The intimacy they have begun to create is not insular and does not depend for its survival on the exclusion of the world outside. The generally disruptive "increase of noise" and the sounds of traffic interrupting conversation serve to extend rather than to end his expectations: "The vistas which opened before him seemed to have no perceptible end. . . . It was a mood that took such clear-eyed account of the conditions of human life that he was not disturbed in the least by the gliding presence of a taxicab, and without agitation he perceived that Katharine was conscious of it also" (301).

The description anticipates the taxicab in *A Room of One's Own*, which "glided off as if it were swept on by the current elsewhere." There as here a sense of what is most real grows mysteriously out of its antithesis: "Nothing came down the street; nobody passed. A single leaf detached itself from the plane tree at the end of the street, and in that pause and suspension fell. Somehow it was like a signal falling, a signal pointing to a force in things which one had overlooked."[15] The inclination to question society's fundamental values emerges increasingly for Woolf's protagonists in such moments of suspension.

Ralph, however, is not ready for this confrontation. Once Katharine has engaged the cab and left him, a galling sense of deprivation returns. Only the hierarchical thought of Rodney's comparative inferiority—"that gibbering ass with the face of a monkey on an organ"—serves to fill the void and restore a valorizing self-confidence. Become once again the romantic lover, Ralph rushes home to write Katharine a long letter, calling her back to singularity, imploring her not to desert him, "not to do what would destroy for ever the one beauty, the one truth, the one hope" (303).

For Katharine and Ralph to connect requires a change in the way they perceive their surroundings as well as each other. Setting them next in London's most diverse park, Woolf recreates the ambience of her recently published story "Kew Gardens." There a rich array of merging sights and sounds once more affects Ralph's needs and expectations; "the very trees and the green merging into the blue distance became symbols of the vast external world" (331). He remains for a time "arbitrary, hot-tempered and imperious" in Katharine's eyes—"He had asked her to come to Kew to advise him; he then told her that he had settled the question already" (335)—but under the impact of Kew such tendencies dissolve. Soon we find him recommending an experiment, a new

compact of friendship in which each party, retaining independence, remains under no obligation to the other. The nature of what is to come, like their walk through Kew, is left
largely undefined. That love and marriage are but one of many
possibilities that might evolve from such a contract offends
society no less than Rodney. Free of the marriage context,
Katharine comes alive to Ralph more fully than ever, and in
her own way.

Again that afternoon, when she leaves him alone, he does
not feel impelled to retain or possess her. The incident marks
two important realizations: that her being is in no way dependent on his needs and expectations, and that he loves her.
The order of priorities is central: "He forgot her absence, he
thought it of no account whether she married him or another;
nothing mattered, save that she should exist, and that he
should love her" (386).

From this point on in the narrative, Ralph and Katharine
largely desist from their guarded predilection to fathom each
other. If, as Katharine puts it somewhat later, "we see each
other only now and then," the impact of what occurs between
such moments becomes suddenly more critical for both. Perception, mirroring life, is an aspect of time as well as of space.
Resisting the mutual temptation when Ralph calls on her to
describe him, Katharine proclaims instead Woolf's existential
aesthetic: "'Tell me what you see,' he urged. But she could
not reduce her vision to words, since it was no single shape
coloured upon the dark, but rather a general excitement, an
atmosphere" (422). Her words recall the author's subsequent
description of the mythical Mrs. Brown and of the modern
writer's obligation to "steep oneself in her atmosphere."[16]

The unsettled nature of their growing affection for each
other appears in stark contrast to the expectations of Katharine's parents and to the conventional form of loving that Rodney and his newly chosen fiancée, Cassandra, choose. Though
convention—"the proper way to behave," in Mr. Hilbery's

words (475)—ensures a common ending for all potentially disruptive impulses, it is precisely a fashionable marriage Katharine and Ralph resist. True to a new sense of complexity, they will not reduce their future to one thing. Since "marriage" remains the enemy, Katharine's first impulse is to live without it: "Why, after all, isn't it perfectly possible to live together without being married?" (482) Though their resolution proves finally less extreme, it nevertheless affirms Mary's heresy when she decides antithetically not to marry: "There are different ways of loving" (447).

The confusion of Katharine's emotions reflects more than a capitulation to love. When we recall that this novel is set around 1910, it should not surprise us that Woolf conveys the variations of the new age or that Katharine, like the heroines who follow her, should feel and celebrate this ambience of change. The streets of London occasion both a widening and deepening of Katharine's liberated instincts: "The great torrent of vans and carts was sweeping down Kingsway; pedestrians were streaming in two currents along the pavements. She stood fascinated at the corner. The deep roar filled her ears; the changing tumult had the inexpressible fascination of varied life" (439).

That she expresses an exhilarating sense of anonymity shortly before telling Ralph that she loves him still further reflects her authenticity: "The blend of daylight and of lamplight made her an invisible spectator, just as it gave the people who passed her a semi-transparent quality. . . . She stood unobserved and absorbed, glorying openly in the rapture that had run subterraneously all day" (439). True to her own feelings, she sheds, as Rodney cannot, society's prescriptive roles. Woolf reflects this openness in her diary some few years after *Night and Day* appeared in 1919: "I become anonymous, a person who writes for the love of it." [17]

Rodney's aesthetics remain comically absolutist. "Have you ever noticed," Cassandra asks Katharine, "how exquisitely he

66

finishes everything? Look at the address on that envelope. Every letter is perfect" (433). The lack of proper ending in art and life strikes him, as it does the equally good-natured Mrs. Hilbery, as inevitably unattractive. The thought of Katharine living unmarried with Ralph Denham is as "dreadfully ugly" to her as the algebraic formulas her daughter finds so pleasing.

Katharine's mother hovers over her with no less force than the outraged Mr. Hilbery. Through her influence Ralph and Katharine are brought back into the fold, although their continued resistance is evident to her as well as to her husband. Serving as the "ambassador" of love, and with a magical wave of her arm, she resolves the contradictions that threaten to prevent this festive comedy from achieving its intended climax. For Katharine as perhaps for Woolf, authority still resides in the controlling mediation of matrons such as she. Not until *To the Lighthouse* do the Mrs. Ramsays lose that sustaining influence Woolf seems compelled to build into the concluding pages of *Night and Day:* "Katharine looked at her as if, indeed, she were some magician. Once more she felt that instead of being a grown woman, used to advise and command, she was only a foot or two raised above the long grass and the little flowers and entirely dependent upon the figure of indefinite size whose head went up into the sky, whose hand was in hers, for guidance" (485).

Even so, her successful intervention cannot obscure the feeling that such resolutions are at best pro forma. As her husband presides with restored urbanity at the dinner table—"He poured out wine; he bade Denham help himself" (501)—the recollection of his fears that "civilisation had been very profoundly and unpleasantly overthrown that evening" (477) informs the reader's mind if not his own.

Ralph and Katharine, committed as they are to an "impending future, vast, mysterious, infinitely stored with undeveloped shapes" (493), resist by all indications what their author will describe irreverently in *Mrs. Dalloway* as society's call for Proportion and Conversion. However tentatively their story ends, it retains an inflection of hope: "Together they groped in this difficult region, where the unfinished, the unfulfilled, the unwritten, the unreturned, came together in their ghostly way and wore the semblance of the complete and the satisfactory. The future emerged more splendid than ever from this construction of the present" (506).

Chapter Four

ON THE
MARGINS OF CONSCIOUSNESS
Jacob's Room

Woolf's first diary entry regarding *Jacob's Room* envisions "a
new form for a new novel," one thing opening out of another.
While her words express the need to "enclose the human
heart," she stresses in this early conception an alternate approach, "entirely different this time: no scaffolding; scarcely a
brick to be seen; all crepuscular." Broadening her canvas, she
intends to allow room for both "gaiety" and "inconsequence."[1]

One comes to appreciate in *Jacob's Room* and the novels
that follow the degree to which a contiguous, often inconsequential setting determines our perception of character. The
defining features of Woolf's personae unfold sporadically with
each new intrusion from the external world. Building on the
method introduced in "Kew Gardens" and "The Mark on the
Wall," in this, her first experimental novel, she uses interruption to describe and define the condition of confronting
others.

Jacob's Room represents Woolf's first sustained assault on the omniscient narrator. Stripped of scaffolding, her narrator finds no Archimedean point from which to appraise, much less to move, the world. If for one moment the protagonist of her story appears discernibly real, "the moment after," the narrator quickly adds, "we know nothing about him. Such is the manner of our seeing" (72).[2] All she can record is the unending flow of things. Acknowledging the bewildering variety of human beings, she feels compelled to leave out virtually no external detail, to include what may appear to be the most marginal of incidents. Woolf emphasizes that the reality she confronts is largely ignored by such contemporary writers as Arnold Bennett, who chastised her for creating characters in *Jacob's Room* that "do not vitally survive in the mind."* Replying in perhaps her best-known essay, "Mr. Bennett and Mrs. Brown," Woolf creates the fictional Mrs. Brown, "an old lady of unlimited capacity and infinite variety," whose character varies according to the social context in which she is seen. The essay concludes with Woolf's plea that her readers resist those works of literature that ignore the decisively modern vision of human character: "You have gone to bed at night bewildered by the complexity of your feelings. In one day thousands of ideas have coursed through your brains; thousands of emotions have met, collided, and disappeared in astonishing disorder. Nevertheless, you allow the writers to palm off upon you a version of all this, an image of Mrs. Brown, which has no likeness to that surprising apparition whatsoever."[3]

In his review of *Jacob's Room*, Arnold Bennett had complained that writers such as Woolf were more interested in "states of society" than in individuals. Woolf responds that the reality of an individual is in fact determined by surround-

*Robin Majumdar and Allen McLaurin, eds., *Virginia Woolf: The Critical Heritage* (London, 1975), p. 113. But compare Desmond MacCarthy, describing Jacob: "This blank void is circumscribed with such precise lines, shapes, colours that I receive therefrom a kind of substance and reality." *Criticism* (London, 1932), p. 173.

ing social details. She goes on to remind him that it was the great Russian novelists who undermined older notions of character. Raskolnikov, Mishkin, Stavrogin, and Alyosha "are characters without any features at all. We go down into them as we descend into some enormous cavern."[4] Woolf invokes the same image in describing her own literary discovery: "How I dig out beautiful caves behind my characters." "Characters," her diary adds a few days later, "are to be merely views: personality must be avoided at all costs. . . . Directly you specify hair, age, etc something frivolous, or irrelevant, gets into the book."[5] Although such comments look toward her next novel, *Mrs. Dalloway*, they apply even more strikingly to *Jacob's Room*, where figures like Jacob and Betty Flanders emerge from the text largely without face, figure or, for that matter, chronological past.

Friends as well as adversaries, reacting similarly to an absence of defining features in the characters of *Jacob's Room*, appear to have missed her underlying intention. Leonard Woolf's initial criticism is recorded in her diary: "He says that the people are ghosts; he says it is very strange: I have no philosophy of life he says; my people are puppets, moved hither & thither by fate."[6] For Rebecca West, Jacob's very existence seemed a matter of "hearsay," and Frank Swinnerton, like Bennett, found it difficult to remember any character at all. Directing our attention to the background of discourse, Woolf has begun openly to advocate a more sociological perspective. Simultaneously this strategy would lure her readers into a less prescriptive state of mind.

Jacob's Room opens on a Cornish beach. Betty, writing a letter to Captain Barfoot, finds that her gold-tipped pen has stuck at the end of a sentence, making a blot on the paper. The pale blue ink continues to spread, causing the period to lose its form and significance. Momentarily suspended between words, Betty finds her thoughts slipping back in time to the accident that killed her husband, Seabrook, two years earlier. In a novel full of punctiliously described details, this is one of the few pieces of chronology the narrator supplies about Betty with any exactness. Even her age is given somewhat vaguely as "half-way between forty and fifty" (15).

Left to raise three young children with no heroes in sight—Captain Barfoot may suggest romance, but he will fulfill a different narrative function—Betty is preoccupied with daily life. She is introduced to us through a series of mundane events: we see her writing a letter home, addressing the envelope, searching her bag for a postage stamp, voicing concern over Jacob's whereabouts, wondering what to cook for dinner. These minor details invite readers to confront, if not to share, activities that many consider for the most part irrelevant. However, such undramatic moments inevitably interrupt narrative expectations even more fully in *Jacob's Room* than they did in *Night and Day*.

Betty's simple actions overlap and fuse with an impinging world the narrator is quick to honor and extend: Mr. Connor's little yacht; the lighthouse; Archer's voice complaining that Jacob "doesn't want to play"; Charles Steele painting Betty's picture. Nothing seems fixed, least of all Betty Flanders. Pressing her heels deep into the sand as if at odds with the sea, she seems intent on withstanding an impending fluidity that affects her mind no less than the reader's. Her "great experiment," namely, "coming so far with young children," appears an act of folly. "There's no man to help with the perambulator. And Jacob is such a handful" (11). On the beach, the act of writing constitutes for Betty a means of modifying the effect of her experiment. Seeking metaphorically to stem the tides, she tries through her disingenuous words to Captain Barfoot to convince them both that in actuality everything is satisfactorily arranged.

The novel begins at the moment Betty's pen sticks, and this sense of arrangement collapses. The disruption, stirring recollections of Seabrook's death, simultaneously invites chaos. As the ink blot spreads and her tears distort her vision of things, the surrounding world slips momentarily from her grasp: "The entire bay quivered; the lighthouse wobbled; and she had the illusion that the mast of Mr. Connor's little yacht was bending like a wax candle in the sun" (7). Blinking her eyes, she regains control of things. Intent on establishing her place as a mother since she is no longer a wife, Betty follows "the old road to the old end."[7] She has, it would appear, no other way to turn.

Though the need to find Jacob, get the children home, and prepare food seems reasonable enough, Betty pursues such duties compulsively. As a consequence, all sense of life outside her own intentions appears suddenly to threaten her. Even the waves at sunset, and "this astonishing agitation and vitality of colour," occasion thoughts "of responsibility and danger" (11). Walking over the beach, "clutching her parasol, holding Archer's hand" (10), she struggles to keep her faculties centered on one thing. The continuity she would sustain—a world of uninterrupted moments—constitutes for Woolf a familiar temptation. The old story she recounts to Archer on the beach about how Mr. Curnow lost an eye supplies, like the structure of her letters, that very "scaffolding" of Western culture Woolf seeks to rearrange.

In those rare instances when Betty relaxes control, the narrator extends the margins of her consciousness. One such instance occurs as Betty acknowledges having forgotten something she was to do before dinner: "And who shall deny that this blankness of mind, when combined with profusion, mother wit, old wives' tales, haphazard ways, moments of astonishing daring, humour, and sentimentality—who shall deny that in these respects every woman is nicer than any man?" (11) Whether "this blankness" is in fact a creation of the narrator's often exuberant imagination or an accurate rendering of the state of Betty's mind remains disturbingly unclear.

A similar obfuscation takes place some weeks later as Betty stands before her husband's tombstone in Scarborough. The inscription—"Merchant of this city"—suddenly impresses her (or is it the narrator?) as absurdly inappropriate. The thought that "she had to call him something [as] an example for the boys" seems her own, since it extends an identifiably maternal duty. But the following impassioned question—"Had he, then, been nothing?" (16)—hangs unplaced between two voices. Here, as elsewhere, Woolf opposes the reader's inclination to isolate and fix the speaker. Instead we are urged to revise our manner of seeing and of knowing. Events that barely touch Betty's mind remain in some mysterious way constituents of her being. One is led to assume that at any moment her more personal vision of things may expand to include a conjoining world she shares in common with others, a world accessible, moreover, only through a combination of perspectives.

On the whole, Betty is unwilling to revise the contours of her daily life. Despite her trip to the seaside, she proves no more capable of innovation than Lily Briscoe at the dinner table with Charles Tansley, a fact that in either case we do not really censure. The pressures to conform are too strong. Intent on preserving those traditional values through which her children may survive and prosper, Betty falls back on the only method she knows. Her instruction to the three boys as they climb up the hill from the beach expresses metaphorically the narrowness of her options: "Don't lag, boys. You've got nothing to change into" (11).

Throughout her exclusions we are reminded of that profusion of impinging sights and sounds waiting to enter and enlarge her senses. Back in Scarborough, seated at the top of Dods Hill, she appears too busy stitching her son's trousers to allow her eyes to wander over the scene below. The narrator interjects that she "should have noted" the myriad surrounding details: houses, moors, clouds, pleasure boats, banjos, flowerbeds, bonnets. But Betty is not unique. While the people below are at play, they, too, seem unaware of the richness of their surrounding world. Reduced to an impervious singleness of purpose, "the pale girls, the old widow lady, the three Jews lodging in the same boarding-house, the dandy, the major, the horse-dealer and the gentleman of independent means, all wore the same blurred, drugged expression" (18).

A sense of inevitability and entrapment marks Betty's friends and neighbors as well. Barfoot, married to a woman he cannot love, limps punctually to have tea with Mrs. Flanders, while leaving his invalid wife trapped at home in her bath chair. Mrs. Jarvis, the clergyman's wife, walks the moors in desperation, seeking a freedom she can neither feel nor define. Betty's life remains, as we have seen, submerged in the needs of her children. Uninterrupted routines lull them, like the pier walkers, ever more deeply into sleepy acquiescence. Predisposed to avoid disruptive experience, they rarely if ever venture from goals others have established for them. Somewhat later, in the streets of London, the narrator extends the theme to include a larger social reality, expressing the malaise: "As frequent as street corners in Holborn are these chasms in the continuity of our ways. Yet we keep straight on" (96).

In *Jacob's Room* even children seem disinclined to relax their hold on things. Lytton Strachey's charge that its author had succumbed to romantic instincts seems misapplied, at least in this regard.[8] Jacob's early explorations, while suffused with innocent exuberance, reflect what is also for Woolf a no doubt socially derived impulse to possess each new object on the beach. First the large rock, one of many that "emerge from the sand like something primitive" (9), moves him as it might any Western child to mount and to grasp its treasure. Plunging his hand into the small tidal pool at the top—the verb anticipates "the beak of brass" passage in *To the Lighthouse*—a younger Mr. Ramsay, perhaps, extracts his trophy. The sexual parallel is compelling. The first of many peaks that he will conquer in his short life, this small triumph makes him feel "rather heroic."

A few moments later, when he has lost sight of his mother—the image of her he has discerned by the sea turns out to be another rock—a white and shiny bone lying some distance away proves an alternative means of self-realization. Holding the skull in his arms, Jacob discovers the next best thing to being found and protected. He has learned like his mother to fix his attention on one subject.

In the society Woolf's novels document, intelligence is described as this process of exclusion, the ability to focus the mind on a single matter. If children, like women and narrators, display at times a certain preference for digression, it falls largely on men and their institutions to ensure that education modifies such tendencies, especially in young men destined, as their sisters are not, to rule.

At first glance, Cambridge seems to invite an unstructured state of mind. Sitting near the river after a prosaic luncheon at his tutor's home, Jacob, now a young man, is observed slipping into a world of his own. In fact, this need for escape is occasioned more by the nature of the subjects discussed than by the dullness of the proceedings. "Summing up his discomfort" later, Jacob reveals an early disposition to resist new ideas as well as an older generation: "Such a thing to believe in—Shaw and Wells and the serious sixpenny weeklies! What were they after, scrubbing and demolishing, these elderly people? Had they never read Homer, Shakespeare, the Elizabethans? He saw it clearly outlined against the feelings he drew from youth and natural inclination" (35). Jacob's notions about politics and literature are impervious to influence or to change.[9] Filled with boyish confidence, at the Plumers' he is as certain about his tastes as he is about his identity: "I am what I am, and intend to be it" (36). His tutor's wife, con-

Jacob's Room

fessing her own incapacity to come quickly to the truth, draws the brunt of his scorn.

As we have seen, narrative interruption is one device Woolf employs to counter human egotism, the tendency to regard one's insight and utterance with finality. Disposed to reduce other people to his own contours, Jacob, at the Plumers', remains callously indifferent to the social forces that have shaped their values. However sound his critique of what Woolf termed in *Night and Day* "the mechanism of behaviour," it remains for the narrator to intrude, albeit omnisciently, with a feminist aside. If Mrs. Plumer has given way to mechanical routine, it is for good reasons: "How could she do other than grow up cheese-paring, ambitious, with an instinctively accurate notion of the rungs of the ladder and an ant-like assiduity in pushing George Plumer ahead of her to the top of the ladder?" (34)

She goes on to elaborate those unstated doubts Jacob's hostess has presumably suppressed for the sake of her sanity: "What was at the top of the ladder? A sense that all the rungs were beneath one apparently; since by the time that George Plumer became Professor of Physics, or whatever it might be, Mrs. Plumer could only be in a condition to cling tight to her eminence, peer down at the ground, and goad her two plain daughters to climb the rungs of the ladder" (34–35).

While one may fail to see the deprivations that form Betty's myopic view of life, here the narrowness of women's choices is made acutely clear to the reader if not to Jacob. He is soon immersed in the "Biographies of Great Men" (39); his "extravagant enthusiasm" will not extend to underprivileged women, particularly if they are middle-aged and not notably attractive. Mrs. Plumer and her uncharismatic husband are more than they appear, but not to a bored young man whose confidence in his own attributes was never higher.

Jacob's custom following Sunday luncheons, we learn, is to eradicate "this same shock-horror-discomfort" by a trip to the river, where the natural surroundings rejuvenate him through a similar process of exclusion. Nature reflects and reinforces the sense of self he has retained from the past, more specifically from childhood recollections of the sort just described. Now as then, he draws from objects like the sheep skull a sense of wholeness and "steady certainty" (36). While the narrator (here more the romantic than her author) revels in his attractive exuberance, we are invited to perceive how Jacob has expunged other people from his vision as thoroughly on the river as he has at the Plumers'.

It is a different aspect of Cambridge that enlists Jacob's sympathies and ironically the narrator's as well. As he sits in King's College Chapel, swept up by the martial rhythms of the church service, his impressions merge once more with a narrative voice: "What sculptured faces, what certainty, authority controlled by piety, although great boots march under the gowns. In what orderly procession they advance" (32). And since order in Cambridge reflects a fusion of mind and ritual, so the rhythm of Professor Huxtable's thoughts as he reads reenacts the military cadence of the church service: "As his eye goes down the print, what a procession tramps through the corridors of his brain, orderly, quick-stepping . . . as the march goes on" (40).

Everything appears "upright"; the thick wax candles never bend, the young men in white gowns walk with esprit and confidence, "buttressing human faith." Not surprisingly, Jacob winces on this occasion at the presence of faculty wives, whose participation mars a symmetry the narrator has marked and celebrated no less enthusiastically. One presumes correctly that Jacob's aesthetics will go largely unchallenged in the course of an education that long has buttressed Western values.

Above all there persists here distaste for women. "Sopworth summing things up," surrounded by young men, despises their presence in art as in life. The impact of such feelings is predictable. While Erasmus Cowan sips his port with the same pleasure as he recites Virgil and Catullus, the subordinate Miss Umphelby worries about her clothing and the subjects she dares not broach in print or for that matter in conversation. At home in this world where "a man could say anything" (41), Jacob, smoking his pipe by the window and looking down on the court of Trinity, appears to the narrator as "indeed masterly," the rightful "inheritor" of the world around him (45).

The process of education through which Jacob is destined for leadership extends beyond the halls of his college. We see him next on summer vacation quarreling with Timmy Durrant as the two of them are boating off the Scilly Isles. Forced by his own lack of training to occupy a subordinately dependent role on board, Jacob finds he can neither read nor daydream. Timmy's sophistication extends, moreover, from seamanship—he navigates, the narrator observes, with the sort of composed authority that "would have moved a woman"—to the world of business. Looking through binoculars, he identifies the destination and cargo of every passing steamer as well as the probable dividend each line pays its shareholders. The problem, as we are informed, is that "Jacob, of course, was not a woman. The sight of Timmy Durrant was no sight for him, nothing to set against the sky and worship; far from it. They had quarrelled" (47).

Engrossed first in petty disputes and after Jacob's swim, in the question of Timmy's "scientific observations," both men are largely oblivious of the surrounding sights. As Jacob's thoughts tramp forward with a cadence that recalls Professor Huxtable, this grand setting remains at best a theatrical backdrop: "What was the coast of Cornwall, with its violet scents and mourning emblems, and tranquil piety, but a screen happening to hang straight behind as his mind marched up?" (50). But for the first time that day, Jacob, "having grasped the argument," wins Timmy's respect. Rising momentarily in rank and status, "becoming master of the situation" (50), he finds his spirits reviving.

The details from shore have entered the text in that interval between two disputations when Timmy, pulling his friend back on board, leaves the ship unmanned. As the sail flaps and a small volume of Shakespeare is knocked overboard, the narrator intercedes with a non sequitur—"Strangely enough, you could smell violets, or if violets were impossible in July, they must grow something very pungent on the mainland then" (48). There follows a shower of details—white cottages, rising smoke, the cry of a man on the street, cabbage fields, stone walls, coast guard stations, hills, and chimneys—before the narrative resumes: "No doubt if this were Italy, Greece, or even the shores of Spain, sadness would be routed by strangeness and excitement and the nudge of a classical education" (49).

The Cornish hills have made Jacob sad (so the narrator speculates) because they represent a mundane world he, much in the manner of young Stephen Dedalus, would transcend. Through Cambridge and the classics he will learn the art of avoiding dull occupations, "settling down in a lawyer's office and wearing spats" (50), and the no more attractive world of Mrs. Pascoe on shore, described (concurrently) scrubbing clothes in her tiny scullery to the cadence of a cheap clock ticking on the mantelpiece.

The problem for Jacob is that to master life much less others offends a deep-rooted if romantic sense of pristine innocence. To surpass Timmy, to become capable "of sailing round the world in a ten-ton yacht" (50), he must descend into an arena he finds distasteful. When some days later, at a dinner party, the first words he hears from Mrs. Durrant are, "Did you take command or Timothy?" (58), his sole defense is a sustained silence.

Only the vague outline of her beautiful daughter sitting opposite offers, like the ocean earlier, an evasion. First at the dinner table, then later in the garden, Clara tempts him to other pursuits. Standing angelically above him on a ladder in the vineyard, she seems almost the creation of his own aesthetic needs: "She looked semi-transparent, pale, wonderfully beautiful up there among the vine leaves and the yellow and purple bunches, the lights swimming over her in coloured islands. . . . 'I have enjoyed myself,' said Jacob, looking down the greenhouse" (62).

Despite his egotism, however, we sense throughout these pages that Jacob is still young enough to change, that at any moment he may in fact become more receptive to that world outside his own. When Clara writes in her diary of this meeting and of Jacob's attractive unworldliness, she describes his candor: "He gives himself no airs and one can say what one likes to him." The entry closes, however, with the informing qualification that "he's frightening" (71).

The poetic fusing of women with nature, however innocently clothed in a familiar rhetoric of loving, is less benign than the narrator supposes. Like the softness of the sea and river, Clara remains Jacob's refuge from a discomforting world. No wonder he hopes, in an extended romantic cliché, that the evening "would never end," that the adored Clara might remain perpetually adoring.

When, in the course of time, Jacob's women prove no less reliable than men, classical art offers a reassuring alternative. First literature, later the classical statues of Greece, fulfill his aesthetic inclinations for something more constant. His needs have evolved with education from Byron to the Elizabethans to Plato, and the time he spends in the British Museum after coming down from Cambridge is devoted to the other forms of literature. Needless to say, "he never read modern novels" (122).

The deities inhabiting Plato's *Phaedrus* move eternally; motion without end for their untouchable truth, without form or color, proves accessible to reason alone. Plato's words, as Jacob reads them later in his London flat, march straight on, leaving him oblivious of the rain, the cab whistles, the drunken woman in the mews below crying to be let in, sounds that conspire like some irreverent chorus to distract and capture his attention. "Falling into step," his thoughts become "(so it seems) momentarily part of this rolling, imperturbable energy, which has driven darkness before it since Plato walked the Acropolis" (110).

The cacophony of sounds rising from the street remains, as with Betty at the top of Dods Hill, on the margin of consciousness, ready to intrude and reshape the present between the acts of business. Only after the dialogue has ended, when "for five minutes Jacob's mind continues alone," does this new world intrude upon the old. Getting up and walking to the window, "he parted the curtains, and saw, with astonishing clearness, how the Springetts opposite had gone to bed; how it rained; how the Jews and the foreign woman, at the end of the street, stood by the pillar-box arguing" (110).

It is the narrator, however, extending the window image, who will perceive the tentativeness of all such uncentered experience: "Then, at a top-floor window, leaning out, looking down, you see beauty itself; or in the corner of an omnibus; or squatted in a ditch—beauty glowing, suddenly expressive, withdrawn the moment after. No one can count on it or seize it" (115). For Jacob, the catalogue of common and unrelated events unfolding on the street below his room neither engages his mind nor elicits his fears.

In *Jacob's Room*, as in *Night and Day*, London after dark serves Woolf as a paradigm for the unknown. No discernible pattern informs the nomadic movements of anonymous human beings under ill-lit street lamps. The gestures and voices of strangers, "angry, lustful, despairing, passionate" (81), erupt with frightening irregularity. Only buildings seem fixed and solid. The sounds abroad are like those of "caged beasts at night," but as the narrator acknowledges, these inhabitants are neither caged nor beasts. Then, "What does one fear?" Her reply comes promptly: "The human eye" through which "the chasm deepens" (81).

When Jacob leaves the confines of his own family, we move with him into this unguarded world. On the train to Cambridge another passenger, convinced with some validity that "men are dangerous," tries vainly to dissuade him from entering her compartment: "'This is not a smoking-carriage,' Mrs. Norman protested, nervously but very feebly, as the door swung open and a powerfully built young man jumped in" (30). Not until "the infallible test of appearance" discloses Jacob to be a species of her own tribe does she regain her composure. The details of his face, the loose and random appearance of his clothing, his youthful indifference, strike a familiar note in her mind. The same age as her son, evidently also a Cambridge undergraduate, he is no longer perceived as the sort of person to attack a defenseless elderly woman.

Only the threat of such an assault, however, can arouse Mrs. Norman's imagination to venture into the chasm. Unsettled by the first appearance of this large, unknown man, she conjures up a battle scenario; she would defend herself by throwing a bottle of perfume with one hand while tugging the communication cord with the other. As the sense of threat diminishes, she appears to have no further basis for association. To connect, she must allow an image of this young man to emerge that might support neither her fears nor her assurances. To speak to him—simply to tell him he might in fact smoke—would require, moreover, a disruptive act of her own. Since "he seemed absolutely indifferent to her presence...she did not wish to interrupt" (31).

Bound as she is by appearances, Mrs. Norman's choice limits Jacob's as well as her own opportunity to extend the boundaries of their worlds. Jacob's indifference presumably expresses his good manners; decorum demands silence, just as it requires that he open the door and help her disembark. Respecting conventions, the two passengers take leave of one another without contact. No collaboration takes place, no figurative marriage of minds through which Woolf hopes, androgynously, for different forms of human intercourse. Only the narrator's voice interrupts astutely to complain: "Nobody sees any one as he is, let alone an elderly lady sitting opposite a strange young man in a railway carriage. They see a whole—they see all sorts of things—they see themselves" (30–31).[10]

This failure to communicate remains oppressively familiar. The details Mrs. Norman musters in visualizing Jacob again recall "Mr. Bennett and Mrs. Brown" and Woolf's state of mind in the presence of strangers. Sitting in a London train, she acknowledges "being uncomfortable, like most people, at travelling with fellow passengers unless I have somehow or other accounted for them."[11] Similarly, we recall the narrator of "An Unwritten Novel" creating Minnie Marsh almost exclusively from her own imaginative needs, and the crisis of identity that occurs once this image collapses: "Well, my world's done for! What do I stand on? What do I know? That's not Minnie. There never was Moggridge. Who am I? Life's bare as bone."[12] Struggling to resist and revise the more accustomed ways our knowledge of the external world evolves in the mind, Woolf comes to reject even the satisfaction of an authorial summation as a betrayal of her own artistic vision. So we share with her characters the sense of an external universe where meaning can only be inferred, and no single perspective can hope to supply comprehensive answers to existential questions. What is real is open-ended.[13]

Inviting the reader into a world where nothing is ever decisive or final, the narrator of *Jacob's Room* interposes: "It is no use trying to sum people up. One must follow hints" (31). The repetition of these exact words toward the end of the novel (154) suggests she has learned with her author to "grope &

experiment."¹⁴ But neither Jacob nor Mrs. Norman seems inclined to experiment. Unwilling to interrupt one another,
they allow the moment to slip away, just as years later, on the
streets of London, Jacob's first Latin teacher will lose the opportunity to make something out of nothing. Having loved
Betty Flanders, and now encountering her son, he is tempted
to approach him: "'I gave him Byron's works,' Andrew Floyd
mused, and started forward, as Jacob crossed the road; but
hesitated, and let the moment pass, and lost the opportunity"
(173). Each man, enclosed in his own private world, is affected by these failures to intrude.

In an early description of London, the narrator speaks of
adjacent buses locked together on Oxford Street, a figure that
will recur at the end of *Jacob's Room:* "Mr. Spalding going to
the city looked at Mr. Charles Budgeon bound for Shepherd's
Bush. The proximity of the omnibuses gave the outside passengers an opportunity to stare into each other's faces. Yet few
took advantage of it. Each had his own business to think of.
Each had his past shut in him like the leaves of a book known
to him by heart; and his friends could only read the title"
(64–65). The passengers' faces recall the drugged expression
of the vacationers on Scarborough pier. Only after "the policeman holds up his arm" and the buses jerk forward again do
they regain their composure, their lives again becoming "tol-
erable."* Neither the thrill of renewed motion nor the change
of scene sets them at ease, but rather an expectation that it
will all soon be over; "every single person felt relief at being a
little nearer to his journey's end" (65).

*Law and order may appear at times a welcome if inauthentic alternative
to the novelist's demanding vocation, pictured appropriately in these pages
as the art of "enclosing vacancy" (155). The policeman, in company with
"banks, laboratories, chancellories, and houses of business," serves to "oar
the world forward": "When his right arm rises, all the force in his veins flows
straight from shoulder to finger-tips; not an ounce is diverted into sudden
impulses, sentimental regrets, wiredrawn distinctions. The buses punctually
stop" (156).

Like Hermann Broch's novel *The Sleepwalkers* (1932), *Jacob's Room* probes the psychology of a society prepared for war and for death. The discovery at the end of the book that Jacob is one of its reified victims should come as no shock. As she will do later in *Three Guineas*, Woolf describes the disposition toward war as an essential aspect of patriarchal culture, a disposition, moreover, that she presumes affects us all. Those who run the country, statesmen and bankers, businessmen and soldiers, move with a singleness of purpose that inspires support if not devotion. "There is something absolute in us," the narrator confesses, "which despises qualification" (144), which draws us, she might have added, to martial order.

Military influences arise early in Jacob's life, most notably through Captain Barfoot who, in the absence of Mr. Flanders, serves as a surrogate for Jacob as well as for Betty. He is described as the sort of man women look to for support, someone capable of taking charge in time of crisis: "Women would have felt, 'Here is law. Here is order. Therefore we must cherish this man. He is on the Bridge at night,' . . . buttoned in his pea-jacket matched with the storm, vanquished by it but by none other" (28). Even his manner of standing and walking suggest "something military" (26).

Largely through Barfoot's inquiries, Jacob begins his proper education in the use of power: he goes up to Cambridge.[15] The captain surmises early that Jacob is destined for leadership. A few years later in Greece, the historically erudite Evan Williams also recognizes his promise. "Here is a fellow," he acknowledges at the very time Jacob appears to have captured his wife's affection, "who might do very well in politics" (146). Lacking himself the most important attribute of great leaders, namely, the ability "to impose his own personality" (143), Williams perceives in this time of crisis that England has need of men such as Jacob.

The details describing Jacob's tastes reveal an increasing impatience with phenomena he cannot master. Even pigeons

in Versailles ("Those silly birds, directly one wants them—
they've flown away"; 130) appear as objects to be overcome.
They are not unlike the countries he would conquer: "After
doing Greece he was going to knock off Rome" (136). His
grand tour takes on the inflection of a military operation, a
tone that affects his writing as well as his thoughts. Indeed, in
the company of men, Jacob's very bearing seems to become
more martial. Twice he appears to friends like "a British Admiral" (145, 165); and a stallkeeper approaching him in company with Timmy mistakes him "for a military gentleman"
(76). With the sense that they are no longer initiates, he and
Bonamy stride proudly through a world that has become "our
ship" (90).

Contemplating an essay he will write on civilization after his
trip to Greece and Italy, he imagines describing it to Bonamy:
"A comparison between the ancients and moderns, with some
pretty sharp hits at Mr. Asquith—something in the style of
Gibbon" (136). But Bonamy will declare his preference for
"sentences that don't budge though armies cross them" (140).
Jacob's intention, however, is not to flatter his homosexual
friend so much as to dominate him. "Magnanimity, virtue"
and other Latinate words "when Jacob used them in talk
with Bonamy meant that he took control of the situation;
that Bonamy would play round him like an affectionate span-
iel" (165).

Jacob's tendency to stare "straight ahead of him, fixed,
monolithic," expresses for his admiring friend the essence of
masculine beauty. But much to Bonamy's regret, Jacob's attention has been captured by classical Greece and more particularly by Williams's attractive wife, Sandra. For Jacob, the
beauty of one coincides with the beauty of the other.

The Greek temples Jacob sees each morning fill him as they
do the narrator with a pleasing sense of permanence: "The extreme definiteness with which they stand, now a brilliant
white, again yellow, and in some lights red, imposes ideas of

durability. . . . Perhaps it is beauty alone that is immortal" (148). In contrast to the vulgar sounds of people chattering on the street, the Acropolis answers Jacob's need for something impervious to change. Craving solidity, "he seldom thought of Plato or Socrates in the flesh; on the other hand his feeling for architecture was very strong; he preferred statues to pictures" (149).

The image of Sandra's beauty moves Jacob, her husband, and the narrator to sculptural similes. Riding opposite the two men in a carriage, Sandra is described as sitting straight and "dominant, like a Victory prepared to fling into the air" (147). A few days later Jacob admires a stone goddess holding the roof of the Erechtheum on her head and is reminded immediately of Sandra. Like the statue, she requires no emendation. In his mind her beauty is complete.

In classical days such symmetry inspired epic ventures. No longer infatuated, and for that matter no longer even young or ambitious, Evan Williams is resigned to a life of unheroic expectations. Jacob, by comparison, has just begun to move upward. Like the *Phaedrus,* Sandra—or at least Jacob's idea of her—calls him to higher things, thereby feeding his proclivity toward romantic love, which the narrator, in a Byronic vein, is moved to mock:

> Then the hook gave a great tug in his side as he lay in bed on Wednesday night; and he turned over with a desperate sort of tumble, remembering Sandra Wentworth Williams with whom he was in love.
> Next day he climbed Pentelicus.
> The day after he went up to the Acropolis. (149–50)

Not surprisingly, the young hero's thoughts rise once more to visions of conquest and sovereignty. Seated like a pagan god "overlooking Marathon," Jacob finds himself thinking about the ways in which countries should be ruled. But his plans for writing "a note upon the importance of history" are interrupted by a flamboyant group of noisy Frenchwomen, one of whom points her Kodak directly at him. "'Damn these women—damn these women!' he thought. . . . 'How they spoil things'" (151).

Jacob's discontent results from existential distraction. The women are no more real to him than the sounds and smells that drifted from shore at Land's End, or the qualities of Sandra's mind and personality he will come shortly to recognize and censure. In contemplating the statues of the Erechtheum—actually fixing his eyes steadfastly on them—Jacob would "annul" exactly that "grand" and "fleshy" vibrance the narrator describes and celebrates as Madame Lucien Grave jumps down from the ruins in a posture of "luxurious abandonment." Jacob, filled with grief at the loss of his aesthetic moment, sees none of this. His mind cannot extend to entertain any such plurality of tastes. Beauty remains for him a singular experience of classical decorum; the truth of Sandra and the statues is one and immutable. His disappointment, moreover, "is generally to be expected," the narrator interjects, "in young men in the prime of life, sound of wind and limb, who will soon become fathers of families and directors of banks" (151). The narrowness of these options reflects for Woolf both the tragedy of Jacob's fate—he will die soon on the battlefields of France—and the tragedy of the culture that surrounds and sustains him.

Jacob's relationship with the woman he presumably loves is similarly exclusionary. Attracted by Sandra's exquisite good taste, he takes her ideas with no more seriousness than does her husband, who suspects his wife of being "brainless." After their first meeting, Jacob complains in a letter to Bonamy that she has lent him Chekhov's short stories. The incident follows a dinner party with Sandra at which she had asked him whether, if forced to choose, he would keep the literature of France or the literature of Russia. It would appear that like any good hostess she was simply keeping up the conversation. Her question is one of many: "Whether he'd seen the theatre by moonlight; whether he knew Everard Sherborn; whether he read Greek?" (144) If Evan is bored, Jacob seems ready and willing to play the game, or so his words to Bonamy suggest: "And now I shall have to read her cursed book" (144).

Sandra would in fact lure Jacob into the shade for a number of motives, not all purely sexual. Disposed, like the Russians Woolf prized, to a plurality of things, Sandra sees everything as having meaning: "one must love everything," she counsels the young man.[16] It is presumably such remarks as these that give rise to Evan's doubts about his wife's intelligence, if not her fidelity.

In contrast to Jacob, who is up early in the morning identifying Parthenon statues in his Baedeker, she is described as "ranging the world before breakfast in quest of adventure or a point of view" (145). The disposition for doing nothing productive suggests again something more than the narrowness of women's options. Conscious, as her men are not, of a surrounding world of movement and diversity, "turning, turning in mazes of heat and sound," she remains, in her own words, "sensitive to every side of it" (153).

Less restrained, moreover, by formal barriers, she is capable of transgressing those decorums that define her station in life. This is a side Jacob cannot readily acknowledge, for to do so would destroy the harmonious synthesis he seeks, the merging of England and classical Greece. In Jacob's eyes, she performs each ceremony with a dignity that inspires him both to serve and to seduce her.

Through establishing his own ends, extending from literary texts to beautiful countries and women, Jacob hopes to circumvent a growing sense of external irrelevancy. Like Betty on the beach at the start of the novel, he struggles to avoid interruptions from a world that borders his narrow intentions. The myth of Sandra's perfection that he creates becomes the measure of his own value. In a self-fulfilling enterprise, success depends on the degree to which he proves capable of rising, hierarchically, to such largely projected expectations.

When Jacob first sees Sandra on the terrace after dinner, she impresses him as beautifully "arranged." Seated before her, he is aware of "the extreme shabbiness of his trousers" (145). She, on the other hand, finds him "very distinguished looking," or so she tells her husband. The remark seems designed to honor rather than to threaten him; how could his wife respond favorably to a man on any other grounds? In reality, though Jacob attracts her for obvious reasons, she seems drawn to him as she has no doubt been drawn to others in the past out of an impulse for risk and adventure. Evan's innocuous remark as they sit in the dining room—"Those pink melons are sure to be dangerous" (143)—expands in her mind to include Jacob as she first sees him walk through the door. As with Mrs. Norman, a sense of threat invites innovation. What emerges, however, is an old scenario.

Employing her knowledge of masculine vanity, Sandra initiates a flirtation that, through no failure of her own, never becomes an affair. Describing herself as having "been left motherless at the age of four," she effectively evokes protective desires. "Jacob thought that if he had been there he would have saved her" (146). Once a certain intimacy is achieved, Sandra questions her intentions as he does not: "What do I want from him? Perhaps it is something that I have missed" (159). From Evan's comments on "affairs" (143) we may assume that she is referring to something more than sex with a handsome young man. It is not ends she desires but beginnings, and to begin she must become part of Jacob's designs. She does so by proposing that they climb the hill to the Acropolis alone and by night.

Where in Dante the invitation to climb is symbolic of man's aspiration for paradise, in Woolf it depicts the modern compulsion to transcend and escape the randomness of life. Like work and war, moreover, mountains serve as "an outlet for manly qualities, without which," Woolf claims in *Three Guineas*, "men would deteriorate."[17] The narrator recognizes

Jacob's need. "Perhaps if one strove hard enough to reach the top of the hill it need not come to him—this disillusionment from women in middle life" (159).

Climbing is a recurrent figure in the novel. Its young protagonist first appears climbing to the top of the beach rock; Betty, taking on a number of paternal roles, is described as plodding up the hill as she urges her children back to their accustomed routines; Barfoot marches up the hill like a soldier to Betty's cottage; Mrs. Plumer goads her unattractive daughters to climb the rungs of the ladder; and the first description Sandra hears of Jacob is that "the young gentleman had left at five to climb the mountain" (143).

The "unseizable force" that pushes Jacob and Sandra toward the Parthenon promises a verifiable end, an experience achieved, something "hard and durable to keep for ever"—or such at any rate remains Jacob's romantic expectation. If the ending proves ultimately illusory, it is the narrator who extends this sense of unreality: "There was the Acropolis; but had they reached it? The columns and the Temple remain; the emotion of the living breaks fresh on them year after year; and of that what remains? As for reaching the Acropolis who shall say that we ever do it?" (160–61)

The copy of Donne's poetry Sandra finds on her dressing table the next morning serves, like one of Madame Grave's photographs, perhaps the one of Jacob, to authenticate the event, to make it all less illusory. She will place it among other mementos—"There were ten or twelve little volumes already" (161)—from which at times "she would suck back again the soul of the moment" (161). But on this occasion the sound of the clock ticking on the landing moves Sandra instead to question: "What for? What for?" The passages he had marked so assuredly in the volume of poems make it clear that "Jacob never asked himself any such questions." Having triumphed, the young warrior no doubt slept well, or so the narrator speculates: "He was young—a man. . . . At forty it might be a different matter" (161). Jacob, however, like

Woolf's first heroine, will die prematurely. The young have no future in a society so narrowly confined.

In an important sense, Jacob at this point in his life has fewer options before him than Rachel or, for that matter, Sandra. Where Sandra can withdraw to the outskirts of power, he is bound ever more firmly by peremptory ends as he steps from college toward the professions. The statue of Ulysses Fanny Elmer visits in the British Museum to recall the absent Jacob ironically signifies his captivity. He returns home the conqueror, but Jacob's "trips" are in fact over. Fully initiated, he finds his way "manfully determined" by a culture bent on imposing "coherency upon Rajahs and Kaisers and the muttering in bazaars, the secret gatherings, plainly visible in Whitehall, of kilted peasants in Albanian uplands; to control the course of events" (172).

Like Saul Bellow's narrator at the close of *Dangling Man,* Jacob appears ready for conscription. Sitting in Hyde Park toward the end of the day, he is annoyed by the slightest intrusion. "What a nuisance you are," he grumbles, while counseling the park attendant to take his tip and "get drunk." Generosity feeds a misanthropic "contempt for his species" (170).[18] When he rises to leave, the act of tearing his park ticket to pieces conceals for one last time an alternative dimension of time and space. "The long windows of Kensington Palace flushed fiery rose as Jacob walked away; a flock of wild duck flew over the Serpentine; and the trees were stood against the sky, blackly, magnificently" (173).

There is no one to deter his movement, least of all his old Latin tutor rushing by in Piccadilly Circus. Swept up by the rightness of things, Jacob moves alongside other patrons of the opera with the same unseeing unanimity. It remains for the narrator to address the malaise before submitting, however sarcastically, to social imperatives:

Under the arch of the Opera House large faces and lean ones, the powdered and the hairy, all alike were red in the sunset; and quickened by the great hanging lamps with their repressed primrose lights, by the tramp, and the scarlet, and the pompous ceremony, some ladies looked for a moment into steaming bedrooms near by, where women with loose hair leaned out of windows, where girls—where children—(the long mirrors held the ladies suspended) but one must follow; one must not block the way. (174)

Outside Covent Garden cars continue to swerve; on the curb two barrel organs serenade the populace; Wortley, "always urbane, always in time for the overture," still buttons his gloves with care while Fanny Elmer worries about her complexion.

The novel ends with an expanding view of such inconsequential actions. In Cornwall Mrs. Pascoe, standing among her cabbages, watches seagulls on the bay. In Scarborough Betty Flanders is preoccupied with the chickens, Rebecca's toothache and, following the notification of her son's death, the mundane question of how to dispense with his shoes: "'What am I to do with these, Mr. Bonamy?' She held out a pair of Jacob's old shoes."

As at the beginning of the novel, Betty Flanders turns to a man for direction, but now the sense of closure seems strangely less confining. Perhaps it is the widening array of connotations the impact of "old shoes" inevitably evokes that serves to interrupt all sense of an ending. Against the background of this liberating chaos—"Such confusion everywhere!"— even Jacob's death, devoid of outline, slips, it seems, into irrelevance.

Chapter Five

THE UNGUARDED MOMENT
Mrs. Dalloway

Seated in her drawing room, mending the dress she will wear that evening at her party, Clarissa Dalloway falls into the rhythm of sewing: "Quiet descended on her, calm, content, as her needle, drawing the silk smoothly to its gentle pause, collected the green folds together and attached them, very lightly, to the belt" (58).[1] The scene, culminating with the unexpected appearance of her former fiancé just returned from India, embodies Woolf's appreciation of artistic accomplishment and the accompanying temptation to enclose herself within the serenity of a thoroughly satisfying moment. Clarissa's motions, like those of some primordial weaver, are described as if reenacting the lives of all created beings rising and falling much as waves on a beach: "So on a summer's day waves collect, overbalance, and fall; collect and fall; and the whole world seems to be saying 'that is all.'" A sense of fulfillment builds in the passage to the antithetical shock of the doorbell ringing and Peter Walsh's crucial interruption.

Mrs. Dalloway

What Woolf comes to see in the course of writing *Mrs. Dalloway* is how fully the creative impulse tends to isolate the signifier from the source of all rejuvenation, namely, his or her external world. Lulled into a wholeness free of imperfection, Clarissa seems to slip, with the narrator of "The Mark on the Wall," deeper and deeper away from the surface of modern life. In each instance Shakespeare supplies a modicum of control. His steadying influence occurs as she reads the lines from *Cymbeline* displayed in a London book shop window: "Fear no more, says the heart. Fear no more, says the heart, committing its burden to some sea, which sighs collectively for all sorrows, and renews, begins, collects, lets fall" (59).

Unlike Woolf's earlier narrator, however, and unlike her own earlier version of Clarissa, the heroine of *Mrs. Dalloway* responds to interruption in the very midst of indulging the most ecstatic vision of closure. Even as the movement of her arm sewing follows a Shakespearean cadence, her attention remains open and receptive to a radically disruptive rhythm:

And the body alone listens to the passing bee; the wave breaking; the dog barking, far away barking and barking.
"Heavens, the front-door bell!" exclaimed Clarissa, staying her needle. Roused, she listened. (59)

In Virginia Woolf's first sketch for what was to become *Mrs. Dalloway*, Clarissa appears walking down Bond Street with the aristocratic assurance one might expect from a woman of her class. Thoroughly at home in a world of smart shops, well-groomed pedestrians, and the governing establishment—couriers are scurrying with messages between Fleet Street and the Admiralty—the proud Clarissa remains, on this June morning a few years after the end of the First World War, like young Jacob Flanders at Cambridge, fresh and "upright." A sense of wholeness pervades the scene; "for Mrs. Dalloway the moment was complete." The flag waving above Buckingham Palace (signaling the return of the king and queen), the policeman confidently directing traffic, Big Ben striking the time of day, inspire, moreover, a condescending ethnocentricity: "It was character she thought; something inborn in the race; what Indians respected."[2]

Woolf's satiric intentions seem clear enough. If, as she puts it somewhat later, she wants "to criticize the social system, and to show it at work,"[3] Mrs. Dalloway appears the vehicle of her reproof. And yet, in the course of this short story, she emerges as something more than a static object of satire.[4] The crux of Woolf's sketch, unsettling Clarissa's classbound self-assurance, anticipates the revisions that will transform her from a stiff and tinselly society matron into her author's most famous heroine.

Having stepped into a glove shop (for here it is gloves rather than flowers that call her outdoors), Mrs. Dalloway of the sketch finds herself quite unexpectedly sympathizing with a shopgirl's less privileged life. "When we're in the country thought Clarissa. Or shooting. She has a fortnight at Brighton. In some stuffy lodging."[5] We can assume that the wife of a distinguished MP generally resists such speculations; crossing the boundaries of class invites impulsive, and potentially compromising, acts. Ironically, the fashionable shop has served in the past to allay disruptive emotions. If passion must exist in human life, let it be for gloves. And how better are we identified than by what we wear? "A lady is known by her gloves and her shoes, old Uncle William used to say."[6] On this visit, however, the setting provides a different sort of connection. Probing the affairs of someone outside her world, Mrs. Dalloway discovers a new and wider basis for relationship, derived from an experience shared by all women. Yet even as she is imagining a working girl's discomfort (standing as she must all day behind the counter) on "the one day in the month" when the strain might prove particularly agonizing, something more fundamental than the barriers of class momentarily complicates—in terms of this study, interrupts—her inherited expectations. Clarissa's imaginative adventure results in contradictory responses: both a generous impulse to help and a no less powerful sense of reservation. "Dick had shown her the folly of giving impulsively."[7]

In "The Russian Point of View," published in the same year as *Mrs. Dalloway*, Woolf praises writers such as Chekhov for confronting existential issues that prove elusive and inconclusive. English readers, she argues, are inclined to find such questions a threat to the very basis of their social and literary practice. She suggests further that English novelists, pressured to accept the hierarchical order of a class-structured culture, are "inclined to satire rather than to compassion, to scrutiny of society rather than understanding of individuals themselves."[8] She may well be describing her own struggle with the earlier Mrs. Dalloway.

Once Clarissa questions her own favored status she invites what is to become with each revision an increasingly liberating form of discord. In the glove store a series of doubts arises to challenge the ground of her belief: faith in God ("one doesn't believe, thought Clarissa, any more in God"); life's smoothness ("It used, thought Clarissa, to be so simple"); and most centrally, social decorum itself ("Lady Bexborough, who opened the bazaar, they say, with the telegram in her hand—Roden, her favourite, killed—she would go on. But why, if one doesn't believe?").[9]

Mrs. Dalloway falls back on noblesse oblige in answering these questions. One goes on for the sake of the underprivileged. The shopgirl, she would convince us and herself, "would be much more unhappy if she didn't believe." Bound by the limits of her class, Mrs. Dalloway in Bond Street gives up the adventure before it has begun.

While scholars differ over the nature of that "depth" Woolf sought to illuminate through her tunneling discovery, most agree that an altered sense of time past distinguishes her final revisions. *Mrs. Dalloway* is perhaps best described in this regard by J. Hillis Miller as "a novel of the resurrection of the past into the actual present of the characters' lives."[10]

Mrs. Dalloway in Bond Street is revived by that sense of common history she shares with members of her class. In the final version, however, the past intrudes in the form of less hierarchical and more personal relationships to interrupt her experience of the present or at the very least to complicate it. What was previously exceptional in this novel becomes the norm. But it is more than the disruptive immediacy of suppressed or disregarded desires, past and present, that transforms Clarissa from an object of social satire to an existential heroine. The personal recollections disclosed by Woolf's tunneling process take on new significance when seen against the kaleidoscopic background of her more public world.

The dynamic of disjunction has a liberating effect. Loosening her hold on old supports, Clarissa finds herself with Septimus metaphorically at sea or, to employ a no less applicable cliché, up in the air. Called on to redefine the moment, she transcends, however tentatively, the constraints of gender, class, and hierarchy.

Instinct anchors Mrs. Dalloway in Bond Street to a world of unchanging roles: "There is this extraordinarily deep instinct, something inside one; you can't get over it; it's no use trying."[11] From the opening pages of the novel, however, Clarissa's mind freely ranges over and through inherited assumptions, creating as she does "every moment afresh." If she is not serenely at home in the present, it is because, however timidly, she anticipates change with a mixture of dread and pleasure; even in recollection, as when in Bourton she recalls the solemnity and excitement of something unexpected "about to happen."

Though she remains loyally aristocratic, the reader is invited to other perspectives. Her gestures as well as her words take on a new transparency. So initially Woolf picks up the term "upright," which recurred frequently in the short story, and

transforms the essentially static image into one of birdlike propensity for flight. On a street corner, "there she perched, . . .
waiting to cross, very upright" (4). This quality, observed by
her neighbor, adds ambiguity as well as range to her thoughts,
an ambiguity Clarissa prizes throughout the novel.

The opening pages develop Woolf's analysis of existential
anxiety as an added aspect of Clarissa's willingness to question
the given. The experience of emptiness and silence in the
midst of London traffic—"a particular hush, or solemnity; an
indescribable pause"—at once suspends and renews her sense
of place and person. Where Mrs. Dalloway's advisers, the un-
named and impersonal "they," describe the experience as
symptomatic of illness, Woolf quickly honors the effects of
Clarissa's angst. When, in the next instant, clock time (Big
Ben) begins again its heavy beat, so irrevocable and final, she
seems more attuned to what Woolf, describing the ambience
of Chaucer's *Canterbury Tales,* terms the "immense variety" of
life.[12] Clarissa's perceptions have in fact widened. She responds
to the high and the low, the snobbish Hugh Whitbread, a fat
lady passing in a cab, a dejected and destitute human being
sitting on a doorstep. The events that typified Mrs. Dalloway
in Bond Street's narrow, self-justifying response are no longer
the source of aesthetic pleasure. Now she celebrates a largely
classless pageant: "In people's eyes, in the swing, tramp, and
trudge; in the bellow and the uproar; the carriages, motor
cars, omnibuses, vans, sandwich men shuffling and swinging;
brass bands; barrel organs; in the triumph and the jingle and
the strange high singing of some aeroplane overhead was what
she loved; life; London; this moment of June" (5).

Unlike her predecessor, Clarissa derives neither assurance
nor stability from her revelatory insights on the streets of London. Such moments—"What she loved was this, here, now,
in front of her"—pass as quickly as they appear. Since the
given remains perpetually inconclusive, existential encounters call for ever-renewed acts of re-creation. No less an aspect

of time than the mind that creates them, words must never be allowed to sink into opaque singularity. Throughout Woolf's fictional world, language as well as personality resists the reifying intentions of a society bent on possession. It is in this light that she praises Sir John Paston, along with Chaucer, for having "the instincts of enjoyment rather than of acquisition."[13] By contrast, the age's passion for "scientific" definition will appear as a symptom of collective social madness, an aberration that ironically overshadows Septimus's madness.

Toward the close of *A Room of One's Own*, Woolf discusses an instinct of something "real" that inspires her as a writer to look more deeply into her own convictions as well as the appearances of people and of things. The result is often unsettling. Great novelists—Hardy, Proust, Dostoevsky—by disrupting the reader's harmony with his world, in an important sense challenge the very conditions of sanity. Injuring our vanity by upsetting our order, such writers seldom tell us the "truth" we want to hear.[14]

While Septimus and Clarissa represent two contrasting visions of truth, "Mrs. D. seeing the truth, Septimus seeing the insane truth,"[15] both reflect what will remain central aspects of Woolf's iconoclastic assumptions. The truths they witness and enact oppose the conforming aesthetics of what remains for her a parochially narrow culture.

With the publication of Woolf's diaries, it has become evident how spells of insanity or, more precisely, her recollections of those spells, helped form an aesthetic intention. The visual distortion that occurs when her mind's hold on things is threatened prompts her to revise the given. Septimus, reflecting as he does a central and traumatic part of the novelist's own personal history, sees the truth, however incoherently, in artistically prophetic terms. His tragedy is that he cannot finally affirm and communicate the explosive immediacy of such visions. He has received one shock too many.

To communicate depth in an age systematically incurious

about its own social and personal motivations presupposes a disposition "to go down boldly and bring to light those hidden thoughts which are the most diseased." Woolf's essay on Montaigne, with its familiar plea, "Communication is health; communication is truth,"[16] informs the theme of *Mrs. Dalloway*. The confrontation with disease, however, does not lead her to affirm the ego's power to face and transcend infirmity. In an important sense, illness itself offers, as we have seen, a means of renewal. Whether such an assumption pertains to her personal life as well as to her art remains an open question.

"On Being Ill," we recall, suggests the advantage one may derive even from a slight case of influenza: "How tremendous the spiritual change that it brings, how astonishing, when the lights of health go down, the undiscovered countries that are then disclosed, what wastes and deserts of the soul, . . . what ancient and obdurate oaks are uprooted in us by the act of sickness." The mind, as if on some imperialistic campaign "to cultivate the desert, educate the native," seeks in health to civilize the body, to maintain its sovereignty over the senses. "With the police off duty," the senses are free to roam. Seeing with the eyes of children, "we cease to be soldiers in the army of the upright."[17]

If such excursions prove "unprofitable," they urge the mind from the elevating abstraction of pure thought to a less refined existence replete with sights and sounds and smells. D. H. Lawrence and even F. R. Leavis must surely approve Woolf's plea for a "reason rooted in the bowels of earth." The robust society she envisions will suspend its own "dominating" predilections in the expectation that "life is always and inevitably much richer than we who try to express it."[18]

On the streets of London, in the grip of his hallucination, Septimus, like Clarissa, responds with childlike pleasure to phenomena that the crowd would reduce to objective clarity. The plane skywriting an advertisement urges a multitude of prospective customers to decipher the message. Eager to comply, they seek answers compulsively. "They were advertising toffee, a nursemaid told Rezia." Overhearing the woman spelling out the letters, "K... R...," Septimus responds to a different rhythm: "'Kay Arr' close to his ear, deeply, ... like a grasshopper's, which rasped his spine deliciously and sent running up into his brain waves of sound which, concussing, broke" (32). Her voice—it is his newest discovery—"can quicken trees into life." Septimus experiences the fullness of being and time as those around him cannot. Even the space between events strikes him as important.

Like some foreign visitor, Septimus the outsider sees familiar objects as if for the first time.[19] At this point of the narrative, his only possibility of communication is with the omniscient reader, who, Woolf presumes, shares and relishes his insights; however disoriented and isolated, his world comes alive for us. We are reminded again of "On Being Ill" and its somewhat rash pronouncement that "the Chinese must know the sound of *Antony and Cleopatra* better than we do."[20] The play is one that Septimus, with the ear of a common reader, earlier learned to love. But that was when he could still share his emotions; with Miss Pole he had discovered Shakespeare.

Septimus is not always open to external things. Whereas Clarissa allows the objects she perceives to grow in her mind, Septimus, fearing the collapse of meaning, often freezes the moment, chooses, in effect, to see and hear no more. To allow himself to tolerate the excitement of unmediated experience is to risk going mad. Moreover, his incongruous perceptions prove destructive because he appears unwilling to translate them into an idiom others can tolerate, much less appreciate. If we gain access to his richer vision, Rezia does not. His wife confesses she cannot even sit beside him once he has started to distort familiar objects; he makes "everything terrible," she complains, not without cause. Following the advice of the doctor, she urges her husband to take notice of "real things," of matters not so organically connected with his own feelings. This therapy of self-forgetfulness proves destructive of life as well as of art. As a growing indifference prevents relationship, his sense of alienation becomes all but intolerable: Septimus pictures himself as a half-drowned sailor alone on an ocean rock; his problem is that he feels not too much, but too little.

On the battlefront Septimus cultivated the same immovable and sustaining indifference that Mrs. Dalloway in Bond Street displayed before the "explosion" of a backfiring car. Trench warfare itself was a study in immobility. Between 1914 and 1918 the Allied lines on the Western Front, with few exceptions, remained essentially fixed, shifting only slightly, and no more than a few hundred yards from the Germans. Four years after the Armistice, the frozen reality of trench warfare still haunts the British imagination. A victim of this debilitating stasis, Septimus moves through the unreal streets of London like the characters of *The Waste Land,* without motivation or passion.

The first image of Septimus in the novel describes his sense of being blocked by the crowds, unable to pass since "everything had come to a standstill." We recall with irony Clarissa's closing thought in the sketch: "Thousands of young men had died that things might go on." The movement his wife Rezia urges on him—"Let us go on"—is denied him by a world in which movement and change appear aspects of sacrilege. Perception no less than bodily motion seems mesmerized by the ruling deities of state and business, anticipating the sister goddesses Proportion and Conversion who appear later. So the multitude cannot help looking at the prime minister's car (Rezia confesses as much) any more than it can resist the blandishments of advertising. When the car has passed, leaving "a slight ripple. . . . all heads were inclined the same way" (25), toward a shop window promoting its wares.

Septimus remains the victim of shock as long as he resists his own chaotic insights, insights that both tempt and terrify him. Schooled in the values of his age long before he became a soldier, Septimus cannot be blamed for relying on its authority. (Ironically, his best chance for survival resides, as we shall see, in tolerating more eccentric visions of himself and others.) His prewar employer, Mr. Brewer, concerned in part by Septimus's health, counsels him in his fatherly way to more manly interests; in place of reading, "he advised football" (130). The war completed Septimus's education. In the trenches he learned to be a man, winning the respect of his superiors ("he was promoted") and, more significantly, of his closest companion, Evans.

We may presume that on the front he had someone with whom to share his thoughts and at appropriate times, perhaps, even his feelings. The reader learns little of Evans, however. Rezia, having seen him once, describes him as quiet, strong, and "undemonstrative in the company of women" (130). The two men "had gone through the whole show" together. The end of Evans, who is killed just before the Armistice, complementing the end of the war, leaves Septimus in fact with neither a sustaining environment nor an ongoing relationship. The battlefront had, after all, established with brutal simplicity the basis for human survival, the distinction between life and death and the nature of what must be done or, no less relevantly, what must not be done, if one is to go on living.

Thrown back on himself, Septimus discovers one evening, with panic, "that he could not feel." Not coincidentally it is the evening on which he has proposed marriage to Rezia. The loss of one refuge leads him rather quickly to seek another. Septimus marries, he makes it quite clear, not out of affection but out of the need for "safety." No less pertinent, the panic has hit him at a time of transition, although at this point what succeeding "show" can inspire the young man to renewed motion is not clear. Moreover, a particular time of day inspires unrest: "These sudden thunder-claps of fear," we hear, come "especially in the evening" (131). Septimus fills the empty time by taking a wife. And what attracts him most in Rezia is her assured activity. Making hats with the other Italian girls— "It is the hat that matters most"—seems as divinely authorized as the deployment of armies. The sense that the girls are impelled by something other than feeling or thought for the moment quiets his deeper fear "that the world itself is without meaning" (133).

Devoid of associative feeling, Septimus does not see, as he will later, that Rezia's vocation is in fact an expression of love. From the first description of her hands moving over each hat "like those of a painter" (132), the beauty she experiences and urges Septimus to see is an aspect of the objects she creates. Not until he can begin to participate in her artistic creation does Septimus move toward health; the doctors, however, make short shrift of that.

Like some Lawrentian antihero, the early Septimus appears stirred by the idea people represent to him rather than by their presence. First Miss Pole serves to reinforce his expectations of literary success ("Was he not like Keats? she asked"; 128). His government appears quick to utilize this romantic attachment to support a larger and more ominous abstraction. Septimus goes to war to make England safe for Miss Pole. Evans appears almost totally in abstract terms, his life no less theoretical in Septimus's mind than his death. Rezia represents the idea of sanctuary. In the course of the novel, Septimus is shaken, tragically, from his idea of her, and thereby finds both the beginning and the end of his life.

At those moments when Septimus overcomes fear and allows a vision of exquisite diversity to invade his being, his perceptions, while filtered through the author's consciousness, take on a creatively poetic form: the quivering of a leaf in the wind, flying swallows, flies rising and falling, the sound of a motor horn, "all of this, calm and reasonable as it was, made out of ordinary things as it was, was the truth now; beauty, that was the truth now. Beauty was everywhere" (105). Keats has reemerged. But as in the poet's odes, the temptation is to freeze the moment and escape time's uncompromising slide through life toward death. Septimus, like Clarissa, "could not look upon the dead" (105). The sayings he writes on the backs of envelopes acknowledging life and change seek also to create a shockproof world, permanent and self-sufficient, complete as the wholeness that Mrs. Dalloway in Bond Street expresses on her morning walk.

The very act of writing would appear an attempt, again like Jacob's, to fix the moment, to find coherence and sanity in wholeness and stasis. The world, however, continually interrupts his artistic and psychological effort to create a haven; Rezia in particular "was always interrupting," urging him to "look," urging him into a future he has chosen to avoid. It is no accident that Septimus breaks down completely as his wife makes plans for children of their own. Septimus shuns the future as he shuns death. Afraid of change, afraid to effect change, he capitulates as often as he resists: "Nothing could rouse him. Rezia put him to bed" (137). The doctor she sends for initiates a therapy of self-control, which only reactivates his fear of life. The final diagnosis of Bradshaw (a specialist on war-inflicted trauma) is to insist on total separation from all sources of future shock, most notably from Rezia: "The people we are most fond of are not good for us when we are ill" (223).

Between the acts of Bradshaw's intended scenario, before Septimus is to be placed in a rest home, he breaks through to the reality of Rezia's presence. Husband and wife wait in what appears to be a "pocket of still air," on "the edge" of some forest, where "warmth lingers, and the air buffets the cheek like the wing of a bird" (218). In this suspended moment when, as with Clarissa in that interim before Big Ben strikes, the processes of civilization are disengaged, Septimus comes to life.[21]

Driven literally and metaphorically to the edge of history, he finally acts to deny those civilizing forces that would convert him to "reason." Before he jumps through the lodging-house window to his death, Septimus relaxes his will to re-main sane. Lying on the sofa, he allows the very images of his madness, a bubbling variety of sights and sounds, to pour like water on him: "The sound of water was in the room and through the waves came the voices of birds singing. Every power poured its treasures on his head, and his hands lay there on the back of the sofa, as he had seen his hand lie when he was bathing, floating, on the top of the waves" (211).

For the moment he surmounts his fears. With new courage he begins cautiously "to open his eyes, to see whether a gramo-phone was really there" (215). Then, all but miraculously, as he accepts the chaotic reality of things in themselves, things that do not rely on his intellectual jurisdiction for their being in space, he begins to talk with Rezia, responds to her words and her work. The hat she is making for Mrs. Peters, he ven-tures, is too small: "an organ grinder's monkey's hat." Par-ticipating in her art, Septimus takes up the ribbons and beads and artificial flowers and creates a design, which Rezia happily sews into a hat. The action, if commonplace (and it is after all the smallest of events), signifies life at its fullest. For Woolf as well as Forster, connection is all.

The police, however, are not long inactive. Civilization re-turns with a vengeance to stamp its image on the faces of the weak. And Septimus will have none of it. His suicide is an act against those like Bradshaw who "make life intolerable." Clarissa's instinctive dislike of this overbearing man leads her finally to identify with Septimus. Both struggle to preserve a vague and ill-defined sense of goodness against those "doctors and wise men" who have long since decided about the nature of truth.[22]

Despite her capacity for imaginative flight, Clarissa, like her counterpart, is tempted continually to crystallize the pres-ent, to make something more permanent of those unsettling moments that arise in the midst of daily routine. The temptation affects Woolf's notion of art as much as her character's notion of life. In either case, to poeticize the moment invites closure.

Clarissa, looking at the passing car at the same time as Septimus, renders the image into an "enduring symbol of the state" (23), still the soul of her social identity. The sight of the seal the footman holds, "white, magical, circular" (24), conveys a profound basis for the faith of all who watch—all but the dislocated Septimus. Mrs. Dalloway, standing outside the flower shop, "stiffened a little" at the thought of her own proximity to this source of majesty. That night she will preside at a grand party. The prime minister will be among the guests. Yet there, at her moment of crisis, when she must face the reality of Septimus's death alone, it will be the absence of patriarchal models, Peter and Richard as well as the prime minister, that leads to her recovery. Here on Oxford Street, as the many clocks strike eleven and as Septimus wanders in isolation through an unfamiliar world, bound to a sovereign he cannot see, the object of Clarissa's devotion remains reassuringly immanent. The religion she shares with the crowd of onlookers lifts her "beyond seeking and questing" into a world "all spirit, disembodied, ghostly" (42), a world mirrored in the stillness of St. Paul's Cathedral, where the casual visitor may confront and glorify permanence. If there is no noise of traffic within, one may presume an extended metaphor; in the presence of authority everything outside, we recall, "had come to a standstill" (20).

Clarissa's sense of belonging as she enters her house is drawn in no less clerical terms: she feels, we are told, like a nun returned from the lordly to a more private realm of worship, where death as well as life has lost its sting. "The hall of the house was cool as a vault" (42). She feels cold and disembodied, her life shaped by the rhythm of a liturgy that would dull the mind to all but its own calming influence:

Mrs. Dalloway

Fear no more the heat o' the sun,
Nor the furious winter's rages.

Even Shakespeare, reduced to opiate, entices the mind to rest.* Surrounded once more by "familiar veils" and "old devotions"—the sounds of the Irish cook whistling from the kitchen, a member of the family typing—she feels at once "blessed and purified." She bends over the hall table, "bowed" as if in prayer, to give thanks to the powers who have allowed this special moment to flower "for her eyes only." If she does not believe in God, she knows to whom to give thanks: "above all to Richard her husband, who was the foundation of it." The table with its message pad, however, interrupts her liturgy: "The shock of Lady Bruton asking Richard to lunch without her made the moment in which she had stood shiver, as a plant on the river-bed feels the shock of a passing oar and shivers; so she rocked: so she shivered" (44).

Like Septimus in madness, Clarissa's inclination is to withdraw from shock. Having read the note, she retreats to the privacy of an upstairs bedroom. We learn that she has been sick, and that her husband "insisted, after her illness that she must sleep undisturbed." Doctor and husband counsel separation as the remedy for disrupted feeling.

But as she is retiring Clarissa's mind, tunneling into past and present, widens the context of her world. In motion she is no longer one thing. If she is a "nun withdrawing," she is also "a child exploring." As on her walk, a variety of incidents arises to engage her attention. She pauses to indulge each new experience—a flash of green linoleum, the sound of a dripping faucet—and her sense of identity expands again to include

*Critics are inclined rather to view these lines from *Cymbeline* (IV, ii) as an expression of art's timeless essence. Joan Bennett, for example, discusses them as aspects of "that deeper level at which the mind apprehends timeless values." *Virginia Woolf: Her Art as a Novelist* (Cambridge, Eng., 1964), p. 100.

that which is not herself. In loosening her hold on things, "seeing the glass, the dressing table, and all the bottles afresh" (54), Clarissa finds she has all but forgotten her grievance against Lady Bruton.

Though her role as wife to Mr. Dalloway is by definition limiting (despite Richard's objection, what can she *do* short of giving parties?), Clarissa has the special talent "of making a world of her own wherever she happened to be" (114). Whether, as Peter Walsh surmises, this is identifiably a "woman's gift," it anticipates the question of art's relationship to social function. Women, existing largely outside the world of power, can come in Woolf's view to acquire a more disinterested (as distinct from indifferent) respect for things in themselves. Clarissa's willingness continually to revise her relationship to the extended world of past and present challenges all who surround her to similar acts of re-creation. Her reconstituted moments challenge the presumptive formulations of an age that rarely questions itself. The safe alternative is parodied in that paragon of good taste, Hugh Whitbread, who, avoiding depth, spends his day placidly brushing surfaces.

In the attic room to which she has retired, Clarissa by contrast faces her own presuppositions, ranging from disappointment to envy, and the complexities these emotions bring to consciousness. If her husband has prompted isolation, a narrowing of exposure to others (reflected in the narrowness of her separate bed) as the basis for recuperation, she acknowledges a certain coldness of spirit within herself that tempts her from relationships; she prefers reading memoirs.

Her relationship with both men and women speaks of a lack of "something central which permeated; something warm which broke up surfaces and rippled the cold contact of man and woman, or of women together" (46). More than sexual, the failure she confesses involves the inability to move out of herself into the existence of others, to leave the safe confines of her familiar past and present and risk the future. She lacks the "abandonment" of spirit that allows foreigners and only a few Englishwomen (she has in mind her friend Sally Seton) to say and do anything they please. And that, presumably, is why she married Richard rather than Peter in the first place. Or was there another motive?

As Clarissa tunnels into her past, we are struck by her willingness to raise those fundamental issues her society tends to avoid. She questions the meaning of "love," "life," and finally "death," struggling to face these realities as they confront her own existence. "This question of love" leads, in her attic room, to the insight that her feeling for Sally, unlike her feeling for a man, has been "completely disinterested" (50). In contrast to detachment, disinterest presumes a passion for the thing in itself and the capability (Keats termed it a virtue of negation) of allowing what is other to remain so—to connect without imposing. Clarissa's objection to Peter's assertive egotism reflects Woolf's larger critique.

Had she married Peter she never would have known that dignity, the gulf between husband and wife, that underlies one of the author's fundamental convictions about human relationship. So particularly in marriage "a little independence there must be between people living together day in day out in the same house" (10). This Richard has given her.

Rezia angers Septimus when, intruding on his serious thoughts, she exhorts him to take notice of other things or to share his insights with her; she was, we remember, "always interrupting" (36). Clarissa, reflecting on her former life at Bourton, recalls how Peter intruded on "the most exquisite moment of her whole life," when Sally had kissed her. The shock of his insensitive comment—"Star-gazing?"—was understandably a source of grievance. "Oh this horror! she said to herself, as if she had known all along that something would interrupt, would embitter her moment of happiness." But even here a widening of thought takes place as Clarissa acknowledges: "Yet, after all, how much she owed to him later" (53).*

Peter, like Septimus, takes himself with guarded seriousness. Where fantasies invade the consciousness of either man, they remain largely self-sustaining romances, controlled and directed by the needs vanity prescribes. The important exception for Septimus is the one instance when he breaks through to Rezia. So Peter, pursuing an attractive woman in Trafalgar Square, remains omnisciently above the self-indulgent scenario he envisions. His adventure leads him finally to stasis, to dream in Regent's Park of some spectral nurse, "champion of the rights of sleepers," who rules and protects him from the "fever of living." If move he must, "let me walk straight on to this great figure, who will, with a toss of her head, mount me on her streamers and let me blow to nothingness with the rest" (87). In company with Jacob, Peter moves toward dissolution.

But Clarissa's disruptive presence, when Peter visits her home on this same June morning, will awaken him to a renewed desire for experience. Jarred into "idiosyncrasy," Peter finds himself appreciating an infinitely rich and changing environment as he walks through the London streets: "intangible things you couldn't lay your hands on—that shift in the whole pyramidal accumulation which in his youth had seemed immovable" (246). Only when he arrives at the Dalloway party will he revert to old and guarded ways. But this is to come later, after he has intruded on Clarissa's privacy.

Clarissa's memories of Peter's continued assault on her defects—"How he scolded her"—similarly disturb her inclination to fall into thoroughly derivative and settled roles. Peter, undermining definition as he does, contributes to the healthy ambiguity Woolf develops in her protagonist. After thinking of her relationship with him, Clarissa "would not say of anyone in the world now that they were this or were that. . . .

---

*By contrast with the scene in *The Voyage Out* when Hewet disturbs Rachel at the piano, here Woolf's tolerance for interruption appears greater.

She would not say of Peter, she would not say of herself, I am this, I am that" (11). So when he makes his unexpected entrance, interrupting her sewing, she resists the compulsion to reduce his being to the contours of a past grievance or, for that matter, to the reality of his own abrasive ideology.

Reacting to Peter rather than to her idea of him, Clarissa allows her impulses freedom to enlarge in the ensuing interview. While the moment is largely fictional—"It was as if the five acts of a play that had been very exciting and moving were now over and she had lived a lifetime in them and had run away, had lived with Peter, and it was now over" (70–71)—her vision is only half made up. Free of grievance or judgment, she responds with enchantment to those substantial sounds and gestures that reveal her old friend. If Peter and Clarissa, separated as they are by time and circumstance, touch each other only tentatively—"as a bird touches a branch and rises and flutters away" (64)—we are moved by their groping effort to reach one another.

What is to be loved or hated in another is often in Woolf a composite based on the most fragmentary of details: Clarissa's recollection, for example, of Peter's half-opening a penknife. Typically for Woolf, human intercourse occurs on the boundary of the mind's knowledge, some obscure communion deeper than ideology and more fundamental than sex. The experience tends to point beyond language itself and, insofar as it remains susceptible to description, urges her toward a special rendering of the novel as a vehicle for communication. In this regard, *Mrs. Dalloway* anticipates *The Waves*. Along with her heroine, Woolf considers the English language rich and flexible enough to convey radically disparate notions of human authenticity. Clarissa's "offering"—the sense, however vague, of her party-giving—seeks a more spontaneous basis for talk as well as for other forms of social relationship. Inspired to bring people together for no reason whatsoever, Mrs.

Dalloway could imagine neither Peter nor her husband acting with such unpremeditated abandon.

The disposition of the party in Mrs. Dalloway and Clarissa's role as hostess have led many readers to emphasize its author's satirical intention. If Woolf and her Bloomsbury friends had a preference for parties, and of course they did, only Clive Bell (many of whose personal qualities can be seen in Peter Walsh) had a taste for high society. Can one imagine any character present at the Dalloway party comfortably included at a Bloomsbury Thursday evening? Even so, Clarissa's motives in giving parties, the reality she seeks to create and share, reflect a number of important Bloomsbury assumptions. With G. E. Moore, Clarissa would call her guests to celebrate "the pleasures of human intercourse and the enjoyment of beautiful objects,"[23] which is to say the value of things in themselves. No less crucial, art remains for her an intrinsic good rather than the means to an end. Through her revised protagonist, the novelist struggled to formulate the proper role for the artist, a task that led directly to her representation of Lily Briscoe in To the Lighthouse and beyond that to her most experimental novel, The Waves.

The problem of making a successful party, like the problem of making a good book, is to create the conditions that will inspire mutuality. The good hostess, like the good writer, while technically in charge, remains unnoticed. Things start to move at the Dalloway party when Clarissa, standing at the top of the stairs, steps back and allows the random talk of people to move at its own course. But first her intention to control events must be thwarted; once again the catalyst is Peter Walsh. The thought of his criticism throws her into confusion: "It was extraordinary how Peter put her into these states just by coming and standing in a corner. He made her see herself" (255). Peter's wandering away just when Clarissa would speak to him increases her frustration. At the same time she realizes a failure in her role: everything about the party is "going wrong . . . falling flat." The guests appear walking about aimlessly, bunched in corners and, worst of all, like "Ellie Henderson, not even caring to hold themselves upright" (255). The familiar word signals Clarissa's retreat. Ellie in her "weaponless state," deprived of self-assurance, has cause for poor posture. It is Richard who moves to talk with her as Clarissa, under the spell of grievance, remains stationary.

At this point the narrative directs us to a yellow curtain, designed with exotic birds, that is blowing out gently from an open window. In her earlier meeting with Peter, the first recollection of the past they share is "how the blinds used to flap at Bourton" (62). Now, mysteriously, as if the space outside somehow affects the moment, the party suddenly comes to life. What seems to motivate this change is merely the image of one undistinguished guest, Ralph Lyon, beating back the curtain as he goes on talking. The gesture is as unpremeditated as Lily Briscoe's impulsive act of drawing a line across the center of her canvas at the end of *To the Lighthouse*. Clarissa's sense—"It had begun. It had started"—is accompanied by a new impulse that holds her back: "She must stand there for the present" (259).

At Bourton, Peter predicted "she would marry a Prime Minister and stand at the top of a staircase" (9). The image fulfilled in his mind her role as "the perfect hostess." So he sees her at this moment (although Richard Dalloway, not even in the cabinet, has fallen far short of such expectations). But he misreads Clarissa's impulse. Far from some majestic desire to oversee the party, she is affected by the demand to let things be. She has created the festivity; now her task is to allow the party to develop a life of its own.

Descending to her guests, this time in the guise of anonymity, Clarissa celebrates the movement that surrounds her; "one felt them going on, going on" (260). No longer stiffly self-conscious, she moves with less severity; "her prudery, her woodenness were all warmed through now." Woolf emphasizes

Clarissa's unbridled motion as she glides, or more precisely "floats," from one group to the next. Like a mermaid, "lolloping on the waves and braiding her tresses she seemed, having that gift still; to be; to exist . . . all with the most perfect ease and air of a creature floating in its element" (264).

If Clarissa finds it difficult to define the meaning of "this thing she called life," she has, with Septimus, broken through to the reality of "something not herself." At the close of the novel, she can imagine his suicide as "an attempt to communicate," because she extends, as Mrs. Dalloway in Bond Street could not, the narrow limits of her social role. Unlike the young guests at her party, Clarissa will not solidify. Having relinquished command, she entertains a world of motion and change.

Chapter Six

A VOID AT THE CENTER
To the Lighthouse

From the outset of her literary career, Woolf responded to "a zone of silence" she came repeatedly to recognize "in the middle of every art."[1] Reappearing in varying forms—the stillness of the Amazon forest; a sense of chasm in *Jacob's Room;* the "indescribable pauses" Mrs. Dalloway acknowledges half guiltily on the streets of London—such moments loosen, as we have seen, the prescribed order of things.[2]

The culmination of Lily Briscoe's vision in *To the Lighthouse* occurs as she draws a line through that "awkward vacancy" at the center of her canvas. In the course of a decade she has resolved first to fill and then to avoid this empty space. As Avrom Fleishman points out, her action confronts two problems: "It is a personal emptiness as well as visual space that must be filled or accommodated by the imagination."[3]

Recently published autobiographical writings reveal more fully how *To the Lighthouse* reflects Woolf's own effort to deal with the sense of void occasioned by her mother's premature death. If her first impulse was to focus on her father—"The centre is father's character, sitting in a boat, reciting We per-ished, each alone, while he crushes a dying mackerel"⁴—the figure of her mother rises quickly to displace him. Far more than Leslie, it is Julia Stephen who marks Virginia's recollec-tion of a time when life appeared unalterably "there." "Why is there not a discovery in Life?" the novelist asks as she writes the first section of *To the Lighthouse*. "Something one can lay hands on & say 'This is it?'"⁵

The inaccessibility of things becomes, ironically, the center of her novel and the medium for growth. A passage from her diary, describing the effort of beginning the "Time Passes" sec-tion, makes this clearer: "I have to give an empty house, no people's characters, the passage of time, all eyeless & feature-less with nothing to cling to. . . . Why am I so flown with words, & apparently free to do exactly what I like?"* Nothing-ness, an important aspect of interruption, moves her to re-shape and revise her own past experience as well as the basis of her art.

In retrospect, the impact of radical loss inspires a wider vi-sion of external reality. "My mother's death," she writes in "A Sketch of the Past," "unveiled and intensified; made me sud-denly develop perceptions."⁶ After meeting her brother Thoby at Paddington shortly before the funeral, she recalls how the station, "glowing yellow and red" in the evening light, ap-peared suddenly more vast and magnificent than ever before: "It was surprising—as if something were becoming visible without any effort." A similar experience at that time occurs in Kensington Square while she is reading a poem: "It was as if it became altogether intelligible; I had a feeling of trans-

*Woolf, *The Diary of Virginia Woolf* (New York, 1980), 3: 76. The light-house is no less accessible. "I meant *nothing* by the lighthouse," she wrote in a letter to Roger Fry. "One has to have a central line down the middle of the book to hold the design together." *The Letters of Virginia Woolf* (New York, 1978), 3: 385.

parency in words when they cease to be words and become so intensified that one seems to experience them."[7]

Contrasting images recur in this sketch: one of surrounding space, vast and inviting, conveying, like Keats's famous letter to John Reynolds on the many-chambered Mansion of Life, mysterious possibilities for being; the other an obsessive evocation of her mother standing more firmly than her father at the center of everything. Comparing Julia Stephen in an early reminiscence to "some wise Fate" watching "the birth, growth, flower and death of innumerable lives," it is easy to understand why her presiding image invites idolatry. "All lives directly she crossed them seemed to form themselves into a pattern and while she stayed each move was of the utmost importance."[8]

To the Lighthouse probes those moments when human volition flags. One of many such lulls occurs as Lily Briscoe and William Bankes, pausing in their walk to watch the Ramsay children playing ball on the lawn, experience in the moment between the throw and the catch "a sense of things having been blown apart, of space, of irresponsibility" (111).[9] As they lose sight of the ball in its trajectory across the sky, the usual course of events is suspended and transformed for the two observers and for the reader: "It seemed as if solidity had vanished altogether" (111).

However trivial, such lapses serve to interrupt household patterns. Not until Mrs. Ramsay restores order by recalling social decorum can Mr. Ramsay resume his comic speculations on Hume "stuck in a bog." Voicing concern that two of her guests, Paul and Minta, may be walking on the beach unchaperoned, her first words—"Haven't they come back yet?"—and subsequent inquiry—"Did Nancy go with them?"—reestablish surveillance. The description of her "bringing Prue back into throwing catches again, from which she had escaped" (112), conveys a narrowing mediation if not a hint of despotism.

To the Lighthouse

By breaking the spell of this interim experience, Mrs. Ramsay guards Prue's future as well as her own. The suspension of domestic roles—the activity of raising children and supporting husbands—constitutes a dangerous submission to things vague and volatile: "She felt this thing that she called life terrible, hostile, and quick to pounce on you if you gave it a chance" (92). Regretting that people—more particularly her own children—must ever grow up, she is aware at times of compulsiveness: "She was driven on, too quickly she knew, almost as if it were an escape for her too, to say that people must marry; people must have children" (92-93). Ironically, it is the danger of Prue's escape from a domestic world whose ethos is marriage that underlies Mrs. Ramsay's subsequent intervention on the lawn.

Where her husband, preoccupied with his own thoughts and desires, remains studiously uninterested in William and Lily walking in the garden, Mrs. Ramsay, oblivious of any other basis for their intimacy, all but determines their future: "They must marry" (109). Ignoring her friend's artistic inclinations—"One could not take her painting very seriously" (29)—she pictures Lily Briscoe's happiness almost exclusively in the terms imposed by society. Mrs. Ramsay's very presence restrains Lily's impulse to experiment, most notably at the dinner table, when Lily's small rebellion, anticipating the children's compact to resist their father, virtually dissolves under Mrs. Ramsay's influence. "There was something frightening about her," Lily reflects. "She was irresistible. Always she got her own way in the end" (152).

This analysis applies to the proposed lighthouse expedition as well as to Mrs. Ramsay's matchmaking, which is to say, her power affects family as well as friends. Mr. Ramsay's small triumph regarding the aborted excursion—we must assume the weather did in fact turn—pales by comparison. So strong is her influence that ten years later he will feel bound to complete the interrupted trip. Without the "circle of life" she

weaves about him, his accomplishments seem barren. Her assurance alone relieves the lingering anxiety that he has not in
fact climbed high enough.

Holding young James on her lap, Mrs. Ramsay creates life-
sustaining patterns for her children as she does for her husband: "Flashing her needles, confident, upright, she created
drawing-room and kitchen, set them all aglow; bade him take
his ease there, go in and out, enjoy himself" (59). Only the
poet Augustus Carmichael, distrustful of such benevolent
overtures, resists. As he shuffles away from her offer of aid, his
irritating noncompliance only increases the discontent still
lingering from her argument with Mr. Ramsay. For the moment she pauses, uncharacteristically, to question whether
the motive "to give, to help, was vanity. For her own self-
satisfaction was it that she wished so instinctively to help, to
give, that people might say of her, 'O Mrs. Ramsay! dear Mrs.
Ramsay...Mrs. Ramsay, of course!' and need her and send for
her and admire her?" (65). Her reflection, however, turns facilely toward a less incriminating conclusion that all human relations are at best "self-seeking."

If Lily cannot act with similar autonomy in her presence—
Mrs. Ramsay professes to admire her friend's independent nature (29)—she is aware how readily Mrs. Ramsay, presuming
as she does that her pity alone permits them to survive, pa-
tronizes men: "It was one of those misjudgments of hers that
seemed to be instinctive and to arise from some need of her
own rather than of other people's. He is not in the least piti-
able. He has his work, Lily said to herself" (128). Suggestively, this small resistance inspires an alternative effort: "She
remembered, all of a sudden as if she had found a treasure,
that she had her work. In a flash she saw her picture, and
thought, Yes, I shall put the tree further in the middle; then I
shall avoid that awkward space" (128).

The intuition is short-lived. She cannot escape society's

prescriptions any more than Jacob could, and Mrs. Ramsay in charge requires that Lily be insincerely pleasant to Charles Tansley, whose injured vanity has driven him into a potentially disruptive silence. Like any good conductor, Mrs. Ramsay directs her players with a glance: "For the hundred and fiftieth time Lily Briscoe had to renounce the experiment—what happens if one is not nice to that young man there—and be nice" (139). But in performing "the usual trick," she pays the price of sincerity, and the possibility of communication ends. "She would never know him. He would never know her" (139).

Mrs. Ramsay's dinner party draws everyone willingly into its protective circle: "They were all conscious of making a party together in a hollow, on an island; had their common cause against that fluidity out there" (147). Like Mr. Ramsay, who ultimately wins his naval victory—accomplished through the seamanship of his son grown older—Mrs. Ramsay, confronting a similar antagonist, guides her ship artfully to a safe harbor: "Inside the room, seemed to be order and dry land; there, outside, a reflection in which things wavered and vanished, waterily" (147). While such events shimmer with a certain Victorian authenticity, they remain for Woolf essentially reactionary celebrations of a paradigmatic wholeness that denies every premise of modernism.[10]

Throughout her novels, windows usually welcome the external world; here they preclude it. Fragile "panes of glass" hold back an oceanic darkness that seems to threaten everyone but Lily. Noting that the windows are "uncurtained" and how candlelight has made everything appear unreal, she compares the feeling with "that moment on the tennis lawn, when solidity suddenly vanished, and such vast spaces lay between them" (147). Now, as then, the intuition arises through a break in design, occasioned by the absence of Paul and Minta. They are late for dinner. "Unable, she felt, to settle things,"

Mrs. Ramsay finds herself fluctuating between uneasiness and expectation, while Lily, animated by the disruption, revels in the sense that "anything might happen" (147).

Shortly after the couple appear at the table, their hostess expresses similar feelings but for ironically different reasons. The inspiration of a match between Lily and William Bankes institutes a change of tactics: "Foolishly, she had set them opposite each other. That could be remedied tomorrow. If it were fine, they should go for a picnic. Everything seemed possible" (157).

Mrs. Ramsay's visions of the future remain but an extension of past decorum. The meal she offers her guests commemorates in her mind Paul and Minta's eternal union—or so at any rate she conceives their marriage vow. She would help William and Lily to a similar "piece of eternity," which is to say, to a history "immune from change." However disposed to agnostic principles, Mrs. Ramsay seems to consider marriage the last vestige of Godhead.

Dipping down into the abundance of the "huge brown pot," a resolved confusion of colors and smells, the reader shares its rich perfection. Nourished, however, by a culture that honors romantic epiphanies, we tend to celebrate not the unfolding event but the achievement, Woolf would emphasize, of our own acquisitive goals, "something one can lay hands on." Such sovereign moments fulfill a predilection for closure by lifting us above existence. If the meat is delicious and tender, the image of eternity it arouses in Mrs. Ramsay's mind remains hard and gemlike: "There is a coherence in things, a stability; something, she meant, is immune from change, and shines out (she glanced at the window with its ripple of reflected lights) in the face of the flowing, the fleeting, the spectral, like a ruby" (158).

A jewel, like any family heirloom, ensures coherence through possession. When Minta loses the brooch her grandmother has passed on to her, the loss threatens her well-being. On the beach, Nancy senses something more at stake: "It might be true that she minded losing her brooch, but she wasn't crying only for that. She was crying for something else. We might all sit down and cry, she felt. But she did not know what for" (117).

Paul's intention to go secretly to Edinburgh at dawn and "buy her another, just like it but more beautiful," not only gives him something to do, but also anticipates his role as her provider. Through Lily's eyes, his exquisite profile, again "like a gem's" (154), pervades her own ambiguous thoughts on love and marriage, urging her for an instant to join in the search for the lost brooch. She resists such calls. Her ultimate choice in the novel remains for less-crystallized and transfixed forms of work and play.

It is industriousness as much as intrusiveness that motivates Carmichael's displeasure: "One could not imagine Mrs. Ramsay standing painting, lying reading, a whole morning on the lawn. It was unthinkable" (291). At least once, however, she expresses a preference for doing nothing. On that occasion, having fulfilled her domestic chores, she indulges the thought of her personality shrinking to "a wedge-shaped core of darkness," free from all forms of human duty and intercourse. But as she entertains such thoughts of disengagement, her fingers remain dutifully employed, first putting away the pictures James has cut out from an illustrated catalogue, then in the more familiar "upright" occupation of knitting. On the one occasion on which she pauses in her daydream to look outward, it is to merge with the stroke of the lighthouse; "in this mood, always at this hour one could not help attaching oneself to one thing" (96–97).

With her daily responsibilities over, she feels "free for the strangest adventures. When life sank down for a moment, the range of experience seemed limitless. . . . This core of darkness could go anywhere, for no one saw it" (95–96). Like her husband's scholarly expectations, which invite an alphabetical paradigm—he had reached the letter Q; he braced himself for the pursuit of R (53–55)—Mrs. Ramsay's modest dreams remain suggestively derivative. There are still a number of places she has not seen: the plains of India, a church in Rome. Only figuratively do her horizons seem still "limitless" (96). From one perspective, at least, the motivation for such inward voyages proves no less conventional and programmatic than Jacob's pursuit of other countries.

More important, Mrs. Ramsay experiences in these crystalline moments a sense of privacy all but immune from interruption. Drawn to inanimate, single objects, she divulges through her fantasies a narrowing rather than an expanding sense of reality: "Losing personality, one lost the fret, the hurry, the stir; and there rose to her lips always some exclamation of triumph over life when things came together in this peace, this rest, this eternity" (96).*

The peace she acquires is a victory over time and space. In this instance, attaching herself to the steady beat of the lighthouse beam, "she became the thing she looked at" (97). Mr. Ramsay walks by her as she knits, and struck by "the sternness at the heart of her beauty," he for once appears to honor her solitude: "He would not interrupt her. She was aloof from him now in her beauty, in her sadness. He would let her be" (100). But it is not in fact respect for privacy that holds him back; it is a sense of aesthetic perfection: "She was lovely, lovelier now than ever he thought" (100). When Mrs. Ramsay, in submitting to his needs, finally speaks, it is to reassure him that despite their argument, he remains her lord and protector.

---

*This passage can be read as a celebration of Mrs. Ramsay's capacity to suspend conventional roles. In view of her rise here to a controlling omniscience, I read "losing personality" ironically.

Just as Mr. Ramsay looks to his books and students for some measure of immortality, so Mrs. Ramsay looks to the matching of Paul and Minta to flatter her "where she was most susceptible of flattery, to think how, wound about in their hearts, however long they lived she would be woven" (170). As she recalls how she had preserved her parents' design, her thoughts of the Rayleys marrying, taking up this tapestry, ensure her own survival.

The notion of life "going on" outside the range of her encompassing domain is as perplexing and unsettling to Mrs. Ramsay as the idea of non-being. When Mr. Bankes, interrupting her reminiscence about old mutual friends, reports on their most recent activities, she finds it "strange and distasteful" that the Mannings should exist "all these years when she had not thought of them" (133).

A contingent, external world disturbs Mr. Bankes with no less impact as he sits talking with his hostess. If her remarks about Carrie Manning make him feel less parochially enclosed—"He never let himself get into a groove" (133)—Mrs. Ramsay's breaking away in the middle of his sentence to address the maid offends him unduly: "That was why he preferred dining alone. All those interruptions annoyed him" (133).

Deprived of her attention, having nothing to do, he becomes first mechanically courteous, then sullen. His irritation grows in proportion to Mrs. Ramsay's diminishing attention: "At this moment her presence meant absolutely nothing to him: her beauty meant nothing to him. . . . He felt uncomfortable; he felt treacherous" (134).

Such moments anticipate, as we have seen, discomforting questions: "It was in this sort of state that one asked oneself, What does one live for? Why, one asked oneself, does one take all these pains for the human race to go on? Is it so very desirable? Are we attractive as a species? . . . Foolish ques-

tions, vain questions, questions one never asked if one was occupied" (134–35).

Mrs. Ramsay's job, at the dinner table as in her household,
is to ensure continuity. Once Lily has been conscripted in this
endeavor, Mrs. Ramsay can entertain what at first glance
would appear a different impulse: "She could return to that
dream land, that unreal but fascinating place, the Mannings'
drawing-room at Marlow twenty years ago; where one moved
about without haste or anxiety, for there was no future to
worry about. She knew what had happened to them, what to
her. It was like reading a good book again, for she knew the
end of the story" (140).

In reading as in fantasizing, however, Mrs. Ramsay retains
control of her subject matter.[11] The satisfaction she draws
from each recalls Jacob reading the *Phaedrus* and climbing
mountains. Reciting a line of poetry while sitting with her
husband after dinner—the scene of her last triumph—"she
was ascending, she felt, on to the top, on to the summit"
(181). As she stands omnisciently above the world, free of "all
the odds and ends of the day," the text becomes her jewel:
"She held it in her hands, beautiful and reasonable, clear and
complete, the essence sucked out of life and held rounded
here—the sonnet" (181).

We notice that such aesthetic tastes, literary and otherwise,
are derived at least in part from her husband. Early in the
novel, standing with Charles Tansley before the bay, she responds it would appear spontaneously to the beauty of the
scene, only to acknowledge quickly: "That was the view . . .
her husband loved" (23). At the close of the dinner party, Mr.
Ramsay's rendering of "Luriana Lurilee" similarly authenticates her own deepest feelings.[12] Even in the midst of disagreement and grievance—he has after all damned her—she submits willingly to a reading that affirms "the folly of women's
minds." Like the commander of Tennyson's light brigade—
"Some one had blundered"—hers is not to reason why, a dic-

tum Mrs. Ramsay appears only too willing to honor: "There was nobody whom she reverenced as she reverenced him. She was quite ready to take his word for it. . . . There was nobody she reverenced more. She was not good enough to tie his shoe strings, she felt" (51).

While poetry conveys ideology, it is also a means of escape for Mr. Ramsay as for his wife. The impulsive suggestion that he may be wrong about the weather sends him scurrying angrily toward the privacy of literature to enjoy a world free of unreasonable interruptions. Repeating the line "Some one had blundered" as he glares—"without seeming to see them" (31)—at Lily and William, he avoids the impact of others. Since he hungers no less ardently for unbroken sequence, such petulance seems inspired by metaphysical as well as personal doubts.

If, at the outset of the novel, Mr. Ramsay overreacts to the question of the weather, it is no doubt because his wife's unreasonable expectations represent a more fundamental threat to the coherence of mind and language. This was a time, Woolf recollects in her sketch of the past, when "no sooner has one said this was so, than it was past and altered."[13]

Beginning with a question we never hear, the rhythm of discourse in *To the Lighthouse* moves to the recurring beat of qualification: "'Yes, of course, if it's fine tomorrow,' said Mrs. Ramsay. 'But you'll have to be up with the lark,' she added" (9). Like the sound of the waves, the prepositional conjunction "but" is heard throughout the narrative. Under its impact life as well as thought becomes by necessity less self-contained, in a manner of speaking less privileged. The revelation constitutes an early shock for James, who believes with childish faith that the expedition is "bound to take place." When Mr. Ramsay rudely interrupts his expectations by saying that "it won't be fine," his mother replies no less assuredly: "But it may be fine—I expect it will be fine" (11). Shifting in voice from "it may" to "it will," her opposition marks as much an advocacy of her own omniscient design as a defense of her son's feelings.

While James playfully cuts out photographs, his mother's thoughts and actions remain, as we have seen, fixed on the lighthouse. Impatiently knitting a stocking for the child of the keeper, rounding up old magazines, finding the tobacco, she persists in the belief that others cannot survive without her intervention, that they exist largely through her mediation. More important, the suspended trip leaves Mrs. Ramsay with no discernible end and with the possibility of "sitting all day with nothing to do." Her concern for "those poor fellows" in the lighthouse, deprived of a visit, masks this deeper anxiety.

As the impact of nothingness continues to disrupt routines in the novel, Mrs. Ramsay's resistance, like some rear guard action, seems equally futile and defensive. If her troops remain loyal, her presiding influence appears increasingly anachronistic. Anticipating not only the death of an age but her own death as well, Mrs. Ramsay's precipitous retreat after her triumphant dinner party occasions both confusion and dispersal: "Directly she went a sort of disintegration set in; they wavered about, went different ways" (168).

Moments earlier the recitation of Charles Elton's poem and the gallant gesture of Augustus Carmichael in bowing to her as he recites the last words—"Luriana, Lurilee"—removes the final obstacle: "She felt that he liked her better than he had ever done before" (167). Then, hesitating at the door through which he has just departed, as if to transfix the history of this triumphant moment in her own mind, she leaves the dining room with a certain sense of foreboding: "With her foot on the threshold she waited a moment longer in a scene which was vanishing even as she looked, and then, as she moved and took Minta's arm and left the room, it changed, it shaped itself differently; it had become, she knew, giving one last look at it over her shoulder, already the past" (167–68).

To the Lighthouse

It is the shock of time passing that drives her so abruptly from the room, not, as Lily mistakenly speculates, "something that had to be done at that precise moment, something that Mrs. Ramsay had decided for reasons of her own to do instantly" (168). As she pauses on her way upstairs, the reassuring sight of a clump of elms she glimpses through the window anchors her thoughts once again:

So she righted herself after the shock of the event, and quite unconsciously and incongruously, used the branches of the elm trees outside to help her to stabilize her position. Her world was changing: they were still. The event had given her a sense of movement. All must be in order. She must get that right and that right, she thought, insensibly approving of the dignity of the trees' stillness. (169)

Straight and steadfast as these trees, her being is grounded in the very substance of all that is most real to her. Encouraged by the thought that "it was all one stream," and that "Paul and Minta would carry it on when she was dead" (171), she returns to minister first to her children, then for one last time to her husband, reading downstairs. As she sits before him, "like a tree which has been tossing and quivering and now, when the breeze falls, settles" (177), she assumes an assured quietness. The image evolves as she too takes up a book, her eyes moving randomly from line to line "as from one branch to another" (179). Reading together, husband and wife conjoin in a final apotheosis of Victorian domesticity.

Predictably, Mrs. Ramsay's disappearance from the text creates a void no one seems eager to occupy. So completely has she filled the first section of To the Lighthouse that as "Time Passes" opens, we find ourselves waiting with the others for her reappearance. Without her the world loses shape and form. Anticipating The Waves, the syntax of these first lines spreads and disperses like a wave on the beach until Prue intervenes:

"Well, we must wait for the future to show," said Mr. Bankes, coming in from the terrace.

"It's almost too dark to see," said Andrew, coming up from the beach.

"One can hardly tell which is the sea and which is the land," said Prue.

"Do we leave that light burning?" said Lily as they took their coats off indoors.

"No," said Prue, "not if every one's in."

"Andrew," she called back, "just put out the light in the hall." (189)

As one by one the lamps are extinguished in the house, only Carmichael, reading Virgil by candlelight, remains awake, a last bulwark against the encroaching darkness. Inspired perhaps by this example, the narrator employs a somewhat different literary model in defense against the void.

From the classic to the romantic a similar intention informs literary endeavor, namely, to bring order to a world in which "divine promptitude" is either distorted or absent. The threat of a world deprived of Mrs. Ramsay's governing influence moves Woolf's narrator to deploy language as a means of softening the shock of non-being. Weaving nothingness into a romantic tapestry, her words seem designed to distract and comfort us. Like children at the feet of Mrs. Ramsay, we find our fears of the unknown allayed and bracketed by the contours of a melodious hyperbole. "Creeping in at keyholes and crevices," stealing "round window blinds," invading bedrooms, "the profusion of darkness" becomes "airs": "Almost one might imagine them, as they entered the drawing-room questioning and wondering, toying with the flap of hanging wall-paper, asking, would it hang much longer, when would it fall? Then smoothly brushing the walls" (190).

Until the caretaker intrudes, the narrator remains safely and omnisciently above her own fable. With no one to interrupt, all aspects of life are subsumed by her single voice. Just as Mrs. Ramsay has enjoined us to yield before the perfection of her design, so the narrator's comforting refrain, a liturgy in praise of beauty, lulls us into acquiescence:

So with the lamps all put out, the moon sunk. (189)

So some random light directing them. (191)

So with the house empty. (194)

So loveliness reigned and stillness. (195)

Mrs. Ramsay conceals the bareness of the pig's skull hanging in her children's bedroom by wrapping a shawl around it. Words offer the narrator, as I have suggested, a similar means of softening the impact both of space and of time passing. Since for Woolf "it is the nature of words to mean many things," all such narrowing intentions remain suspect. However artfully accomplished, this poetic idiom appears no less a cliché than Mrs. Ramsay's words, "We are in the hands of the Lord," which slip out as the rhythm of her thoughts merges with the beam of the lighthouse (97).

Once the narrator has narrowed and objectified the inhuman forces of nature, her language collapses frequently into a baroque and sentimental idiom: "The little airs mounted the staircase and nosed round bedroom doors. But here surely, they must cease. Whatever else may perish and disappear, what lies here is steadfast. . . . At length, desisting, all ceased together, gathered together, all sighed together; all together gave off an aimless gust of lamentation" (191).

The personification of the seasons that follows illustrates the same disposition. Winter deals out the nights "with indefatigable fingers" as if they were playing-cards, while autumn gives rise to a medley of romantic alliteration: "The autumn trees, ravaged as they are, take on the flash of tattered flags kindling in the gloom of cool cathedral caves where gold letters on marble pages describe death in battle and how bones bleach and burn far away in Indian sands" (192).

133

Like an early Keats poem or the succulence of Mrs. Ramsay's Boeuf en Daube, such offerings seem designed to tease us out of thought. Ironically, a no-less-romantic allusion serves to interrupt the narrator's monologue. The decrepit Mrs. McNab, "tearing the veil of silence with hands that had stood in the wash-tub," enters the novel with a markedly Wordsworthian amble.

If she is called on to set things in order, to stem the corruption of time passing, she does so with animal tranquility. Through her plebeian eyes the insensible forces of nature, resisting all aspects of caretaking, remain a source of distracting pleasure. Even after the notice, ten years later, that the house must be made ready for the Ramsays' return, her toil seems oddly irrelevant. As she first appears opening all the windows, dusting and singing some "old music hall song," she moves, it seems, irreverently, which is to say, without compulsion.

Mrs. McNab's attention, affected by years of servitude as well as old age, is distracted both by recollections of the past and by the objects that emerge around her. Through her presence nonhuman phenomena take on, moreover, a new integrity for the narrator and concurrently for the reader. Dropping her guard, she allows this new perspective to alter if not to reshape her tale.

The image of friends walking together by the sea as they have done at the close of Mrs. Ramsay's dinner party now gives us a widening, if less assured, realization of things. "Into a scene calculated to stir the most sublime reflections and lead to the most comfortable conclusions" there intrude small children playing war games on the beach, a passing ship bound perhaps for France, "a purplish stain" floating ominously on the water.[14] "It was difficult blandly to overlook them; to abolish their significance in the landscape; to continue, as one walked by the sea, to marvel how beauty outside mirrored beauty within" (201). Deprived of such consolations, the narrator, between the acts at least of her own scenario, confronts a world of broken sequence:[15] "To pace the beach was impossible; contemplation was unendurable; the mirror was broken" (202).

Slipping figuratively into the minds first of Mrs. McNab, then of George and Mrs. Bast, the narrator is inundated by unmediated detail: the shawl swinging in the wind, thistles between the tiles, nesting swallows, straw and plaster on the floor, bare rafters, rats behind the walls, butterflies on window-panes. The narrator luxuriates for a moment in the turbulence of this new vision: "Let the wind blow; let the poppy seed itself and the carnation mate with the cabbage. Let the swallow build in the drawing-room, and the thistle thrust aside the tiles, and the butterfly sun itself on the faded chintz of the arm-chairs. Let the broken glass and the china lie out on the lawn and be tangled over with grass and wild berries" (208).

The fear of dissolution, however, reoccasions hyperbole. "If the feather had fallen, if it had tipped the scale downwards, the whole house would have plunged to the depths to lie upon the sands of oblivion" (209). Mrs. McNab, combining work with play, interrupts the cliché: "But there was a force working; something not highly conscious; something that leered, something that lurched; something not inspired to go about its work with dignified ritual or solemn chanting. Mrs. McNab groaned; Mrs. Bast creaked. They were old; they were stiff; their legs ached" (209).

The good life the narrator no doubt enjoys in company with the Ramsays and their friends is sustained by such in-elegant labor. Moved outside the perspective of her class, the narrator expands her art to include such unattractive visions—this "laborious birth"—before self-interest inevitably resurfaces. She describes the rows of decaying books—"black as ravens once, now white-stained, breeding pale mushrooms and secreting furtive spiders." But the pargeting elegance of such language cannot sustain itself in a world of "intermittent music which the ear half catches but lets fall; a bark, a bleat;

irregular, intermittent, yet somehow related; the hum of an insect, the tremor of cut grass . . . the jar of a dorbeetle, the squeak of a wheel, loud, low, but mysteriously related" (212).

This new pageant of sounds builds to its climax with the appearance of Lily reentering the narrative, however parenthetically, unbracketed: "(Lily Briscoe had her bag carried up to the house late one evening in September)" (213).[16] Ten years have passed but the reconvening of their house party tempts the narrator once more to adorn the darkness. It is a regal and patriarchal figure she employs to describe the beauty of the night, "flowing down in purple; his head crowned, his scepter jewelled" (213).

With Lily falling quickly to sleep in her old room and Carmichael reading by candlelight, history seems, as Mrs. Ramsay had hoped, at the point of repeating itself; "it all looked, Mr. Carmichael thought, shutting his book, falling asleep, much as it used to look": "Indeed the voice might resume, as the curtains of dark wrapped themselves over the house . . . so that they lay with several folds of blackness on their eyes, why not accept this, be content with this, acquiesce and resign? The sigh of all the seas breaking in measure round the isles soothed them; the night wrapped them; nothing broke their sleep" (214). "Time Passes" ends, however, with Lily Briscoe "awake," ready in the absence of Mrs. Ramsay to ask questions of her own in a voice of her own.

While the "Lighthouse" section opens with Lily asking, "What does it mean, then, what can it all mean?" her mind, displacing the narrator's voice, turns to acknowledge the derivative nature even of such existential thrusts: "a catchword that was caught up from some book . . . to cover the blankness of her mind" (217). In the course of this small crisis, she will embrace her own artistic idiom as the means of confronting the nothingness Mrs. Ramsay's absence still occasions, a "blankness" that remains, then as now, uniquely

Lily's. For the time being, walking from the bedroom to her place at the breakfast table, she adopts old routines.

Outside the house, the reorganized trip to the lighthouse has been delayed. Neither Cam nor James is ready, Nancy has forgotten to order sandwiches, and no one seems to know what gifts to take, causing Mr. Ramsay to march back and forth on the terrace in a rage.

Sitting alone over her empty coffee cup, Lily struggles unsuccessfully to relive the past. With Mrs. Ramsay dead, it appears "as if the link that usually bound things together had been cut," and Lily along with the others now drifts aimlessly "up here, down there, off, anyhow" (219). A sense of frightening unreality—"Anything might happen"—startles her as it did years before when Paul and Minta were late for dinner. Whereas earlier the exciting possibility merged with Mrs. Ramsay's confidence in the ordained decorum of things—"They must come"—here, ten years later, it inspires Lily to begin painting. This sense of chaotic irresolution spurs her creative impulse, just as shortly it will affect the structure of her composition. Lily will employ art not to cover and conceal nothingness, but to convey its ever-expanding impact.

For now, the recollection of an old problem—how to bring together "the grey-green light on the wall" with the opposing "empty places"—moves her to begin again. "It had been knocking about in her mind all these years" (220). Significantly, only after Mr. Ramsay interrupts "the frail shape she was building," demanding attention and sympathy, does Lily's vision widen to include a more immediate sense of external things.

Following their short, unplanned conversation about boots, she finds him to be more than just the egotistical widower selfishly demanding time and attention. It is the most trivial of details—"He tied knots. He bought boots"—which she has presumably ignored, that brings him to life in her eyes. Where she could feel nothing for the absent Mrs. Ramsay, the sight of

Mr. Ramsay bending gallantly over her shoes, sharing his invention concerning shoelaces, inspires her with passion: "The blood rushed to her face, and, thinking of her callousness (she had called him a play-actor) she felt her eyes swell and tingle. . . . Thus occupied he seemed to her a figure of infinite pathos" (230).

What causes this transformation is a new perspective arising from a moment of mutual self-forgetfulness; they are saved by something outside themselves. If the patriarch has not in fact changed—he must lecture and instruct her still in the art of tying shoelaces—a sense of liberation pervades the entire scene. On this "blessed island of good boots," this space between human intentions, communication does occur. However short-lived, such unguarded moments form the basis of Woolf's anarchist faith.

Inspired by Mr. Ramsay's "sudden recovery of vitality and interest in ordinary human things" (233), Lily finds his abrupt departure toward the lighthouse nonetheless unsettling. Free to return to her painting, she responds ambivalently: "So they're gone, she thought, sighing with relief and disappointment" (233).

As she stands in front of her easel, her renewed sense of absence extends to include the unmarked canvas before her. At the far edge of the lawn, the definite sight of Cam and James following their father's "firm military tread" in pursuit of Mrs. Ramsay's goal only increases her feeling of anxiety: "She looked blankly at the canvas, with its uncompromising white stare" (234). With no mark on the wall to foster confidence, and no tangible spot from which to take stock, she falls back on the memory of things past, specifically on the structural problem that prevented her from finishing the painting ten years earlier. Employing the most recent detail at hand, the image of Mr. Ramsay lecturing on shoelaces, she visualizes it as a knot to be untied: "But there was all the difference in the world between this planning airily away from the canvas, and actually taking her brush and making the first mark" (234–35).

The consequences of the latter impress her immediately. To begin without assurance means to venture alone, to create a meaning for which one is solely responsible: "One line placed on the canvas committed her to innumerable risks, to frequent and irrevocable decisions" (235). As if plunging into the waves, she makes "her first quick decisive stroke." Immediately her motions become fluid. The rhythmical movement of her brush, the brown pigment running down the canvas, all serve to enclose a "space" that strikes her as the most "formidable" of realities. Its unsettling impact will not leave her in peace but rouses her instead to perpetual confrontation: "This formidable ancient enemy of hers—this other thing, this truth, this reality, which suddenly laid hands on her, emerged stark at the back of appearances and commanded her attention" (236).

The naked revelation of what is in effect no thing seems almost too much to bear. Longing for "worshipful objects" (236), she regresses once more. The sight of the house, still and upright in the early morning light, steadfast as the elm trees, recalls Mrs. Ramsay: "Life stand still here, Mrs. Ramsay said. 'Mrs. Ramsay! Mrs. Ramsay!' she repeated. She owed it all to her. . . . She hoped nobody would open the window or come out of the house, but that she might be left alone to go on thinking, to go on painting" (241).

Simultaneously the thought of Mr. Ramsay's departure impels her to walk toward the end of the lawn, where she can better watch the small expedition's progress. As the sailboat moves ever farther out on the bay, her effort to fix and distinguish it by stretching "her body and mind to the utmost" (308) once again recalls her dead friend, this time on the beach identifying floating objects in the sea: "'Is it a boat? Is it a cork?' she would say" (255). Reduced finally to a speck on the horizon, the sailboat, like this recollection, loses form and substance. No longer simply the enemy, the resisting expanse of space evokes a sense of gratitude: "Heaven be praised for it, the problem of space remained, she thought, taking up her brush again. It glared at her. The whole mass of the picture was poised upon that weight" (255).

Where in "A Sketch of the Past" Woolf described the centrality of her mother in terms "of that great cathedral space which was childhood" (81), here she employs the same image to convey Lily's liberation from all such dependent needs: "Lily, painting steadily, felt as if a door had opened, and one went in and stood gazing silently about in a high cathedral-like place, very dark, very solemn" (255).

Her independence extends beyond the medium of art. She is psychologically free to subvert Mrs. Ramsay's designs, and she thinks of Paul and Minta and Mrs. Ramsay's plan that they should wed. But the marriage has in fact been a failure and Lily "would feel a little triumphant, telling Mrs. Ramsay that the marriage had not been a success" (260). Realizing how close she had come to a similar fate—"She had only escaped by the skin of her teeth though, she thought" (262)—Lily suddenly sees Mrs. Ramsay's mania for marriage as limited and absurdly "out of date." However disapproving, Lily seems willing with her author to accept some relativity of preference: "They're happy like that; I'm happy like this. Life has changed completely" (260).

A few moments before, the serenity of the house and the recollection of Mrs. Ramsay had impressed her with their air of immutable beauty. Just as quickly she rejects the idea of such finality: "She was astonishingly beautiful, as William said. But beauty was not everything. Beauty had this penalty—it came too readily, came too completely. It stilled life—froze it" (264).

An alternate physiognomy seems lifelike and mobile by virtue of both its complexity and its imperfection: "The little agitations; the flush, the pallor, some queer distortion, some light or shadow, which made the face unrecognisable for a moment and yet added a quality one saw for ever after. It was simpler to smooth that all out under the cover of beauty" (264).

"No age," wrote Woolf in the closing essay of *The Common*

Reader, "can have been more rich than ours in writers determined to give expression to the differences which separate them from the past."[17] Through Lily she enunciates the definitive aspect of her modernist creed. Affirming a vision of unending transformation and disclosure, Lily at the end of *To the Lighthouse* expresses those same doubts Woolf noted more cautiously when first formulating the novel. While the tone of her question remains anxious, the turbulence she describes has become in the course of the narrative paradigmatic: "Was there no safety? No learning by heart of the ways of the world? No guide, no shelter, but all was miracle, and leaping from the pinnacle of a tower into the air? Could it be, even for elderly people, that this was life?—startling, unexpected, unknown?" (268).

The answer to these questions is as clear for James Ramsay at the tiller as for Lily on shore. Both artist and "lawgiver" (251) must frequent a world where no single rendition of outward reality will ever suffice, in which, as Lily speculates, "One wanted fifty pairs of eyes to see with" (294).

That James has successfully navigated his craft to the island and won the praise of his father, or that Lily has finished her painting, seems absurdly irrelevant. The end of each human effort remains inconclusive. Having reached the lighthouse, Mr. Ramsay sits there saying nothing. Lily, contemplating her "attempt," draws a line through the empty center of a painting destined to rest unnoticed and unappreciated in someone's attic. Heedless of authenticating fame, she requires neither converts nor patrons. Relinquishing the day as she has her vision, she retires at the close with a graceful anonymity that recalls Clarissa Dalloway. The absence of a reigning artist at the center of things anticipates again the experimental thrust of *The Waves*.

Chapter Seven

IN PRAISE OF NOTHINGNESS

The Waves

The completion of a novel for Woolf usually resulted in one of two dissimilar responses: a despondency bordering at times on madness, or an excitement about her next project. *To the Lighthouse* proved an exception only in that the two reactions occurred almost simultaneously. Describing what "may be the impulse behind another book," Woolf makes it clear that the mysterious fin she has seen rolling far out in the flooded Ouse Valley—an expansive vision that both frightens and excites her—has emerged "in the midst of my profound gloom, depression, boredom, whatever it is."[1]

Woolf's thoughts about this curious and depressing experience signify far more than symptoms of the madness Leonard Woolf felt justified in excluding from *A Writer's Diary*. Among her more important entries is one dated and written two days before her vision of the fin, at the time she was composing the final pages of *To the Lighthouse*: "Intense depression: I have to confess that this has overcome me several times since September 6th. . . . It is so strange to me that I cannot get it right—the depression, I mean, which does not come from something definite, but from nothing. 'Where there is nothing' the phrase came [back] to me, as I sat at the table in the drawing room."[2]

She is aware that such considerations are suspect, and expresses surprise that during the preceding few weeks she had been able to do as well as think about nothing at all without being sick: "For the first time for many years, I had been idle without being ill."[3] These adventures, however, exact a price. With nothing tangible to grasp, and at the mercy of forces beyond her power to curtail or modify, she compares the disorienting experience to stepping down into a well where "nothing protects one from the assault of truth. Down there I cant write or read; I exist however. I am. Then I ask myself what I am? & get a closer though less flattering answer than I should on the surface—where, to tell the truth, I get more praise than is right."[4]

"At our ordinary level of intimacy and ease," Woolf retains the reassurance and recognition of those who support her, which is to say, she allows family and friends the burden of defining and implementing her place in the world. She remains sanguine by withstanding the vision that calls her to explore threatening terrain. But such choices for "intimacy and ease" seem to constitute an act of artistic if not psychological betrayal: "It is always a question," she acknowledges, "whether I wish to avoid these glooms."[5]

Writing *To the Lighthouse* served to free Woolf from a traumatic reliance on her parents, but not, evidently, from a reliance on the more immediate of their surrogates. A debilitating fear of the unknown, retarding experimental intentions, drove her for a time to replace the enigmatic fin with the more reassuring outline of Vita-become-Orlando.

In deference to those loved ones who would shield her from

disruptive realities, Woolf temporarily submitted. For eighteen months *The Waves* was put aside, but not without her haunting suspicion that the future might depend on her strength to withstand the comforting solidity derived from her fanciful reconstruction of Knole, the Sackvilles' ancestral home. The result was the innovative literary biography, *Orlando*, begun some months after the publication of *To the Lighthouse* and completed about a year before she began writing *The Waves*.[6]

Nigel Nicolson suggests that *Orlando* is Woolf's "most elaborate love letter." What seems evident is that Vita's intimacy, perhaps more than Leonard's during this period, softened "the assault of truth." Less an exorcism of Vita Sackville-West than an opportunity to celebrate and perhaps reclaim her love, *Orlando* represents, from one perspective at least, an important break in Woolf's literary development, an escapade, as she put it later, from the more demanding task of formulating new directions for the novel.[7] The act of reconstituting Vita at the center of history may have served to fill the void of her diminished attention.

Rich as the correspondence between these two close friends and writers is, let me suggest that "love" is not its preeminent feature. Vita enjoyed the role of protectress, and found Virginia's fragile dependence a source of some attraction; Virginia, on the other hand, reveals through frequent and plaintive appeals for affection the desire to be led emotionally if not intellectually. Her letters resound with images of Vita's grandeur and her own insufficiency; "After all," she writes in 1926, "you're abundant in so many ways, and I a mere pea tied to a stick."[8] At one point Vita appears as a surrogate mother whose very presence recalls the contentedness of childhood: "Why do I think of you so incessantly, see you so clearly the moment I'm in the least discomfort? An odd element in our friendship. Like a child, I think if you were here, I should be happy."[9]

Significantly, the alternate state of existence that arises in these moments of declared affection is a world she associates somewhat defensively with the process of writing novels: "You are always charging at the head of an army—but I walk, nosing along, making up phrases, and I'm ashamed to say how wrapped up I get in my novel."[10] Her confession in this same letter—"I often think of you instead of my novel"—echoes more than romantic hyperbole.[11]

Within a short space of time, having completed *Orlando* and the substance of what will appear shortly as *A Room of One's Own*, Woolf returns to "her very serious mystical poetical work," now entitled "The Moths." Contemplating this "next book" in her diary, she appears to shift from thoughts of her novel to the image of these nocturnal creatures beating their wings against the windows of Monk's House, the Woolfs' Sussex home, as evening falls: "The Moths still haunts me, coming, as they always do, unbidden, between tea & dinner, while L. plays the gramophone."[12] Like the translucent "fin passing far out," the event inspires the novelist to look more deeply into that amorphous space between the acts of human intercourse, a dimension Woolf, in company with the philosopher Martin Heidegger, describes frequently at this time as an experience of nothingness.

In another passage omitted from *A Writer's Diary*, Woolf reveals an important state of her mind as she returns to the task of formulating *The Waves*. Acknowledging how Lytton Strachey's *Elizabeth and Essex* has depressed her, she points to the book's failure to move below the surface of things: "One would, in the depths, have got real pleasure."[13] With her parents gone—the entry is written on the day her father would have been ninety-six years old—and Vita no longer an obsession, Woolf seems more confident about confronting unmediated experience. A few months before beginning to write the first draft of her new novel, she is ready and willing to make the strenuous descent: "I must think of that book again, & go down step by step into the well. These are the great events &

revolutions in one's life. . . . I have now earned the right to some months of fiction. & my melancholy is brushed away, so soon as I can get my mind forging ahead, not circling round."[14] The plunge into nothingness now represents a breaking of circularity. Her mind is ready to be fertilized.

Naming this new novel *The Moths* may have been inspired by another experience of moths Vanessa described in the spring of 1927. Writing from Cassis in an atmosphere full of darting insects—"Moths flying madly in circles round me and the lamp"—her sister describes a gigantic one half a foot in length, pounding against the window. She and her friends allow it to enter and attempt to keep it alive.[15]

One month later she writes in her diary of "the story of the Moths," and of her notion of developing the idea of a continuing stream that is "not solely of human thought." She imagines a man and woman talking together at a table with one of them finally letting "the last great moth in." Throughout this intended dialogue on age and "the death of humanity," the moths and subsequently the waves "keep on coming."[16]

When she begins her novel two years later, the first sentence describes "an enormous moth" that has entered the house. The translucent crescents and dark borders of its wings fluttering on the bare wall seem, like the former vision of the fin, ready to dissolve into nothingness at the slightest agitation or shift of perspective.[17] But here the transparency of experienced reality awakens creative instincts. Resisting the temptation to seek something tangible, Woolf allows this disruptive vision to lead her toward the opaque edge of objects.

Woolf started *The Waves* on July 2, 1929, three weeks before Heidegger delivered his inaugural lecture at the University of Freiburg on the question, "What about this nothing?" Her diary entries during these months abound with similar speculations, most of which Leonard omitted from *A Writer's Diary*. The first such deleted entry appears particularly relevant: "The memorable things happen when there is a great space of silence all round them perhaps. I don't know." This is immediately followed by a passage Leonard did include: "Now about this book, The Moths. How am I to begin it? And what is it to be?"[18]

On June 15, having returned from a short trip to France, she notes "a sense of nothingness" rolling through the house, "what I call the sense of 'Where there is nothing.'" Routine has not yet reestablished circularity—"We are not going round in the mill yet"—and with time flapping on the mast, as she puts it, she seems to "see through everything": "Perhaps the image ought to have been one that gives an idea of a stream becoming thin: of seeing to the bottom."[19]

A week later she acknowledges that "the only way I keep afloat is by working," and the impact of "the phantom waves," we find, has invaded all aspects of her conscious life: "I shall make myself face the fact that there is nothing—nothing for any of us. Work, reading, writing are all disguises; & relations with people. Yes, even having children would be useless."[20] Her statement, however, includes a sense of "solemnity" as she emphasizes that at the depth of such immensity lies something more real: "I feel that if I sink further I shall reach the truth." Work and no doubt art acquire in this context a certain ambiguity. On the one hand the process of writing is an evasion, on the other a means of confronting and probing depth. Later that summer, in the passage already quoted, she will speak of the need to return to *The Waves*, to step down into that "well."

Perhaps the most important entry, one that Leonard discerningly included in his diary selections, is made that autumn. She describes how on the streets of London the impact of silence and vacancy subsumes even the consolation of grief: "No one knows how I suffer, walking up this street, engaged with my anguish, as I was after Thoby died—alone; fighting something alone. But then I had the devil to fight, & now nothing."[21] From this experience evolves a new dimension of freedom for Woolf, a sense of both adventure and limitless possibility strangely related to the discomforting loss of omniscience.*

The world Woolf offers in *The Waves* exists precariously on the margins of that non-being she has tried to avoid. This is no place to pin things down. Few planks emerge from the phantom sea, as they do in "The Mark on the Wall," to answer the narrator's recurring plea for "something definite, something real."[22] The moths, like the sounds of nature, come and go at their own oblivious pace.

From the opening page of the first holograph version we plunge with the author into an ever-abundant universe. Woolf opens her senses to all the particularities of a given scene, attempts, as she puts it in her diary, "to give the moment whole; whatever it includes."[23] As in "Time Passes," a flood of images—the huge moth, a crowing cock, the sound of birds and the sea, the jet from a fountain, objects in the room—inundates the senses; the origin of this collage is interruption: "Sight and sound interrupted each other, as if the mind of a very old man or woman, had gone back to the dawn of memory; & without being able to finish any sentence; without being sure or in what order things came; without attempting to make a coherent story."[24]

If in time Percival comes to stand Orlando-like in the midst of this existential chaos, it will be his absence that marks as well as signifies the center of Woolf's completed text. The six voices that constitute *The Waves* must survive without the formulating presence of the friend they love and idolize. As with Woolf's parents and no doubt Vita, the loss of Percival represents both threat and possibility.

---

*Observing a total eclipse of the sun in Yorkshire in June 1927, Woolf compares the plunge into inexpressible darkness to "being at the mercy of the sky." *The Diary of Virginia Woolf* (New York, 1980), 3: 144.

The Waves

In childhood, Bernard, Susan, Rhoda, Neville, Jinny, and Louis exist in a largely indeterminate space whose reality is never a source of narrative speculation, at least not in the main body of the text. The interludes where the author is free to comment more directly on such matters as the cycle of the sun through the course of a day constitute, at least in the final version, a separate portion of the narrative.

A week before beginning *The Waves* Woolf asks herself whether one could "get the waves to be heard all through," an idea that seems to follow her plan for the opening: "the sense of children; unreality; things oddly proportioned." [25] She achieves this ambience, in the course of many revisions, by removing her own omniscient voice. Lacking a traditional narrator to fill in the space between words and actions, the children's world appears to unfold no less randomly than the sounds of morning in the first holograph. The absence of a narrative voice, however, accomplishes more.

While the six children eat meals and do their lessons at a particular time and place, such rituals appear oddly inconsequential. The impressions affecting each of them arise from an ever-expanding horizon of unmediated sights and sounds: the "ring" of a drawer Bernard first sees; Susan's "slab of pale yellow"; Rhoda's birds; Neville's globe; Jinny's tassel. Each image, like the sound of stamping in Louis's ear, seems to exist miraculously independent of the social, or for that matter the narrative, context. [26]

Running through the garden after breakfast, Jinny sees leaves moving through a break in the hedge; just so, their events unfold sporadically, fragments of every fluctuation of time and perspective. The moment of school time they share shifts with the intrusion of each fresh image. Six voices following one another in explosive evocation—"I see a ring. . . . I hear a sound. . . . I see a globe"—convey an experience of a world in which everything seems included and nothing is irrelevant.

The Waves

As the children confront a widening space, experience becomes disruptive of personal identity. Jinny's kiss in the garden shatters Louis's composure, thrusting him as it does into a new and baffling context. Not only Louis complains of the dissolution of boundaries. The merging and confusing of one thing with another appears to Neville as the inevitable consequence of even the slightest interaction, while Bernard characteristically notes that language initiates similar confusions. Seated together, "we melt into each other with phrases. We are edged with mist. We make an unsubstantial territory" (16).

Moved by this atmosphere, they relish the impulse to wander, however vaguely, through a phenomenal world whose limits appear endless. Like the contours of their fantasies this first morning, everything seems possible. White petals floating in a basin become a fleet of ships, words are transformed into colors, leaves of a tree arch into the dome of a cathedral. Swept away from the hardness of definition, the children sink like swimmers (they are also "runners," but we can excuse the youthful storyteller for mixing metaphors) into the new and expansive mystery of Elvedon, where facts and events remain invitingly inconclusive.

Informed by the opening interludes that the sun is rising and that time is passing, the reader is tempted to make comparable clarity of the narrative by rising above it. Such inclinations, however, seem destined to remain even less effectual than the children's fantasies. From the beginning, Woolf honors a translucence she discerns at the heart of life. The center of each thing remains indefinite.

With time the children are taught to grow out of transparency, to become something more definite and useful. The study of Latin allows Neville the exactitude of "well-laid sentences," a sequence and structure he can hope to master. Louis rejoices in the bulk and authority (the two merge in his mind) of Dr. Crane reading a Bible lesson from the pulpit. Susan, in search of something "hard," similarly reduces school time to her own well-defined intention: "'I have torn off the whole of May and June,' said Susan, 'and twenty days of July. I have torn them off and screwed them up so that they no longer exist, save as a weight in my side. They have been crippled days, like moths with shrivelled wings unable to fly'" (53).

This "hard thing that has grown here in my side" shields her from an ever-fluctuating present. Like Jinny's expectation that "one man will single me out" (55), she too excludes diversity. Rhoda, maddened by the intuition of transparent nothingness—"I have no face" (33)—strives for heaviness and centrality by imitating others. The face she seeks must be composed and monumental, worthy of reverence. She will "endow it with omniscience, and wear it under my dress like a talisman" (33).

Bernard, fearing experience, looks toward language to shield him from ambiguity: "I must make phrases and phrases and so interpose something hard between myself and the stare of housemaids, the stare of clocks, staring faces, indifferent faces, or I shall cry" (30). In contrast to the creative anonymity Virginia Woolf affirms in *A Room of One's Own* and elsewhere, Bernard views anonymity in terms of death and artistic failure. For him to stop writing or working threatens the very sense of self-assurance that makes Louis choose to follow him.

Overhearing the cook describing a recent murder, Neville finds himself suddenly immobilized at the foot of the stairs, rooted to the spot, like the apple tree standing outside his house: "The ripple of my life was unavailing. I was unable to pass by. There was an obstacle. 'I cannot surmount this unintelligible obstacle,' I said" (24). The incident recalls "A Sketch of the Past," where Virginia tells us she is momentarily unable to step across a puddle and "the whole world became unreal."[27] The event dovetails with a similar state of mind following the death of her mother.

If death remains an essentially negative force—the enemy against whom hero and moth struggle with equal ineptitude—

there remains for Woolf something solemn about its powerful neutrality. "Massed outside," as she puts it in "The Death of the Moth," "indifferent, impersonal, not attending to anything in particular. . . . Just as life had been strange a few minutes before, so death was now as strange."[28]

While Louis, marked as he is by an Australian accent, may try to convince us that his greatest fear is rejection, or Rhoda that she has no end in view (130), or Neville that other people threaten him the most (22), what underlies and enunciates all their uncertainties about life is death.* And indeed Woolf makes a death the central event of *The Waves*—the death of Percival. That he exists in the novel solely through the response of his six friends seems only to magnify Woolf's view of the force of those patriarchal values he represents. His disappearance from the text constitutes a social crisis. Throughout the novel Percival's significance emerges by way of familiarly sovereign terms. The first reference is Neville's, describing him as "upright among the smaller fry" (35–36). Louis observes that "everybody follows Percival," whose "magnificence is that of some mediaeval commander" (37). At dinner Bernard describes how the group of friends "assume the sober and confident air of soldiers in the presence of their captain" (123). Percival inspires confidence as long as he remains there to lead them. "Look at us," Louis early comments, "trooping after him, his faithful servants" (37).

Ecclesiastical, sporting, and military images spanning history converge in praise of Percival's grandeur. Giant and monolithic (82), he looms at the center of their collective lives like some pagan deity. Neville describes him as "remote from us all in a pagan universe" (36); for Bernard, at the close of the farewell dinner, he is "a God" (136). Jinny, for whom there is

---

*J. M. Haule's concordance to *The Waves* lists over forty entries for "Death/Deaths." Only "Nothing/Nothingness" appears to have an equal number of listings. *Concordances to the Novels of Virginia Woolf* (Oxford, 1981).

"nothing staid, nothing settled in this universe" (46), sees Percival poised before the wicket, infused with the single pur-pose of winning, perpetuating the heroic illusion that he is in-dispensable. Of Percival in India, Bernard speculates that "the Oriental problem is solved" (136); and Neville, imagining Percival riding (like Vita in Virginia's letter) "at the head of troops" (152), thinks that had Percival survived, order and justice might have endured for fifty years.

The need for a leader to protect them from the "monstrous tyranny" of life tempts each of the six characters into postures of dependence. All find through Percival an ideal who far sur-passes their own capacity to emulate him.[29] "I cannot stand all day in the sun," Neville confesses, "and think only of the ball. I shall be a clinger to the outsides of words all my life" (48).

Rhoda, submerged in oceanic fantasies, looks on Percival as on some huge underwater stone around which they can all swim contentedly like minnows (136). His death immobilizes her in a manner that recalls Woolf's personal trauma following her mother's death. "'There is the puddle,' said Rhoda, 'and I cannot cross it'" (158). Without "something hard" to lead her, she is condemned to be blown eternally down endless cor-ridors: "What then can I touch? What brick, what stone? and so draw myself across the enormous gulf" (159). The need for Percival to supply the motive for action reflects again her au-thor's struggle for independence. Rhoda confesses that "we cluster like maggots on the back of something that will carry us on" (162).

More than emulation, it is in fact the passion to merge with Percival's godlike being that describes their common aspira-tion. As Jinny puts it during the first dinner, their moment comes to life because it is made "out of one man" (145). The nature of this meal and the reunion dinner years later retains aspects of the Eucharist and perhaps of those more ancient rites Jessie Weston discusses in *From Ritual to Romance*. There she describes "the central Christian rite" as the actuality of a worshipper partaking of, becoming "one with, his God, receiving thereby the assurance of eternal life." In a pre-Christian context Weston's description of the Mystic Meal, through which initiates of the Attis cult "connected with, and [depended] upon, the death and resurrection of the god," similarly echoes the reunion dinner where Woolf's six characters gather to celebrate and reconstruct their dead friend.[30]

Percival stands at the center of the historical narrative Bernard attempts finally to recount and to summarize. The religious connotation seems clearly intended. Indeed, it may well be the Christianized version of the earlier Grail stories that Woolf undercuts, for at the center of *The Waves*, along with the death of a patriarchal god, reemerges that mysterious "fin."[31] Only after Percival falls does the fin appear, first in the sixth interlude (182), and then as part of Bernard's speculations, where the sequence of his words closely matches Woolf's in her diary: "Leaning over this parapet I see far out a waste of water. A fin turns" (189). Recalling images in T. S. Eliot as well as in Heidegger, the emptiness of land and water becomes a dimension of being itself:

Nothing, nothing, nothing broke with its fin that leaden waste of waters. (245)

Nothing came, nothing. I cried then with a sudden conviction of complete desertion, Now there is nothing. No fin breaks the waste of this immeasurable sea. (284)

Struggling throughout the novel to reconstruct the house Percival has built for them (walls that metaphorically surround and protect them), the six friends resist, like Mrs. Ramsay, the fluidity of time and space. It is a house, as Rhoda comes to perceive, built on contradiction: "We have made oblongs and stood them upon squares. This is our triumph; this is our consolation" (163). Again "consolation" appears as the inauthentic means of triumphing over a modern world devoid of Holy Grails.

Rhoda's commitment following the death of Percival to make a pilgrimage to Greenwich reveals but one incapacity to exist without a sustaining idolatry. Here it is objective time that has replaced the fallen hero. While she affirms her capacity to "relinquish" and "let loose," she remains confined by familiar boundaries: "The structure is visible. We have made a dwelling-place" (164).

Two important sequences in *The Waves*, the farewell and reunion dinners, illustrate both the restricting appeal of Percival's influence and an obscurely liberating significance emerging from his absence. So on the streets of London, as Bernard hurries toward the farewell dinner on the eve of Percival's departure for India, he momentarily avoids the continuity that is in the process of forming his character; Bernard is engaged to be married. Allowing himself to slip into the motion of the crowd, he forgets both engagements and becomes first a child, then an invisible presence, stripped of body as well as purpose. Like Mrs. Dalloway on Bond Street, he speculates that "people might walk through me" (113).

What has appeared to be a largely involuntary act—he has dropped off "like a child from the breast" (112)—grows into an act of resistance against those acquisitive and restrictive impulses that characterize social behavior. Saying "No," he chooses instead to plunge below the surface of things: "No, but I wish to go under; to visit the profound depths; once in a while to exercise my prerogative not always to act, but to explore; to hear vague, ancestral sounds of boughs creaking, of mammoths, to indulge impossible desires to embrace the whole world with the arms of understanding, impossible to those who act" (114).

The impulse shadows Woolf's intention while writing *The Waves* to probe the depths as well as to "saturate" the moment, "to put practically everything in. [32] With Bernard the choice involves a conscious abdication of social identity: "I am not, at this moment, myself" (115).

The Waves

Bernard's resistance, however, appears purely circumstantial; he regains, almost instantaneously, a sense of his own present mission, that part of him remaining imperially above the experience. "I am not part of the street—no, I observe the street" (115). A girl waiting on the sidewalk moves him to begin "a romantic story," to enlist objects of perception for his own artistic and psychological needs. As a result his aesthetic intentions become, in the manner of Woolf's patriarchs of culture, pronouncedly acquisitive.[33] Firmly in control of events like Percival, he does not allow them to exert undue influence.

It is not so much the fragmentary nature of this urban interruption that moves him to return to normal as it is his own unwillingness to allow the moment to exist free of his impositional needs. An arbitrariness in Bernard points majestically toward Percival; Bernard, the artist, would be sovereign of all he surveys: "I conceive myself called upon to provide, some winter's night, a meaning for all my observations—a line that runs from one to another, a summing up that completes" (115).

A king by all worldly criteria requires subjects. Anticipating his final monologue, Bernard confesses the necessity of an audience to authenticate and ensure the validity of his creations and, more important, of his very existence in the world: "I need the illumination of other people's eyes" (116). Hurrying away from this "sunless territory of non-identity" toward the source of true light, he reaches the restaurant to discover that Percival has not yet arrived. The absence affects Bernard's artistry. "Impatient of solitude" (117), he resorts once more to fanciful creations, which move him dangerously toward the margin of experience, until the well-lighted dinner table and the expectation of the honored guest restore what is, from society's perspective, a saner self: "I am engaged to be married. I am to dine with my friends tonight. I am Bernard" (118).

Neville, who has arrived early, anticipates the coming of Percival in language that recalls the Last Supper: "This is the

156

place to which he is coming. This is the table at which he will
sit. Here, incredible as it seems, will be his actual body"
(118). Somewhat later Bernard will describe their celebration
in words that echo the Eucharist. "We are drawn into this
communion by some deep, some common emotion. Shall we
call it, conveniently, 'love'?" (126).

Without Percival, for Neville as no doubt for the others,
the very dining room seems insubstantial. The wavering objects on the table appear to wait for his touch to take on reality and meaning. They endure his absence in the knowledge
that he will ultimately arrive to bring, like the gospels, new
life. Woolf's irony is nowhere more implicit, for it is the old
life in fact that Percival embodies.

Neville observes that "without Percival there is no solidity.
We are silhouettes, hollow phantoms moving mistily without
a background" (122). To be perceived, even silhouettes require some background of light; this Percival supplies. Light is
also a central motif for the Percival of Arthurian romance, the
mysterious light of the Holy Grail in the forest, which inspires
his quest. And in an early review of a production of Wagner's
Parsifal, Woolf described a Percival affected, along with everything else, by an abundance of light: "The Grail seems to burn
through all superincumbences."[34]

Like moths circling a flame, the six characters find it difficult to exist outside the "prickly light" (119) Percival's inten-
sity supplies. Their lives, touched by his presence, resist the
shade. Figures of light abound even in his absence from the
restaurant. To replenish her dreams, Rhoda looks for the radi-
ance of some face, and Jinny appears to Susan as a blazing fire
on the horizon; her laughter curls like "tongues of fire" round
Susan, serving thereby to "light up" her shabby appearance.
Jinny describes herself moving "like a lantern down a dark
lane, bringing one thing after another out of darkness into a
ring of light. I dazzle you; I make you believe that this is all"
(129). Once Percival is seated in their midst, Rhoda observes

that "the light becomes richer, second by second"; even after he leaves, the group appears to Neville as still glowing (135).

While Rhoda and Bernard, more than the others, possess the imagination to venture occasionally into the shadows, such "moments of departure," Rhoda acknowledges, always start "from this table, these lights, from Percival" (139) and his chosen queen. When Percival "takes his seat by Susan, whom he loves, the occasion is crowned" (123). The farewell dinner concludes with Neville's questions: "What can we do to keep him? How bridge the distance between us? How fan the fire so that it blazes for ever?" (147). Darkness remains, in this context, the enemy of existence.

With the loss of Percival, first from the dinner, then shortly after, from life, a consuming darkness, looming on the out-skirts of Bernard's storytelling, threatens to engulf everyone and everything. Above all, his death occasions a sense of soli-tude and emptiness. Percival "sat there in the centre," Ber-nard recalls. "Now I go to that spot no longer. The place is empty" (153). Bernard feels a similar sense of void: "I turn to that spot in my mind and find it empty" (156). Without Per-cival to sustain or oppose his infirmities or, for that matter, his virtues, Bernard must face them alone. Rhoda, forever sen-sitive to the experience of nothingness, fails even to survive. Percival's death elicits the intolerable terror that she will sink into this emptiness "with no one to save her." Submitting pas-sively, she reflects, in the passage already quoted, on the de-structive consequence of her own maggotlike dependence.

Each of the friends, like T. S. Eliot's Prufrock, finds it diffi-cult to begin for him- or herself. Implicit in Rhoda's image is another telling critique on the self-centered quality of their love for Percival. Despite the satisfaction and wholeness each experiences in his presence—again not unlike the pleasures of Mrs. Ramsay's table—their feelings appear to derive more from need than from affection. Like the food they consume, Percival bestows a "moment of ravenous identity" that Ber-nard aptly terms an "egotistic exultation" (143).

The Waves

It is a self-supporting image Bernard and the others choose to re-create following their friend's death, an image that relieves them of creating something new. The inversion of Christian faith is again evident. Louis first suggests, as the friends disperse after dinner, that they retain the broken circle "in our blood," and thereby preserve what Jinny calls "this globe whose walls are made of Percival" (145). Similarly Bernard, having internalized a lost centrality, affirms that Percival "shall remain the arbiter" (155). Retaining his authority, they ensure a world without change. From ritual to romance, the future for Woolf lies not through Percival, but through the antithesis of those values he represents.

By the time of the reunion dinner the friends are middle-aged and have grown apart. Bernard's life, as if by necessity, adopts a familiar form: "I have sons and daughters. I am wedged into my place in the puzzle" (216). Though he claims it is only his body that remains so irrevocably "fixed," that art allows him the freedom to wander, he is not so different from the others. Bernard supposes that his creative philosophy sets him apart, that unlike Louis, who "has formed unalterable conclusions upon the true nature of what is to be known," he does not "cling to life": "I shall be brushed like a bee from a sunflower. My philosophy, always accumulating, welling up moment by moment, runs like quicksilver a dozen ways at once" (218).

In reality, he resembles most writers, Woolf included, who seek with Louis "the solution" capable of linking "all in one" (219). Just as he waited in youth for Percival to arrive, Bernard waits in middle age for a key to the "mysterious hieroglyph" of life.[35] When he too sees a "fin" rising from the waters, the absence of a transcending explanation retards each impulse to begin: "I see far out a waste of water. A fin turns. This bare visual impression is unattached to any line of reason. . . . I note under F., therefore, 'Fin in a waste of waters.' I, who am perpetually making notes in the margin of my mind for some final statement, make this mark, waiting for some winter's evening" (189). When the evening arrives, Bernard will choose once more the allegiance of Percival. Haunted by the dissolving randomness of experience, he cannot ulti-mately free himself from a limiting need for singularity.

With Percival gone, no mediating influence exists to bring the friends together. Time has further fragmented the "ring" (Bernard's first perception of things) that once encircled their world. As they convene at the reunion, "the shock of meet-ing" occasions a disagreeable need to oppose one another. Through their own accomplishment they have all taken on definition, even Rhoda, who is committed to "nothing." As Louis notes, the torture of this meeting is that they are no longer linked in one chain.

Some softening of attitudes occurs as food and wine blunt "the sharp tooth of egotism" (224), and they cease speaking exclusively about themselves, but it is not until all talk ends at the party's conclusion that a devastating lull serves to reunite them. Annulling the proud distinctions each has attempted to make throughout the evening, the moment inundates Neville's "credentials," Louis's business, Bernard's refined phrases. Drop by drop, the fluid silence dissolves their derived solidity, until each becomes "featureless and scarcely to be distinguished from another" (224).

The sustained silence transforms Bernard into a man with-out qualities, and further inspires his thoughts on the unre-ality surrounding and permeating human life, his notion that "the earth is only a pebble flicked off accidentally from the face of the sun and that there is no life anywhere in the abysses of space" (225). That life can cease becomes suddenly no less miraculous than that it should begin. The world that has nourished them and "life" itself can be "stayed" in a time-less void of darkness.

Bernard observes that they have passed momentarily "be-yond life." Then, as on the street before the farewell dinner, he recoils and takes up, this time in company with Neville, a militant posture against the impinging threat. In Bernard's case the resolve appears partly comic: "It is the memory of my nose that recalls me. I rise; 'Fight,' I cry, 'fight!' remembering the shape of my own nose, and strike with this spoon upon this table pugnaciously" (225–26). The event will reappear with added emphasis in his final summation.

Like St. John Hirst on the Amazon, Neville views such irrational violence with distaste and urges a combative defense: "Oppose ourselves to this illimitable chaos, . . . this formless imbecility" (226). His bellicose tone recalls Hirst's "torpedoes" and anticipates the "spear" with which Bernard, in the vein of a more ancient Percival, turns to battle his final enemy. But here at the table, with Percival gone, there is no promise of an eternal recurrence, of law and order. Phrases echoing T. S. Eliot's "A Game of Chess"—"It is time. . . . It is time"—rise appropriately from Louis as he ushers them all outside into an equally impervious wasteland.*

Initially the six walk abreast through Hampton Court as if to withstand "this flood" together. The center, however, no longer holds, and their bodies "stream away, down the unlighted avenues, past the strip of time, unidentified" (227). Trying to recover some aspect of time as he walks, Bernard finds that "with that streaming darkness in my eyes I have lost my grip" (227). Once they relinquish the compulsion to hold fast together, to vanquish what Jinny too describes as "the abysses of space" (228), they triumph, however momentarily, in unexpected ways.

Rhoda, slipping behind the others with Louis, finds the

*Echoes of T. S. Eliot occur throughout *The Waves*. Louis is described as "prim and supercilious" and a "marmoret." Woolf uses the same word to describe Eliot in her diary. Note also Jinny's "jug, jug," derived perhaps from *The Waste Land*, which the Woolfs' Hogarth Press published in 1923. I am indebted to Victor Luftig for this reference. On this subject, note Doris L. Eder's "Louis Unmasked: T. S. Eliot in *The Waves*," *Virginia Woolf Quarterly*, 2.1–2 (1975), pp. 13–26.

walls of her mind becoming transparent, opening to the darkness. Disembodied, free of fear and anxiety, she enjoys a familiar diversity: "What song do we hear, the owl's, the nightingale's, the wren's? The steamer hoots; the light on the electric rails flashes; the trees gravely bow and bend. The flare hangs over London. Here is an old woman, quietly returning, and a man, a late fisherman comes down the terrace with his rod. Not a sound, not a movement must escape us" (230).

The randomness by which such observations unfold and the sense of multiplicity they include contribute to the mood of dislocation. In contrast to the interludes, the cadence of Woolf's prose creates a world without apparent priorities where nothing seems central, not even death. Louis, aware that all appears newly alive, joins the celebration: "I cannot hear death anywhere tonight." Inspired by this rich confusion, he is moved courageously to ask, "How shall we put it together, the confused and composite message?" (230), a question that Rhoda translates into a need for omniscience: "If we could mount together, if we could perceive from a sufficient height" (231).

In retrospect Bernard recalls how Louis and Rhoda preserved this special moment longer than any of the others, a moment free of all discriminations. It collapses, however, more from their friends' intrusion than from the couple's need for transcendent understanding. As the four approach, still undefined, wearing "the ambiguous draperies of the flowing tide in which they have been immersed," they appear to Louis and Rhoda as simply men and women. For Louis, who has allowed the dark vision access into his mind, what was formerly real and natural now strikes him as aberration: "'Something flickers and dances,' said Louis. 'Illusion returns as they approach down the avenue'" (232). Incapable of tolerating such interruption, he reverts to his former stance: "They are on us. The southern sun flickers over this urn; we push off in to the tide of the violent and cruel sea. Lord help us to act our parts as we greet them returning—Susan and Bernard, Neville and Jinny" (232).

The inner and the outer worlds, existing in opposition, appear irreconcilable. Exemplified through the language of the preceding interlude, the artist's function under such aegis is to encircle and protect the moment: "Rimmed in a gold circle the looking-glass held the scene immobile as if everlasting in its eye" (208). Louis, in effect, rejoins an old drama, a script in which each actor's part is eternally fixed; between the acts, one simply endures.

Bernard, awakening at the same time to a world of "must, must, must," supplicates again for an authority capable of mediating contradiction. Although visions of suspended time inspire and enrich his art, he too indulges triumphant thoughts. Where Jinny employs rouge and powder, he employs a language of evasion.[36]

Bernard's long monologue concluding *The Waves* puzzles many critics. The problem, which lies in the final paragraphs, is Bernard's identification with Percival, along with the interlude answering this affirmation with apparent indifference: "The waves broke on the shore."[37]

Narrative episodes in *The Waves* disclose a unique combination of voices. Despite Bernard's claim that he has become many people, that his friends now exist in him (276), the shift to a single utterance seems at some variance with this design. It interrupts a rhythmic continuity Woolf has worked hard to attain, and appears to offer readers a return to narrative omniscience, like the ticket home to Waterloo Bernard clasps so firmly at the close of the reunion dinner. Even the novel's final interlude can be conceived as part of Bernard's rhetorical moment, reflecting as it does his own intention to describe what he perceives "in words of one syllable" (293).[38]

Although it seems fitting that a writer should have the last word, the inception of Bernard's long soliloquy—" 'Now to sum up,' said Bernard" (238)—should arouse suspicion. If we overlook the youthful Jacob Flanders's similar disposition (filtered through a not wholly unsympathetic narrator) to summarize others, we expect a maturer Bernard to have benefited from the earlier admonition: "It is no use trying to sum people up. One must follow hints."[39]

The last episode of *The Waves* picks up the dispersal that marked the scene in Hampton Court. Now, years later, this incident is part of a single "story" enclosed in Bernard's mind. With time, the friends have scattered further, and in their absence Bernard feels bound to re-create them for someone else as much as for himself. It is the need to narrate rather than to find companionship that compels him to seek out a virtual stranger in a restaurant: "I must tell you a story" (238). Choosing someone ignorant of his life, Bernard, much like the Ancient Mariner, becomes sole interpreter of the facts. Although he assures his guest that they will be able to converse freely with each other, no aspect of the stranger's thoughts actually intrudes. Neither physical nor verbal, the "blow" ultimately dealt him involves the incongruously comic realization that his dinner companion continues to exist independently of Bernard's narrative phrases.

The one true story he ultimately tells is exclusively his own, a story insulated from other perspectives. Bernard's re-created friends cannot contradict essentially personal needs. In relating how Rhoda committed suicide, for example, he cannot forebear making her the object of his albeit gentle paternalism: "'Wait,' I said, putting my arm in imagination (thus we consort with our friends) through her arm. 'Wait until these omnibuses have gone by. Do not cross so dangerously'" (281). Admittedly the scenario is self-serving, but Bernard to his credit recognizes his motives. In persuading her not to cross a dangerous street, he confesses, "I was also persuading my own soul" (281).

Bernard knows that his inclination to tell stories is often

induced by the indiscriminate threat of others. He remains adamant, however, in defense of such self-supporting needs. One example is the recollection of Neville touching certain objects and walking in his own characteristic way. Bernard explains to the stranger why he was forced to leave the room: "Everything became definite, external, a scene in which I had no part. I rose, therefore; I left him" (274).

The painful situation merges with the considerable "discomfort" at Hampton Court occasioned by the impact of the others. While Bernard repeats his refrain—"I am not one person; I am many people" (276)—he rejects with telling impatience all that experience in which he has no part to play. Where his author strives to get everything in, Bernard's aesthetics appear at these moments to be essentially exclusive. In this state of mind he tends predictably to fall back on recollections of Percival: "Heavens! how they caught me as I left the room, the fangs of that old pain! the desire for some one not there. For whom? I did not know at first; then remembered Percival. . . . But he was not there" (274).

Before the restaurant meeting Bernard's thoughts dwell nostalgically on the childhood image of his nurse turning pages of a picture book. He recalls the old woman stopping before one illustration to say: "Look. This is the truth" (287). Associated in his mind with the failure to achieve singularity, the memory anticipates his subsequent restaurant narrative: "I was thinking of that picture in the picture-book. And when I met you in the place where one goes to hang up one's coat I said to myself, 'It does not matter whom I meet. All this little affair of "being" is over. Who this is I do not know; nor care; we will dine together'" (287–88). The note of capitulation suggests that Bernard's summation represents a certain choice to desist and withdraw from life.

Bernard allows himself, like Rhoda, to fall passively into nothingness. His visit to the hairdresser, who swathes and pinions him in a sheet, seems to reenact this decision. Death offers a permanence that has eluded him, a fulfillment he has come, moreover, to equate with art.[40] "If there are no stories, what end can there be?" (267).

Following the loss of wholeness at Hampton Court, Bernard tells how an early recollection of boys singing from the deck of a river steamer evoked strong feeling: "The sound of the chorus came across the water and I felt leap up that old impulse, which has moved me all my life, to be thrown up and down on the roar of other people's voices, singing the same song; to be tossed up and down on the roar of almost senseless merriment, sentiment, triumph, desire" (278–79). The image recalls in the reader's mind an earlier incident, when Louis watched a group of cricketers at school "singing in chorus" with Percival in their midst. "The boasting boys," moving together "simultaneously," filled Louis with a sense both of splendor and of unworthiness. Their pride seemed warranted, and their achievements connected with the accomplishments of all those destined for leadership. They marched, singing like troops behind their general, with a precision and confidence that further impressed him: "How majestic is their order, how beautiful is their obedience! If I could follow, if I could be with them I would sacrifice all I know" (47).

Bernard, admitting his own incapacities as a schoolboy for their accomplishments—"I by a fluke make sometimes fifteen" (49)—had professed unconcern and even distaste for success. Now we witness a reversal. Despite disavowals, he chooses to rise and lead through the medium of his art.

In the years surrounding the composition of *The Waves*, Woolf came to scrutinize the narrowness of imaginative forms that cannot reach beyond the immediacy of their authors' more personal vision. Essays like "The Narrow Bridge of Art" (1927) censure particularly those contemporary poets and dramatists who distance themselves from an uncongenial present age. Their forms, as we observe, remain for Woolf acts of concealment. The art toward which she aspires seeks to honor the self-expanding variety of experience that typifies the narrative variety of *The Waves* prior to Bernard's summation. Notwithstanding Bernard's sensitive rendering of modern experience, his poetry discloses a romantic egotism that denies modern life its depth. The modern egotist, Woolf writes in "The Narrow Bridge," having "lost the power of accepting anything simply for what it is," seeks the other merely to verify his own emotions.[41]

Bernard is motivated to acts of artistic transcendence in the conviction that "what is" is at best imperfect and at worst corruptly debilitating: "Lord, how unutterably disgusting life is! What dirty tricks it plays us, one moment free; the next, this. Here we are among the breadcrumbs and the stained napkins again. That knife is already congealing with grease. Disorder, sordidity and corruption surround us" (292).

While such distaste builds to a climax as Woolf's characters age, it grows out of her early suspicion about the quality of life in the larger world. This sense of aversion will reappear in the opening of *The Years* as Colonel Pargiter walks through a poor district of London. The temptation to employ the elevating power of prose to embellish an ugly world no doubt has affected every writer of talent. In *The Waves*, as in *To the Lighthouse*, Woolf continues to resist her own propensity to make art the vehicle of romantic transformation.

In her last revisions Woolf pictures Bernard, looking "down from this transcendency," abstracting aesthetic pleasure from the very things he reviles. Only after the apparent unconcern of his dinner partner has shaken him out of omniscience does a sense of life return.

In the first holograph draft of *The Waves*, the stranger to whom Bernard addresses his final story is described as being young as well as "almost unknown"; the second holograph finds the stranger older but still thirty years younger than Bernard.[42] Both would emphasize the ending of Bernard's life through the contrast of ages. The ultimate text develops the stranger's function more in terms of an absolute ignorance of Bernard's life—"Anything can be said to a complete stranger"—and through the "shock" precipitated by the impact of his or her indifference.* Just as the waiter will disrupt Bernard's solitude—"I would willingly give all my money that you should not disturb me" (295)—so the stranger's very separateness— "Oh, but there is your face" (292)—literally destroys Bernard's artistic intentions. In the second holograph, after reviling the stranger for this "blow" that staggered and awakened him, Bernard goes on to describe his companion: "You who destroyed me, have also revived in me this & that, one thing and another, tick tock tick tock rush, sound, cry. . . . the rising & the falling, the sense of being."[43] Reminiscent of childhood interruptions when Susan or Neville, or both, preoccupied with their own activities, appeared unexpectedly, these thoughts are linked in this holograph with an earlier autobiographical incident, namely, the recollection of "the earliest sound of all, the sea's sound, the beat of the waves as I heard it, when I woke."[44] The "shock" of the stranger's presence recalls "the shock-receiving capacity" Woolf described as the quality that made her a writer.[45] In each case such moments undercut art's reductive tendency.

As it does for Woolf, Bernard's encounter with nothingness occasions both despondency and insight. He recounts for the stranger how the moment occurred one day as he was leaning over a gate when "the rhythm stopped. . . . A space was cleared in my mind." Life revealed itself to be both "imperfect" and "unfinished" (283). Like Woolf before the puddle, he finds no inner self arising to combat and withstand the threat. Engulfed and immobilized by nothingness—no sound breaks the silence, no cock crows, no smoke rises, no train

---

*Jeffrey Ballard, a Stanford undergraduate, first pointed out to me that the sex of the stranger, both in the holograph versions and in the final text, is never clearly stated.

moves—Bernard describes himself as "without a self. . . . A
heavy body leaning on a gate. A dead man" (285):

Nothing came, nothing. I cried then with a sudden conviction of
complete desertion. Now there is nothing. No fin breaks the waste
of this immeasurable sea. Life has destroyed me. No echo comes
when I speak, no varied words. This is more truly death than the
death of friends, than the death of youth. I am the swathed figure in
the hairdresser's shop taking up only so much space. (284)

Not until the stranger appears before him in the restaurant
does Bernard recover and authenticate the world he has lost
by establishing his own narrative centrality.

If Bernard is uncertain of his surroundings—"Is it Paris, is
it London where we sit or some southern city of pink-washed
houses?" (288)—the story he has set before the stranger, "a
complete thing" (289), requires neither qualification nor collaboration. It is single and compact, the description Woolf
employs in the first draft of the novel to describe Bernard at
the close: [46]

> I am sealed,
> shrouded;
> single; compact.

Bernard rises above the world like a hero of the past, and
triumphs for one last time over contingency. The figures he
employs before and after the stranger's disruption stress both
height and religion. The two merge as he describes his body
rising "tier upon tier like some cool temple," reaching a serene
and transcendent station "up above" (290) the world of things.
There the beauty he sees below—pieces of bread, which strike
him as "relics," the peeling of pears, forks laid side by side, his
own wrinkled hand—evoke thoughts of gratification and self-
reverence: "I could worship my hand even, with its fan of
bones laced by blue mysterious veins" (290). The moment expresses a joy also in resolution now that desire no longer urges
him "out and away" (291). Remaining stationary, he takes

The Waves

upon himself "the mystery of things . . . without leaving this place, without stirring from my chair" (291), until at that very instant the stranger's eye breaks like a disinterested wave over the sanctuary he has created and would preserve: "Oh, but there is your face. I catch your eye. I, who had been thinking myself so vast, a temple, a church, a whole universe, unconfined and capable of being everywhere on the verge of things and here too, am now nothing but what you see" (292).

But as the "I," momentarily retrieved from the deluge, slides once more into anonymous irrelevance, Bernard, even in his swan song, allows the truth of what he has rejected to set him in motion. Tumbling him about like a wave, scattering his possessions, the stranger's "blow" reawakens the very reality he would deny: "I begin to perceive this, that and the other. The clock ticks; the woman sneezes; the waiter comes. . . . A whistle sounds, wheels rush, the door creaks on its hinges. I regain the sense of the complexity and the reality and the struggle" (293–94). For this Bernard is thankful, before saying goodnight and regressing almost at once into a world devoid of interruptions, a heavenly solitude in which he tells us expectantly: "No one sees me and I change no more" (294).

Enclosed by Percival as well as by death, the quixotic image of Bernard, riding with "spear couched" (the pun is relevant), crystallizes like a work of art into something permanent.* The frame of this picture, no longer an expanding horizon, is touched with the very voice of its subject. The rhythm of the interludes is now marked by Bernard's unyielding rhetoric. As if in a final act of proud transcendence, Bernard's art stamps its image on the surrounding emptiness. The last aspect of the external world is reduced to a vestige of his own rhetoric, and the world, as it were, dies with him.

*The sense of death as a kind of "crystallization" is a central theme in D. H. Lawrence. The term recurs in his novels, essays, and letters. To give one example: "Life, the ever-present, knows no finality, no finished crystallization." *Phoenix* (New York: Penguin Books, 1978), p. 219.

The Waves

The promise of shining knights destined to lead us out of darkness invokes familiar expectations for Woolf, as it no doubt did for readers of her own culture.[47] If it is an essentially infantile need that postulates a catcher in the rye, the impulse invites too readily a legacy of dependence. For the adult and more relevantly for the maturing artist, such myths, particularly in a secular age, supply at best an artificial coherence. Percival's centrality in *The Waves* partakes of this dimension, an aspect of myth that Woolf's last two novels resist with something more than an intuition of alternatives. Ironically, with *The Years* it is a Christian poet who most contributes to her increasingly anarchist persuasion.

Chapter Eight

TOWARD MUTUALITY
The Years

Like most of Woolf's novels, *The Years* is more than casually concerned with the origins of life and movement. Since at the time of writing its author was studying Dante's *Purgatorio*, it is not surprising to find that the Italian poet affected her treatment of these themes. Just as the narrator of the *Commedia* is called to renewed motion by the divine interruption of worldly pretensions, so the heroines of Woolf's novel recover a sense of movement as they allow similarly unworldly perceptions to disrupt the static insularity of their own class-bound lives. For each writer, movement involves the willingness and strength to break out of a confining circularity: in the case of Dante, the unqualified centering of one's existence on earthly matters; in the case of Woolf, a prescriptive dance around the sacred tree of property and privilege.

Looking out from the window of his London club—it is the spring of 1880—Colonel Abel Pargiter, newly retired from military service, regrets the loss of a determined course of action: "Everybody in the crowded street, it seemed, had some end in view. Everybody was hurrying along to keep some appointment. Even the ladies in their victorias and broughams were trotting down Piccadilly on some errand or other. . . . But for him there was nothing to do" (5).[1]

Unable to revive the past with his club mates through "old jokes and stories," or to seek out his wife for distraction and support—she lies terminally ill at home—the colonel falls back on his mistress. "He had somewhere to go, after all" (6). Mira, however, is absent when he arrives at her flat; and in the interval before she appears, the chaotic impact of the poor neighborhood aggravates his sense of lost privilege. Unpleasant smells from the tenement, wet clothes hanging from a line, sounds of unsupervised children shouting on the street, evoke a disillusion with life that recalls Bernard's disgruntled words. "It was sordid; it was mean; it was furtive" (7).

At home in Abercorn Terrace, the colonel's children, having tea, appear imbued with the same feeling of stasis. Waiting for the kettle to boil, waiting for some distraction to serve as a topic for conversation, waiting for some decisive change in their mother's condition—"She was better today; would be worse tomorrow" (5)—they continue with nothing really to do, which is to say, without impetus. The arrival of their father, still discontent after visiting Mira, only intensifies the situation. With neither the energy nor the inclination to sustain customary family routines he seems to detest, Colonel Pargiter looks impatiently for his eldest daughter, Eleanor, to appear and to occupy the center. Since this is her day for visiting the poor, he must wait with the others for her tardy arrival.

Milly's response once Eleanor does appear proves suggestively misleading: "Thank goodness, there's Eleanor she thought, looking up—the soother, the maker-up of quarrels, the buffer between her and the intensities and strifes of family life. She adored her sister. She would have called her goddess. . . . Protect me, she thought, handing her a teacup" (14).

The Years

From the outset, Eleanor exists in ambiguous relationship with those who look to her for support and compliance. Cheerful by temperament, she seems well suited to preside in her mother's absence. Her talents in fact lie elsewhere. Ill-designed by either nature or intention to fulfill the role of leadership, easily distracted and disposed to stray from the point at hand, she is moved, anarchically, to transgress all boundaries of relevance. From the start, interruption is her medium.

After Colonel Pargiter leaves the table Eleanor refuses, however subtly, to take charge. In the face of family conflict—"There was something strained in the atmosphere" (16)—she allows her attention to wander "absentmindedly" outside an uncurtained window: "The trees were coming out in the back garden; there were little leaves—little ear-shaped leaves on the bushes. The sun was shining, fitfully; it was going in and it was going out, lighting up now this, now—" (16). The vision of motion and change is abruptly interrupted by the youngest of the children, Rose, demanding unreasonably, since the hour is late, to go out-of-doors. Eleanor acknowledges and grants the demand.

Similarly, Eleanor allows the younger children the unusual freedom of peeking through windows to see what goes on outside; her only sacrifice to decorum is that they do so unobserved. As with Rose, her decision seems motivated by the impulse to break free of Victorian protectiveness. The result is a widening of perception. From the window Delia observes uncommon sights for a child of her class: "A woman of the lower classes was wheeling a perambulator; an old man tottered along with his hands behind his back" (18). When a hansom cab comes down the street, Delia finds herself, like the narrator of *A Room of One's Own* and Eleanor at the conclusion of the novel, imaginatively extending this ordinary event: "Was it going to stop at their door or not? She gazed more intently" (18).

This external world proves, like the weather—"It was

an uncertain spring"—to be unpredictable and "perpetually changing." As the hansom passes and a gust of wind blows a scrap of paper across the darkening pavement, Delia drops the blind apprehensively: "There was a wildness in the spring evening; even here, in Abercorn Terrace the light was changing from gold to black, from black to gold" (19). Their servant Crosby, without need of summons, dutifully meets the threat of change. Pulling shut the "sculptured folds of claret-coloured plush," she restores a profound and deadly silence in which everything beyond the drawing room seems "thickly and entirely cut off" (20).

The world outside remains hostile so long as it threatens to disrupt the Pargiters' way of life. Deprived of youth and command, the colonel no longer rides forth to subdue those with mutiny in their hearts. Could he observe Rose venturing disobediently out of the house, his gravest fears would be confirmed. The pockmarked man reaching menacingly toward her as she rushes past on the way to Lamley's store would represent all that is sick and unruly in the changing London scene. Ironically Rose, the potential victim, emerging triumphantly from the house, carries on, imaginatively at least, where the colonel cannot: "'I am Pargiter of Pargiter's Horse,' she said, flourishing her hand, 'riding to the rescue!' She was riding by night on a desperate mission to a besieged garrison, she told herself. She had a secret message. . . . All their lives depended upon it" (27).

Too young and of the wrong sex to uphold the empire, she remains throughout *The Years* a soldier in defense of her own class interests. Despite her struggle for women's suffrage— Rose goes to jail for throwing a brick—the more radically deprived outcasts of society remain as threatening to her as they have been to her father. Safely back home in bed, she is reassured by the knowledge that "Papa would kill him" if any such intruder entered the house. This reflects an insularly dependent state of mind that she will never fully outgrow. Merging with her image of the poor, the pockfaced derelict sustains a mythology through which the impoverished come increasingly to represent a threat more than a consequence.

Though Rose ventures forth from home in the image of her father, she gains, perhaps inadvertently, an experience exclusively her own. Rose's impassioned "I saw... I saw..." with all its unfinished urgency serves in a more important narrative sense to initiate Eleanor's ultimate liberation. The realization that she cannot in fact reach her young sister, much less protect her, inspires first uncertainty and then a subsequent revelation of the emptiness of her own place in the world:

> "I saw," Eleanor repeated, as she shut the nursery door. "I saw..." What had she seen? Something horrible, something hidden. But what? There it was, hidden behind her strained eyes. . . . She paused, looking down into the hall. A blankness came over her. Where am I? she asked herself, staring at a heavy frame. What is that? She seemed to be alone in the midst of nothingness. (42–43)

However alienating this experience, it will form, as with Lily Briscoe and Bernard, the potential for change. Thrust outside the customary line of hierarchy, Eleanor will come to revise radically the premises of her own social being.

Throughout the 1930's Woolf described herself as an "outsider." Although the use of this term suggests in part a concern over her literary reputation (Forster and Eliot were making a greater impact on the reading public), it also reflects a growing ideological intention. If Woolf's earlier heroines respond marginally to the ordeal of less privileged classes, the inspiring donnée of *The Years* involves a closer identification with women like Eleanor, Maggie, and Sara Pargiter who choose to step more emphatically outside the prescriptiveness that characterizes their common background.

In a speech delivered to a Brighton working-class audience shortly before her death, Woolf suggests that such ventures are essential to the survival of literature as well as society. Only

"if commoners and outsiders like ourselves" strike out independently, "trespass freely and fearlessly," she concludes, will
art survive the destructiveness of war. Although the break-
through she envisions is largely a perceptual one—the capacity to extend, as she attempts in *The Waves,* the manner in
which we see the world—*The Years* involves from its inception
more political expectations.

Eleanor's weekly visits to a poor Jewish family—what her
father condescendingly terms "her Grove day"—establish an
important theme. If hope exists for the human race, much less
for the Pargiters, it must arise from a widening of class presumptions that will express some form of synthesis between
Dante and the political egalitarianism Woolf has grown to es-
pouse. The lines Eleanor quotes midway through the journey
of her own life clarify the "bridge" Woolf conceives between
The Years and the *Purgatorio:* [2]

> For by so many more there are who say "ours"
> So much the more of good doth each possess.

The quotation reflects the point of view Woolf transcribed in
her diary some months later while contemplating "a new
book": "'I' rejected: 'We' substituted."[3] The move represents
in her mind a more mutual sense of human behavior grounded
in reciprocity as well as in a loosening of acquisitive intentions.

Eleanor's involvement in the life of the Levys does not satisfy her charitable instincts so much as it extends, at times
painfully, the range and quality of her perceptions. Aware that
this Jewish working-class household, similarly deprived of a
healthy mother, is far more congenial than her own, Eleanor
sees her existence as suddenly wider and consequently more
confused: "So many different things were going on in her
head at the same time: Canning Place; Abercorn Terrace; this
room; that room. There was the old Jewess sitting up in bed in
her hot little room; then one came back here, and there was

Mama ill; Papa grumpy; and Delia and Milly quarrelling about a party" (31).

Such disorienting comparisons free Eleanor to make more independent judgments. Noting how her sisters compete for their father's attention and how Milly feels compelled always to "bring the conversation back to marriage," she senses both the problem and the solution, and has the first of her prophetic insights: "They stay at home too much, she thought; they never see anyone outside their own set. Here they are cooped up, day after day....That was why she had said, 'The poor enjoy themselves more than we do'" (32).

The impulse to extend the boundaries of class involves sacrifices few of the Pargiters' friends and relatives are willing to make. Eleanor's cousin, Kitty Malone, longing for something at least temporarily different from accustomed routines, imagines making love to a man outside her class: "He was not Eton or Harrow, or Rugby or Winchester; or reading or rowing. He reminded her of Alf, the farm hand up at Carter's, who had kissed her under the shadow of the haystack when she was fifteen, and old Carter loomed up leading a bull with a ring through its nose and said 'Stop that!' She looked down again. She would rather like Jo to kiss her" (71).

The pleasures of having tea with Jo Robson's family, however coarse their manner and Yorkshire accent, are essentially romantic escapades, like her trips north to the country once she is married to Lord Lasswade. For Kitty, dependent on the genteel class that sustains her own tastes, such flights exist within a purely inward realm of being, a dimension of time and space relatively untouched by others. The impression following her small sexual fantasy at the Robsons' that "she had given her nurse the slip and run off on her own" (71) recurs twenty-four years later on the train to her country estate when, having literally slipped away from matronly duties, she compares herself to "a little girl who had run away from her nurse and escaped" (270). These moments, if rejuvenating, do not modify Kitty's singular way of life.

When the narrative picks her up again in the "1910" chapter, first in what is apparently a suffragette meeting, then some hours later at Covent Garden, Kitty seems assured and aristocratic. As Virginia did in the presence of Vita, Eleanor feels "like a child again beside this great lady" (180). But Kitty's manner masks a narrowly acquisitive set of expectations. At the opera, as she observes Edward Pargiter—the man she had chosen not to marry—all thoughts center on herself: "He has never married, she thought; and she had. And I've three boys. I've been in Australia, I've been in India" (183). The opera itself excites similar private and self-adulatory thoughts: "The music made her think of herself and her own life as she seldom did. It exalted her; it cast a flattering light over herself, her past" (183).

Siegfried's appearance on stage recalls to her that inconsequential event thirty years earlier when Jo Robson had appeared at tea "with shavings in his hair" (183), an indication that even such small social transgressions have been at most infrequent in her life. Wagner's art, no more real to Kitty than the separate lives of those friends who frequent her box, barely extends her mind, much less her imagination.

As Kitty sits at ease in the circular grandeur of Covent Garden, among ladies and gentlemen "dressed exactly as she was," the effect of the spectacle is to solidify her limited impression both of herself and of her surroundings. Only at the opera's conclusion, when the young man seated next to her responds so enthusiastically to the performance, does her composure falter:

He was leaning over the ledge. He was still clapping. He was shouting "Bravo! Bravo!" He had forgotten her. He had forgotten himself.
"Wasn't that marvellous?" he said at last, turning round.

There was an odd look on his face as if he were in two worlds at once and had to draw them together.

"Marvellous!" she agreed. She looked at him with a pang of envy. (185)

Ignoring the basis of this momentary discomfort, Kitty moves peremptorily to bridge the gap between what is over and what is to follow: "'And now,' she said, gathering her things together, 'let us have dinner'" (185). Her words recall a lull during the performance when the Wanderer has departed and Siegfried has not yet emerged from the wings. Leaning toward the empty stage, Kitty asks with a note of apprehension: "And now?" (184). Her question, surfacing in this moment before Siegfried reappears, narratively extends to include the absence of another hero in the house—King Edward VII, who is on his deathbed. Throughout the opera the royal box remains disconcertingly empty. Only the triumphant Siegfried, sword in hand, seems for an instant to reestablish a lost centrality: "Here he was again. The music excited her. It was magnificent" (184).

It is not Wagner's Ring so much as the refined circle viewing it that would parget—the pun is crucial for Woolf[4]—all aspects of change. Outside the hall in this watershed year of 1910, the motions of ordinary people appear by contrast neither smooth nor continuous.* Starting and stopping like vehicles on the street, the sporadic movements recall the sunlight Eleanor observed in 1880 outside the window of Abercorn Terrace. With the spring weather intermittently shifting—"neither hot nor cold," sometimes bright, sometimes dark (160)—the rhythm of interruption seems everywhere.

Rose, however, reflects no such awareness as she walks toward Hyams Place to lunch for the first time with Maggie and Sara. Although now a defender of minorities and presumably

---

*Woolf even considered entitling the novel "Ordinary People." *The Diary of Virginia Woolf* (New York, 1982), 4: 266.

of the poor, she cannot conceal her rising distaste for her cousins' shabby house and the noisy neighborhood surrounding it. Advancing still in the image of her father, Rose begins her journey determinedly, "as if she were leading an army" (161).

By contrast Sara, sitting upstairs singing at the piano, is attuned to "the swarm of sound, the rush of traffic, the shouts of the hawkers, the single cries and the general cries" (163) ascending from the street below. Both Sara and Maggie work and play "absent-mindedly," the word echoing again an early description of Eleanor. The reminder that "Rose is coming" arouses cheerful resistance in Sara, who seems to laugh throughout the scene. As they predict the formal way Rose will remove her gloves and lay them on the table, and her polite discourse, Sara's rejoinder is to place their guest's chair in direct view of the factory across the street.

Rose is by no means ready for such intercession. Noting how "everything was different from what she expected," she does not feel free to talk until she recognizes a familiar red chair from Abercorn Terrace:

"That used to stand in the hall, didn't it?" she said, putting her bag down on the chair.
"Yes," said Maggie.
"And that glass —" said Rose, looking at the old Italian glass blurred with spots that hung between the windows, "wasn't that there too?"
"Yes," said Maggie, "in my mother's bedroom."
There was a pause. There seemed to be nothing to say.
"What nice rooms you've found!" Rose continued, making conversation. . . . "But don't you find it rather noisy?" (165)

Polite conversation is the strategy Rose uses to avoid a pause through which this nullifying uproar might further disorient her. As she struggles to withstand it, Rose oddly recalls the time as a child when she had demanded of Eleanor: "I want to go to Lamley's" (166). The recollection of that adventure, flooding and distorting the present moment, makes her feel (like Eleanor after visiting the Levys) "that she was two different people at the same time; that she was living at two different times at the same moment" (167).

The ambience of her poor cousins' house generates an uncomfortable widening of perception and, more important, a less defensive need to guard the moment. Once she has relaxed, talk is no longer a problem: "There was no need to say anything clever," she observes, "or to talk about one's self" (170). But the interval proves short-lived. Looking out the same window that inspired Sara's playfulness, Rose retains her hold on reality. At forty, she is too old to change. She once tolerated such neighborhoods—"when I was young"—but now the factory across the street, the public house on the corner, the dingy houses opposite and the incessant noise all assure her there is no advantage in living with the poor.

In "1911," no longer bound to the family house now that her father has died, Eleanor happily anticipates being free to reshape the past. Standing before a mirror just prior to dining with Sir William Whatney at her brother's home, she resolutely confronts "the woman who had been for fifty-five years so familiar that she no longer saw her" (198). The scene prepares the reader for a similar moment of introspection when Kitty, looking into her mirror before journeying north, is overcome with a feeling of blank non-being. Where she flies from the revelation, Eleanor is moved to self-examination: "And what was my good point? she asked herself, running the comb once more through her hair. My eyes? Her eyes laughed back at her as she looked at them. My eyes, yes, she thought. Somebody had once praised her eyes. She made herself open them" (198).

It was Sir William, still the prospective husband, who years before had told Morris, "Your sister has the brightest eyes I ever saw" (301). Breaking free both from her relatives' intention that she settle down and from those who see her simply as "an old maid who washes and watches birds" (203), Eleanor chooses instead to pause or to act as the spirit moves her. Outside on the terrace, she characteristically allows her eyes to wander as the others continue a small talk imbued with class-bound prejudice: "The elm trees had become dead black against the sky. Their leaves hung in a fretted pattern like black lace with holes in it. Through a hole Eleanor saw the point of a star. She looked up. There was another" (208).*

As in the *Purgatorio*, which she will skim later that evening, the twinkling stars invite a widening of perception. Ironically, it is not transcendent other worlds these spots of light convey but new, unwanted neighbors intruding, as Celia has complained, on their privacy: "There's another, Eleanor thought, gazing at a twinkling light ahead of her. But it was too low; too yellow; it was another house she realised, not a star" (208). While the others go on talking, Eleanor, we are told, simply "wondered," with a disposition that describes her own resistance to insularity. Unwilling to be bound like Celia within a world of property or matrimony, she determines to give up both.

Later, reading in bed the lines already quoted from *Purgatorio*, she is filled with still-new wonder by Dante's provocative words. The realization that she will be free to probe the meaning of such texts when she's "pensioned Crosby off" literally inspires a new life: she will neither marry Sir William— "his life was over; hers was beginning"—nor "take another house" (213). The consequence of each decision is to make her more sensitive to the needs of those less fortunate than she.

Two years later, as she prepares to leave Abercorn Terrace

*Note as one example of this class prejudice the discussion of Renny's name:

"You can call him Renny," said Peggy, pronouncing it in the English way.

"But that reminds me of Ronny; and I don't like Ronny. We had a stable-boy called Ronny." (206)

for the last time, her pleasure is marred by concern for their old servant, whose existence has centered on the house and the needs of its inhabitants. For Crosby this day signifies "the end of everything" (216): "Eleanor, holding the door open, looked after her. It was a dreadful moment; unhappy; muddled; altogether wrong. Crosby was so miserable; she was so glad" (217).

Unlike Martin, who continues to support a system he acknowledges to be "abominable" (222), Eleanor, though she is its beneficiary, determines to exist outside its influence. While her brother describes himself half-jokingly as "Crosby's God" (230), he submits, not without a certain satisfaction, to the inevitable flow of human events. In these years and months before the outbreak of the First World War, a deceptive impression of circularity tempts the mind once again to acquiesce. Birds wheeling around country church towers, omnibuses swirling "in a perpetual current round the steps of St. Paul's" (226), convey the sense of timeless order. As Martin sits with cousins in the park, "in a circle of privacy," watching children sailing toy boats, the world appears to him devoid of disruptive influence: "Two of the racing yachts were coming together as if they must collide; but one passed just ahead of the other. Martin watched them. Life had resumed its ordinary proportions. Everything once more was back in its place" (245).

Not surprisingly, we find him in this mood taking on the role of Sara's protector and accepting that evening a place in Kitty Lasswade's grand party. During dinner, "looking at Kitty at the head of the table," Martin confesses: "I only think of 'better families' when I dine in this sort of place" (252). Remaining fashionably critical, he is "there" as Eleanor is not. His sister—notably absent from "1914"—has refused Kitty's invitation, just as she refuses to participate in a patriarchal society indisposed to face its own contradictions. However Kitty may expand under the Yorkshire sky following her party—

"She lay there listening. She was happy, completely. Time had ceased" (278)—such insular pleasure relies on a culti-vated ignorance of a world on the verge of war.

Eleanor, now fifty-nine, reappears in the midst of wartime London, "pausing in the dark street" to wonder where in fact she is. It is the winter of 1917, and she is dining with Maggie and her new French husband in a house somewhat larger, if no less shabby, than the flat in Hyams Place. Examining the prongs of a fork while seated in the basement—where they eat for lack of servants—Renny proclaims with a certain pride that "we are extremely dirty." His Gallic outspokenness and the ramshackle informality of the surroundings impress and stimulate Eleanor from the outset.[5]

Along with everything else, conversation seems erratic and discontinuous, particularly following the narrative flow of "1914." A string of interruptions—Eleanor entering in the middle of an argument, Sara's late and whimsical arrival, a German air raid during dinner—forces the guests periodically to readjust their relationships to objects and to each other. Eleanor first describes the effect: "Things seemed to have lost their skins; to be freed from some surface hardness; even the chair with gilt claws, at which she was looking, seemed po-rous" (287). In contrast to the frozen intransigence of the world and weather outside, everything within radiates life. In this bohemian atmosphere where no introductions are neces-sary, one is free to express one's feelings on a wide range of subjects from war to sex, or to say nothing at all. So, at any rate, it appears to Eleanor before she comes to recognize old values in "Bloomsbury" garb.

Nicholas Pomjalovsky—we learn his surname twenty years later—who first engages Eleanor in conversation, offers him-self as spokesman for the new future. Despite the fact that his ideas seem drawn from Woolf's 1925 essay, "The Russian Point of View," or perhaps because of it, Woolf is quick to undercut his disposition to lecture. Eager, like most men, to serve as woman's protector—his homosexuality does not modify this inheritance—and to retain the opportunity to lecture his compatriots, the Polish emigré wants an audience as badly as did Sir William Whatney.[6] Nicholas is no more receptive to ambiguity than the philistines he censures, and is uncomfortable with situations he cannot oversee. Thus he celebrates change in a manner largely if not wholly rhetorical. A hint of this emerges during a lull in the air attack: "There was profound silence. Nothing happened. Nicholas looked at his watch as if he were timing the guns. There was something queer about him, Eleanor thought; medical, priestly?" (290).

Talk begins after the raid with the same apparent spontaneity, but it all sounds thin and inconsequential after the threat of death. Though Eleanor attempts to recall the subject of their conversation, "there had been a complete break; none of them could remember what they had been saying" (292). The desire to fill this void affects even Sara, who implores Nicholas for "a speech." In the background the continuing gunfire sounds "like the breaking of waves on a shore far away." Under the sustained threat, the Pargiter clan once again falls back on the familiar safeguards of civilized custom.

The world outside their private needs remains as barbarian and potentially disruptive for the Pargiters in "1917" as it had been in "1880." Tightly curtained windows, a requirement of wartime, keep the external world at bay, as the red folds of Abercorn Terrace did. The fact is evident even before the bombardment begins, as Eleanor, parting the curtains, looks out the basement window to see the effect of the sirens. The sight of people scurrying in the street inspires a question no one else answers, or even raises: "Oughtn't we to ask people in?" (289).

As they circle together around a "light in the center," even after the bombing has ended, talk seems to insulate them from foreign events they cannot control. The mood of uninterrupted tranquility persists upstairs, as Eleanor, standing in front of the fireplace and indulging a private moment before the all clear, feels suddenly and irrationally "immune" from danger. This sense of unqualified peace and safety, when "everything seemed to become quiet and natural," ends abruptly as "the others" join her in the room and Maggie pokes the fire.[7]

It is not some natural flow of events that supports Eleanor's well-being, although the bright fire at the time seems to burn without human intervention. Just as Maggie has attended to her sleeping children and now mends their clothing, she periodically sees to the fire, preserving in each case the conditions through which children and guests can dream and play. She has, we recall, no servants.

> Maggie took the poker and struck the wood blocks. The sparks went volleying up the chimney in a shower of gold eyes.
> "How that makes me..." Eleanor began.
> She stopped.
> "Yes?" said Nicholas.
> "...think of my childhood," she added. (294)

Eleanor, indulging a benignly childish view, like Rose in Hyams Place, slips back with Nicholas into private conversation on "the soul," only to find their lofty subject interrupted once again:

> "This is how we live, screwed up into one hard little, tight little—knot?"
> "Knot, knot—yes, that's right," she nodded.
> "Each is his own little cubicle; each with his own cross or holy books; each with his fire, his wife..."
> "Darning socks," Maggie interrupted.
> Eleanor started. She had seemed to be looking into the future. But they had been overheard. Their privacy was ended. (296)

Staring intently at the fire, hoping that Nicholas will continue his speech, Eleanor finds Maggie's words shaking her for the second time from "the burning coals, and that old fancy."[8] "Maggie took the poker and struck the wood and again a shower of red-eyed sparks went volleying up the chimney. We shall be free, we shall be free, Eleanor thought" (297).

With imagination and ingenuity Sara, who has been half-asleep, marks the connection: "'The soul flying upwards like sparks up the chimney,' she said" (297). That the subsequent disclosure of Nicholas's homosexuality does not alter Eleanor's affection for him seems linked with her capacity to follow the sparks. It is as if the latter signified in some strange way both a rising and a widening of consciousness.

As Eleanor walks to the window one last time before leaving, the sight of stars fills her at once with a sense of peace—inspired this time by "immensity"—and an impression of consuming change. Freed suddenly to move beyond the boundaries of her familiar world, she refuses Nicholas's offer of a cab and, in what might appear the least consequential act of all, chooses to take a bus. There among the silent and anonymous public huddled in semi-darkness, she sees the stars reappear through the twinkling eyes of someone less fortunate, if more lively, than she: "She found herself staring at an old man in the corner who was eating something out of a paper bag. He looked up and caught her staring at him. 'Like to see what I've got for supper, lady?' he said, cocking one eyebrow over his rheumy, twinkling old eyes. And he held out for her inspection a hunk of bread on which was laid a slice of cold meat or sausage" (301).

On the two occasions when Maggie pokes the fire, Woolf describes the rising sparks as "a shower of gold eyes" (294), then as "a shower of red-eyed sparks" (297). Flying up the chimney, they extend Eleanor's perception as she looks out the window toward the stars. Her perception of the sky, unlike Kitty's in Yorkshire, becomes simultaneously a private and a public revelation. Similarly, the vitality and humor of the poor man on the bus serve to enlarge and redeem her present moment. Recalling Dante's epic, the image of stars pervades this entire section of *The Years*.[9]

If Eleanor does not choose like Sara to live exclusively among the poor, she nevertheless sees the truth as no Pargiter has before and as few will see it twenty years later. When, in "Present Day," Morris Pargiter's son North returns from Africa after many years, he seems prepared to take on the family role. "You haven't changed," Eleanor comments insightfully as her nephew first steps through the doorway.

Driving to dine with Sara before the clan gathers later that evening in the novel's culminating party, North responds to his cousin's impoverished surroundings with the same words that described his grandfather's discontent at Mira's two generations earlier: "'What a dirty,' he said, as he sat still in the car for a moment—here a woman crossed the street with a jug under her arm—'sordid,' he added, 'low-down street to live in'" (311). Entering the hallway of a house that "had seen better days," he is assailed by the smell of cooking vegetables, the oily brown wallpaper, and above all the succession of anonymous apartments that seem in some unintelligible way to obscure North's sense of himself. "He had a feeling that he was no one and nowhere in particular" (311).

The first indication of Sara's presence, the sound of her laughing on the telephone, annoys him. "He had hoped to find her alone. The voice was speaking and did not answer when he knocked" (312). The "untidy" state of things inside is even more irritating, not least of all a smudge he perceives on Sara's nose as she greets him at the door. Recalling a party at which she wore her skirt "the wrong way round," North still equates such details with the fact that she has never married, or even "attracted the love of men." The analysis unfolds in his mind, we are told, "as if he were writing a novel" (317).

Throughout the evening North employs literary procedures
to avoid or divert potentially anarchic moments. Later, at Delia's party, as Eleanor opposes his notion that "everybody
ought to marry," he turns toward a young couple by the fireplace. Reshaping their story to suit his own scenario, he sees
them as romantic lovers standing together "on a cliff above a
torrent": "He arranged another background for them or for
himself—not the mantelpiece and the bookcase, but cataracts
roaring, clouds racing" (372). When this fantasy is interrupted by Eleanor's persistent claim that "marriage isn't for
everyone," North regains aesthetic composure by placing her
in another outdated, if not exclusively literary, setting. The
cliché he adopts so facilely pictures Eleanor sacrificing a husband, notably Sir William, for the good of the family. This
self-fulfilling insight evokes new affection for her and for the
good life she has helped to preserve. "He felt fond of everyone
at the moment" (372).

Sara's Milton Street flat—the literary allusion proves an
anachronism—is hardly suited to bolster North's classical
tastes, much less his morale. He tries to reestablish old decorums by recalling the more attractive setting they have
shared, but finds the noise outside—a passing lorry, a blaring
trombone, a woman practicing her scales—insurmountable.
Then, submitting for a moment to the disparate sounds of the
musicians, "like two people trying to express completely different views of the world in general at one and the same time"
(316), he begins unexpectedly to laugh along with Sara.

This proves a short-lived interval. The challenge of existing in this detached manner, without a conscious role to play,
drives him, as it did Rose, to assert control. His apprehension,
moreover, that Sara's actions are in no visible way dependent
on his needs or expectations—she slips in and out of the room
as randomly as sounds from the street—recalls again Colonel
Pargiter: "Nothing seemed to be happening. He waited. He
felt an outsider. After all these years, he thought, everyone

was paired off; settled down; busy with their own affairs"
(317–18).

At Delia's party one woman, at least, will serve to revive
North's patriarchal options. He dances with an attractive
guest who confesses, "I don't know anybody here." North's excitement feeds symbiotically on her reliance. "It made him
seem different to himself—it stimulated him. He shepherded
her towards the door" (368).

With no such role to pursue in Sara's flat, he turns for distraction to a volume of Shakespeare. The line he quotes at
random from *King Richard III*—"A shadow like an angel with
bright hair" (318)—merging as it does with Sara's spectral reappearance in the room, hardly contributes to North's needs.
Between the ceremonial activities of waiting for dinner, his
frustration with life continues to build: "Next moment she
came in. But there seemed to be some hitch in the proceedings. The door was open; the table laid; but nothing happened. They stood together, waiting" (318).

The unattractive meal, when it does arrive, is hardly designed to lift North out of the doldrums. Ironically, only Eleanor's interruption, telephoning to remind him of the party,
supplies him with a new, which is to say, an old impetus.[10] Her
reminder becomes a satisfying call to duty.

Fully intending both to go to and to enjoy Delia's affair, but
unwilling to be shepherded or bullied by men or by women,
Sara responds to her cousin's admonition that she "must" at-
tend with a good-humored injunction of her own: "'I must,
must I?' she said, making the coffee. 'Then,' she said, giving
him his cup and picking up the book at the same time, 'read
until we must go'" (338). Having once experienced Sara's literary preferences, North chooses instead to recite "the only
poem he knew by heart," Marvell's "The Garden." The words
of the poem, so much more substantial than the line read earlier, sound "hard and independent" to Sara as they penetrate
the room's growing darkness. North, pausing at the end of the

first verse in anticipation of a continuity that affects Sara as well—"'Go on,' she said"—senses instead two worlds inter-mingling:

> Society is all but rude—
> To this delicious solitude...

he heard a sound. Was it in the poem or outside of it, he wondered? Inside, he thought, and was about to go on, when she raised her hand. He stopped. He heard heavy footsteps outside the door. (339)

The sound of Sara's Jewish neighbor, first walking down the hall, then "snorting as he sponged himself" in the communal bathroom, fills North with new disgust.

Sara's response to this rude intrusion is to weave it into the fabric of their evening together as if thereby to tempt North once more from his past into a more mutual present. What emerges echoes T. S. Eliot's "Gerontion":

> "The Jew," she murmured.
> "The Jew?" he said. They listened. He could hear quite distinctly now. Somebody was turning on taps; somebody was having a bath in the room opposite.
> "The Jew is having a bath," she said.
> "The Jew having a bath?" he repeated.
> "And tomorrow there'll be a line of grease round the bath," she said.
> "Damn the Jew!" he exclaimed. (339)

The thought of grease and hair left in the tub makes North shiver with revulsion. He cannot indulge the interruptions of this sordid world: "'Go on—' said Sara: 'Society is all but rude,' she repeated the last lines, 'to this delicious solitude.' 'No,' he said" (340). With the speaker of Eliot's poem, North gives up their collaboration for the sake of wholeness:

> why should I need to keep it
> Since what is kept must be adulterated?

Unwilling or unable to exist in two worlds or to allow such intrusions to reshape his grasp of reality, he shifts to more prosaic roles. Consulting his watch, like Nicholas during the air raid, North regains some small aspect of authority. "It's time to go," he tells Sara, instructively. "Go and get ready" (343). The comforting boundaries of clock time rather than thoughts of celebration move him, it seems, to leave. "For if one went to a party, he thought, it was absurd to go just as people were leaving. And the party must have begun" (343).

Throughout this section of "Present Day," the narrative shifts back and forth between North dining at Sara's apartment and his sister Peggy conversing with Eleanor. Like her brother, Peggy struggles to retain control in the face of what she conceives to be her aunt's whimsically irregular behavior. Eleanor's tendency to ramble, more pronounced than Sara's, is easier to explain. "It was age coming on, she supposed: age that loosened screws and made the whole apparatus of the mind rattle and jingle" (325).

The continuous effort to keep their conversation on "safe" topics, which is to say, on the past rather than the present, reveals as much about Peggy's compulsions as it does about Eleanor's lack of concentration. Where her aunt enjoys the here and now, Peggy cultivates a protective distance from things her scientific mind has not sufficiently resolved. Peggy's excessive irritation over Eleanor's unguarded and often unmotivated interests makes the younger woman appear at times comparatively old and moribund.

At seventy-nine Eleanor looks forward to new and different encounters with people; Delia's party supplies precisely such opportunity. Her niece, despite breaking into the professions—she is a successful doctor—appears bound, no less than North, by narrowly patriarchal values. Patting her companion's knee in the cab, a gesture that recalls Nicholas's paternal action while lecturing Sara, she enjoys the role of guardian as fully as her brother does. The condescending if genial statement—"I shall never be as young as you are!" (335)—and her subsequent refusal to let Eleanor share in paying for their cab to the party, are means by which she, too, exerts authority.

Accompanying such behavior is a familiar distaste for un-mediated experience. As the two women pause by the window while waiting for the cab that will take them to Delia's, the view of the sky—"like another voice speaking, to fill up the pause"—inspires Eleanor with an exciting recollection: in that space between chimney tops she saw her first airplane. Only after she begins to ramble does Peggy note: "That's old age . . . bringing in one thing after another" (328). Focusing her critical faculties on what others say or do, Peggy rarely ex-presses spontaneous feelings about life. When she does, she is usually motivated by her own grievance.

They arrive early, to find themselves in a room almost de-void of guests. Again in "empty space," this time "in the middle of the room," Peggy is impelled to become the doctor: "What is the tip for this particular situation? she asked herself, as if she were prescribing for a patient. Take notes, she added. Do them up in a bottle with a glossy green cover, she thought. Take notes and the pain goes" (351).*

Continuing the rhythm of her working day, Peggy endures the party. Friends and relatives gain access to her mind like a succession of patients, by virtue of their infirmities: Eleanor's approaching senility; Martin's fear of cancer (Peggy is in fact his doctor); a young poet's unhealthy egotism. Like Eleanor, Peggy probes a culture incestuously fixed on itself, and her di-agnoses are frequently apt. But they fulfill essentially self-centered needs. Aware like monastics of the past that her world is bursting with "tyranny, brutality, torture," Peggy turns elsewhere for solace. "In the Middle Ages, she thought, it was the cell; the monastery; now it's the laboratory; the pro-fessions" (355). Yet the anarchic vagrancies of a pluralistic world move her as much as human misery and injustice to de-

---

*Woolf could be commenting on her own, at times compulsive, note-taking.

vise familiar methods of exclusion: "Why do I notice every-thing? she thought. She shifted her position. Why must I think? She did not want to think. She wished that there were blinds like those in railway carriages that came down over the light and hooded the mind" (388).

Although Eleanor's openness arouses Peggy's resistance, she is aware at moments of something strange and unique in her aunt's makeup. Peggy, in fact, describes succinctly if inadver-tently the prophetic dimension Eleanor brings to *The Years*: "a fine old prophetess, a queer old bird, venerable and funny at one and the same time" (328).

No more palatable to Peggy than to North, such contradic-tions disrupt the equanimity of pose and profession. In poetry as in science, Peggy's taste is sustained by a narrowing of vi-sion. With the narrator of Keats's ode, she avoids contradic-tion, which is to say, interruption, by victimizing thought: "The blue blind that one pulls down on a night journey, she thought. Thinking was torment; why not give up thinking, and drift and dream?" (388). Only "the misery of the world," Peggy claims, "forces me to think" (388). If the choice to drift and wander is often virtuous in Woolf, here it portends a death wish.

Peggy's analysis of her patients' needs and demands reflects her own diminished capacity for movement. Her fatigue all through the evening signifies more than a hard day's work: "Rest—rest—let me rest. How to deaden; how to cease to feel; that was the cry of the woman bearing children; to rest, to cease to be" (355).

Eleanor's enemy, unlike that of her niece or, for that mat-ter, of Bernard in *The Waves*, is not death but her own inclina-tion at times to confront adversity in the authoritarian role of a Pargiter. Moved to employ "the tone of the Colonel's daugh-ter" when a working man has swindled her in "1891," Eleanor finds herself pontificating rather too easily: "You have to bully them or else they despise you" (100).

The danger surfaces in "Present Day" when a more deserv-
ng offender—apparently the photograph of Mussolini gesticu-
lating in the evening paper—becomes the object of her anger:
"'Damned—' Eleanor shot out suddenly, 'bully!' She tore the
paper across with one sweep of her hand and flung it on the
floor. Peggy was shocked" (330). While the incident can be
read as her prophetic warning of a threat Britain has not yet
recognized, the militant gesture reenacts a form of behavior
Woolf sought to modify in herself as well as in her heroine.*
However satisfying to fling inkpots at despots and at fraudu-
lent workmen, such professions of rage, she argues in *Three
Guineas*, tend to narrow and obscure the deeper threat while
falling back on more mannered declamations of the past. "So
she had seen her father crumple *The Times*," Peggy recalls,
"and sit trembling with rage because somebody had said something in a newspaper" (331).

Alternatively, Eleanor's humorous disposition emerges as
Woolf's foil for opposing a stultifying idolatry no less crippling
to human needs in 1937 than at the time of the prophets.[11]
Where patriarchal systems of the past shut up their victims
"like slaves in a harem," Woolf argues in *Three Guineas*, "the
professional system, with its possessiveness, its jealousy, its
pugnacity, its greed, . . . forces us to circle, like caterpillars
head to tail, round and round the mulberry tree, the sacred
tree, of property."[12] She invites her reader to disengage, and

---

*In *Three Guineas* (New York, 1966), the photograph of a foreign dic-
tator—Hitler or Mussolini—is linked to those Church fathers who, centuries earlier, excluded both women and prophets from the ruling hierarchy.
Challenged by such forms of "voluntary and untaught" revelation, these
early patriarchs, Woolf argues, reshaped the text to suit their image of proportion. The choice to adopt hierarchical structures in the early Church signifies a radical perversion of Christianity's egalitarian origin, a time, she reminds us, when the gospels were "open to anyone who had received the gift
of prophecy" (p. 123). "The prime qualification was some rare gift which in
those early days was bestowed capriciously upon carpenters and fishermen,
and upon women also" (p. 122). From this perspective, Eleanor Pargiter's
anger may be read as more profoundly Biblical.

suggests one effective means: "Directly the mulberry tree begins to make you circle, break off. Pelt the tree with laughter."[13]

Peggy calls her aunt a prophetess because she is funny as well as profound.[14] Her eccentricities disclose, more often than not, a cheerfulness fundamentally at odds with all forms of manipulation, hierarchical or otherwise. When Eleanor visits the law courts in 1891 to hear Morris argue his first case, the pompous look of the judge, whose less ceremonial judgments she knows to be suspect, makes her want both to laugh and to depart. Laughter serves actually to move her from the staid court "out into the street" (112).

During Delia's party laughter takes on a discernibly prophetic inflection through Eleanor, Maggie, and—more obliquely—the closing performance of the caretaker's children. So Maggie, as Nicholas puts his hand on her knee and Renny urges her to make a speech, responds in North's eyes to each of their misplaced needs: "No idols, no idols, no idols, her laughter seemed to chime" (425).

A "good party" in Bloomsbury parlance presumed a mixture of talk, irreverence, and above all self-effacing merriment. "It is good to have an unbuttoned laughing evening" Woolf could say even after a boisterous group of partying friends all but disrupted a performance of her play *Freshwater*.[15] More often it was Woolf's playful pokes at other people's pretensions that would occasion the company's uncontrolled laughter.*

Woolf's earlier fiction reflects, perhaps somewhat romantically, an undue faith in the dynamics of the social party. With *The Years* her expectations have become less parochial and

---

*"It was impossible not to help laughing at the extravagance of Virginia," her brother Adrian records, adding that such noisy interjections stopped all conversation. Commenting on her part in the *Dreadnought* hoax, E. M. Forster is one of many friends who realized the force of her comic intentions: "She could surely have hoaxed our innocent praelectors, and, kneeling in this very spot, have presented to the Vice-Chancellor the

more political. Where the parties in *The Voyage Out, Night and Day,* and *Mrs. Dalloway,* to choose three examples, begin by virtue of some shift of emphasis within—Rachel's improvising at the piano, Rodney's loss of text, Clarissa's retreat—Delia's party in an important sense does not come to life until it sustains a radical intrusion from outside its own defining center.

As in the air raid dinner twenty years earlier, the Pargiters remain with few exceptions grouped together, hesitant to venture out of their corner, unwilling to expand into a room filled, as Eleanor will observe, with a variety of different, if socially acceptable, guests. When North does move out to dance with the unknown girl, he is inspired not so much by her difference as by thoughts of extending the Pargiter domain.

North and Peggy find it equally difficult to forget themselves; as a consequence their capacity for laughter, it seems, diminishes emphatically. Only shortly before dawn does the party, chiefly through Maggie, appear to soften North: "She laughed, throwing her head back as if she were possessed by some genial spirit outside herself that made her bend and rise, as a tree, North thought, is tossed and bent by the wind . . . and he laughed too" (425).

Earlier in the evening, uncontrolled influences, however benign, arouse in him, like the sound of the Jew bathing, profound displeasure. The impact of Eleanor asleep on the edge of the dance floor affronts something deeper than social decorum: "Eleanor snored. She was nodding off, shamelessly, helplessly. There was an obscenity in unconsciousness, he

exquisite but dubious head of Orlando." The hoax in question occurred in 1910, when Virginia and her friends, disguised as the Emperor of Abyssinia and his suite, boarded a British flagship and were honored by the thoroughly taken-in officers. The above quotations appear in S. P. Rosenbaum, ed., *The Bloomsbury Group* (Toronto, 1975), pp. 3, 205. Woolf was able to laugh at her own pretensions, as well, in pieces such as "Am I a Snob?"

thought. Her mouth was open; her head was on one side" (378).

North is driven back toward the unmediated origins of life he apparently despises. For him civilization itself seems at stake: "Silence gaped. One has to egg it on, he thought; somebody has to say something, or human society would cease, . . . something with which to feed the immense vacancy of that primeval maw" (378).

Since no one present fills the void, North's discontent grows more pronounced. Turning toward Maggie as Eleanor grunts in the background, he is taken aback to find that she too exists aloofly independent of his needs. As with Bernard, the shock is almost too much to bear: "She smiled. She said nothing. Then half consciously she echoed his question without a meaning in her echo, 'Why?' He was dashed for a moment. It seemed to him that she refused to help him. And he wanted her to help him. Why should she not take the weight off his shoulders and give him what he longed for—assurance, certainty?" (379–80).

Reawakening, Eleanor recognizes at once the advantage of being young, and she laughs at North's complaint that he does not even know what he wants: "Her feeling of happiness returned to her, her unreasonable exaltation . . . with the future before them. Nothing was fixed; nothing was known; life was open and free" (382).

Equally impatient with life, Peggy, as we have seen, finds it even more difficult "to give up brooding, thinking, analyzing," to "enjoy the moment" as Eleanor urges (384). Only once in the course of the party is she really pleased, and that is when she hears of her teacher's praise of her as "my most brilliant pupil": "There, said Peggy, that's pleasure. The nerve down her spine seemed to tingle as the praise reached her father. Each emotion touched a different nerve. A sneer rasped the thigh; pleasure thrilled the spine; and also affected the sight. The stars had softened; they quivered" (362).

A moment earlier, these same stars observed through the window had appeared cold and indifferent, like the young poet she had just dismissed. His egotism, reflecting her own, had filled her with feelings of stasis: "She turned round and stood at the window. Poor little wretch, she thought; atrophied, withered; cold as steel; hard as steel; bald as steel. And I too, she thought, looking at the sky" (361). However, it is not the stars that now invite movement—they inspire her only to "count them"—but Delia, who brings the good news: praise from "her master."

Pressed by Eleanor to join them on the floor, Peggy is perplexed and disoriented by the uncontrolled laughter, almost as much as North had been bothered by Eleanor's snoring. In a corresponding image, Renny's mouth, "wide open," emitting loud grunting sounds—"Ha! Ha! Ha!"—moves her, like North, to intervene. In this case, however, the mediation is unsuccessful: "That is laughter, she said to herself. That is the sound people make when they are amused. She watched him. Her muscles began to twitch involuntarily. She could not help laughing too" (389).

The game they are playing on the floor involves drawing a composite portrait, each supplying independently a different detail. As Peggy, who has not herself contributed to the completed picture, observes the conglomerate of nonsensical features, "She laughed, laughed, laughed; she could not help laughing." The recurring force of uncontrolled laughter serves like some strong drug to suspend her sense of the present: "She felt, or rather she saw, not a place, but a state of being, in which there was real laughter, real happiness, and this fractured world was whole; whole, vast and free. But how could she say it?" (390).

Peggy's impulse to verbalize this experience recalls the recent response to her teacher's praise when she described physiologically the effect of pleasure on her senses. It also reminds us of Woolf's defense of writing in "A Sketch of the Past." The difference is that Peggy seems more intent on leading than edifying. Turning at once to buttonhole her audience, she insists they cease their merrymaking and adopt her perspective. As a consequence she destroys the very moment she would make more real: "'Look here...' she began. She wanted to express something that she felt to be very important; about a world in which people were whole, in which people were free . . . But they were laughing; she was serious. 'Look here...' she began again. Eleanor stopped laughing" (390).

With war imminent, Woolf in the lines quoted from "A Sketch" looks to art as the means of depriving the external world of "its power to hurt me." Even so, the passage builds, with the added recognition that "there is no God," to a less personal crescendo: "*we* are the words; *we* are the music; *we* are the thing itself" (my italics).[16] By contrast, Peggy, moved by the vanity of her thoughts, endeavors like the lecturer of "Why?" to convert her listeners to her own elevated point of view.[17]

Shortly before laughter plummets Peggy too abruptly into a world without self, she begins to perceive things oddly. "From her seat on the floor," which she has assumed at her aunt's prompting, people's shoes take on an unaccustomed prominence. Moving back and forth to fox-trot rhythms, they seem divorced from the bodies and feet that direct them. Voices above her head drift down in small gusts of broken syllables, "inconsecutive" and nonsensical, like the language of sleep or childhood. In such an atmosphere sentences as well as speeches are destined to fail.

Asked by North, somewhat later, about the Greek chorus, the scholarly Edward Pargiter finds himself similarly swept away as "a burst of laughter drowned his words" (427). "Not restrained by barriers," overflowing, flooding, mingling "with the soul of others," the waves of laughter seem to level all prior distinctions, recalling that spontaneity Woolf describes at the heart of Russian fiction.[18]

Eleanor's exuberance remains unbounded as she responds from the floor to the variety and movement flowing about her; at such moments Peggy notices how "the veins stood out on her forehead" and predicts she will be "a wreck tomorrow morning." Correcting Renny's notion that it is the unreal world of sleep that has made her feel so young and alive, Eleanor emphasizes, through word and gesture, the existential source of her inspiration. "'But I meant this world!' she said. 'I meant, happy in this world—happy with living people.' She waved her hand as if to embrace the miscellaneous company, the young, the old, the dancers, the talkers; Miriam with her pink bows, and the Indian in his turban" (387).

Open to the unpargeted diversity of modern life, free of restrictive discriminations involving age, gender, or race, Eleanor embraces a reality impervious to syntheses of the past. If she emerges in the novel's concluding pages as Woolf's most defined heroine, however, she can never fully transcend the compulsions of her culture.

Some minutes before the two working-class children appear at the party, Eleanor, depressed by the realization that her life, like Delia's party, is coming to a close, centers on her own repeated failure to make sense of it: "This is too short, too broken. We know nothing, even about ourselves. We're only just beginning, she thought, to understand, here and there" (428).

Eleanor's fatigue signifies more than age and the lateness of the hour. Just as Peggy had described earlier the strain of continually having "to pick up the pieces, and make something new, something different" (392), Eleanor, like Jacob and Bernard before her, similarly relishes the idea of an ending. Retreating into a family circle, she hollows her hands on her lap in imitation of Rose, who "had hollowed hers round her ears." The act signifies the Faustian threat: "She felt that she wanted to enclose the present moment; to make it stay" (428).[19]

As with Bernard, the external world rises once more to interrupt her intentions. But Eleanor, if similarly resigned to "the endless night; the endless dark," remains open, as he will not, for the advent of some new happening: "She looked ahead of her as though she saw opening in front of her a very long dark tunnel. But, thinking of the dark, something baffled her; in fact it was growing light. The blinds were white" (428).

In Dante the dawn brings an apotheosis of expanding beatitude: "every movement graced with dignity." In Woolf the children appear all but simultaneously with the dawn, to rekindle movement: "There was a stir in the room. Edward turned to her. 'Who are *they?*' he asked her, pointing to the door" (428). Brought up from the basement by Delia for a piece of cake, they resist each invitation to dance, however figuratively, around the mulberry tree. Remaining silent as first Martin and then Peggy urge them to say or do something— "Haven't you got a name? . . . Weren't you taught something at school?"—they are moved to perform not by the promise of money or praise, but rather by what appears to be solely the impulse to enjoy themselves. Nudging one another playfully, they burst into a song designed to resist the too-serious audience. If they must fill the empty center, it will be with no discernible meaning.

Their distorted sounds—"Not a word was recognisable"— disparage language along with sense. "The rhythm seemed to rock and the unintelligible words ran themselves together almost into a shriek. The grown-up people did not know whether to laugh or to cry. Their voices were so harsh; the accent was so hideous" (430).

Eleanor's half-questioning description of the children— "Beautiful?"—and Maggie's quick reply—"Extraordinarily" (431)—serve to document the moment's special status. Even the most formal guests, moving together spontaneously, it seems, to the window, are affected: "The group in the window, the men in their black-and-white evening dress, the women

The Years

in their crimsons, golds and silvers, wore a statuesque look for a moment, as if they were carved in stone. Their dresses fell in stiff sculptured folds. Then they moved; they changed their attitudes; they began to talk" (432–33). The imperial sounds of "God Save the King" playing on the gramophone recall them to a proper sense of closure; simultaneously, Eleanor stands at the window listening to the sounds of pigeons cooing outside, and subsequently to what strikes her as the no-less-extraordinary reemergence of life and movement—a young man and woman stepping out of a taxi—on the street below.

Having acknowledged a preference for "failures, like Morris" (407), she turns appropriately in her final act toward her brother, the least successful Pargiter, to share and celebrate something yet to be defined. The dawn has just inspired Renny to speak of endings: "Now for the peroration" (431). Free of such need and echoing, ironically, Kitty's peremptory control at Covent Garden, Eleanor's last words embrace an uncertain future: "'And now?' she asked, holding out her hands to him" (435). The novel ends with a renewed sense of accord.

Chapter Nine

THE TYRANNY OF LEADERSHIP
Between the Acts

Between the Acts compares art's promise of wholeness with the absolutism of authoritarian leadership, and in terms that at times echo Freud's critique of religion. While planning her new book, Woolf was reading *Group Psychology and the Analysis of the Ego,* and she must have responded sympathetically to Freud's image of God as deified father.[1] Through the devout Lucy Swithin, God appears in the novel as a transcendent and patriarchal leader whose "gigantic ear attached to a gigantic head" discerns harmony where we hear cacophony. Although Lucy is one of three major characters who resist the compulsion to be led, her need for some final authority remains suspect for Woolf, even in this time of national crisis.[2]

The novel was completed as Britain faced the threat of German invasion. During these years the Woolfs' residence in Tavistock Square was destroyed in an air raid and the house they then moved to, in Mecklenburgh Square, was seriously damaged. Aware of their fate if Hitler triumphed, she and

Leonard drew up plans for suicide.[3] That she could continue at this critical point to formulate her critique of patriarchal values at home testifies to her strength and independent mind. By setting *Between the Acts* on a pageant day in a village much like Rodmell, Woolf suggests that it is neither Luftwaffe nor Wehrmacht that constitutes the immediate threat to life and language, but rather good English folk, of all classes and professions, bound intransigently to old ideas. Like Sartre (who actually experienced German occupation), she perceives that a more humane generation will not emerge spontaneously from the defeat of Nazism.[4]

Toward the conclusion of *Three Guineas*, Woolf decides she can best help to prevent war by remaining free of the group petitioning her support. Speculating that "new words" and "new methods" will arise more easily outside those institutions still committed to traditional procedures, she argues that words, like people, need room in which to grow and change.

The same idea appears in a 1937 radio broadcast for a series entitled, appropriately, "Words Fail Me." Exploring the conditions in which "words" best flourish, Woolf's talk, reprinted as "Craftsmanship," applies readily to the theme of her last novel: "Undoubtedly they like us to think, and they like us to feel, before we use them; but they also like us to pause; to become unconscious. Our unconsciousness is their privacy; our darkness is their light."[5]

If language fails at the opening of *Between the Acts*, it is because Woolf's characters resist such invitations to pause. "With the windows [of Pointz Hall] open" (3) on what is by every indication a beautiful summer evening, Lucy's brother Bartholomew continues to dwell on the state of their cesspool.[6]

Though she protests—"What a subject to talk about on a night like this!"—the only woman present, Mrs. Haines, appears no more responsive to the array of unmediated events outside the window. Driven to fill the first break in conversation, she appropriates the external world rather too quickly into exclusively personal terms. "Then there was silence; and a cow coughed; and that led her to say how odd it was, as a child, she had never feared cows, only horses" (3). Next she mistakes the sound of a bird for a nightingale[7] and is corrected by a more imaginative narrative voice supplying the first hint of something more real: "It was a daylight bird, chuckling over the substance and succulence of the day, over worms, snails, grit, even in sleep" (3).

The site of Pointz Hall, we learn from the lord of the manor, Bartholomew Oliver, represents an ancestral resolve "to escape from nature" (8). Tonight, as no doubt frequently in the past, the women of his household seem destined to oppose this family heritage. In the midst of discourse he is interrupted by "a sound outside, and Isa, his son's wife, came in with her hair in pigtails; she was wearing a dressing-gown with faded peacocks on it. She came in like a swan swimming its way" (4). Like old Bart's sister Lucy, Isa is a child of that chaos he and his heirs are bound to restrain.

Surprised to find people sitting there, once the fact of their presence registers on her, Isa allows her attention to drift toward Rupert Haines: "In his ravaged face she always felt mystery; and in his silence, passion" (5). Inspired by something more than sex or boredom, she finds in his eccentric features a means of imaginatively extending the boundary of her own rather narrow domestic scene. Above all, it is the Romantic's disposition for disharmony that seems to move her; "beauty has only a single prototype," Victor Hugo speculates, "the ugly a thousand."[8] Silence, moreover, allows similar freedom, particularly in a world where language is uneventful.

Isa, who is receptive to interruption as the others are not, extends her fantasy to include the lines of Byron that Bart quotes in the midst of a pause: "'She walks in beauty like the night,' he quoted. Then again: 'So we'll go no more a-roving by the light of the moon.' Isa raised her head. The words made two rings, perfect rings, that floated them, herself and Haines, like two swans down stream" (5).

The merging of art and eros in Isa's imagination expresses more than a romantic need for escape. Underlying her dream of circular perfection is a note of resistance, an inclination to trespass, implicit artistically in her response to Bart and sexually in the unstated affront to her husband. In her broadcast talk, Woolf had praised the truancy of the English language in "ranging hither and thither," subsuming bounds of class, race and decorum. Another passage from "Craftsmanship" echoes the phrase from Byron that engages Isa: "Indeed, the less we inquire into the past of our dear Mother English the better it will be for that lady's reputation. For she has gone a-roving, a-roving fair maid."[9]

Lucy fulfills the need to transgress the boundaries of her world through "imaginative reconstructions of the past" (9). Awakened in the predawn by the singing of the birds, she imagines the scene outside her window as it was in the time of primeval Britain, when rhododendrons filled the Strand and mammoths roamed Piccadilly. Grace, intruding with a breakfast tray, meets a glance "half meant for a beast in a swamp, half for a maid in a print frock" (9).

Lucy is rebuked, first by her brother and later by Isa's husband, for her "frivolous" and undisciplined state of mind. "She would have been . . . a very clever woman," Bart thinks, "had she fixed her gaze" (24)—a complaint that recalls Morris Pargiter's description of Eleanor in the opening of *The Years*. Women appear disposed to embellish and confound that objective reality the Oliver men find most accessible in newspapers.

Lucy rarely looks at the *Times*, and Isa reads it almost solely for distraction. On one such occasion, Isa picks up the paper Bart has dropped to find herself inadvertently reading of a woman raped in London. The details she seizes on seem all

but extraneous to the incident, unfolding more like a sequence in a novel than in a news report: "'A horse with a
green tail...' which was fantastic. Next, 'The guard at Whitehall...' which was romantic" (20).

Isa's indifference to the rhetoric of fact ironically makes her
more sensitive to the news of the day, which is to say, to the
nuances of totalitarian behavior. As the words build on each
other, the image of the girl striking her attacker "about the
face with a hammer" dovetails unconsciously with the sound
and appearance of Lucy entering the room "carrying a hammer" (20). Disobeying Bart's orders, she has nailed a placard
on the door of the Barn and earned a familiarly patronizing
rebuke: "'Cindy—Cindy,' he growled, as she shut the cup-
board door. . . . It was by this name that he had called her
when they were children" (21). This year, however, the old
argument, with the same words about the placard and the
weather, is colored in Isa's mind by the girl's resistance, and it
emerges as an act of heroism: "How courageous to defy Bart"
(24).

In a novel so steeped in literary allusion, it is notable that
newspapers, the source of opinion on everything from the
state of the Empire to the state of the weather, serve to guide
almost every inhabitant of Pointz Hall. Like the pageant,
however, literature remains at best a marginal enterprise,
something to pursue literally between the acts.

When Isa's husband, Giles Oliver, comes from London, he
arrives quoting the news report "that sixteen men had been
shot, others prisoned, just over there, across the gulf, in the
flat land which divided them from the continent" (46). These
salient facts motivate his outrage over the family's small talk
and the play (the pun is again evident) he must endure. Our
sympathy with him diminishes as we recognize a familiar egotism at the heart of his concern. Giles is not in the best of
spirits on pageant days. For a man of action, plays, like books,

are a source of discomfort. As Isa notes, "Her husband hated this kind of talk this afternoon. Books open; no conclusion come to; and he sitting in the audience" (59).

The pageant cannot begin until the question of rain is resolved. The newspaper's forecast of fair if variable weather forms the basis for their decision: "They all looked at the sky to see whether the sky obeyed the meteorologist" (22). Later in the afternoon the *Times* no less accurately predicts Britain's future once the threat of foreign invasion is met and mastered: "Homes will be built. Each flat with its refrigerator, in the crannied wall. Each of us a free man; plates washed by machinery; not an aeroplane to vex us; all liberated; made whole" (182–83).

Through the journalist, art and society appear reassuringly unambiguous. Though the local reporter cannot obtain a "synopsis" of the play from its author-director (plot, we note, coincides with interpretation), he can record those scenes whose meaning remains undeniably clear: "Mr. Page the reporter, licking his pencil, noted: 'With the very limited means at her disposal, Miss La Trobe conveyed to the audience Civilization (the wall) in ruins; rebuilt (witness man with hod) by human effort; witness also woman handing bricks. Any fool could grasp that'" (181).

Page's story ensures that, unlike the spectator of Miss La Trobe's play, his reader is never "left asking questions" (200). The sense of stability such writing imparts reflects and reinforces for Woolf exclusively institutional values. Every newspaper, she submits in *Three Guineas*, "is financed by a board. . . . Each board has a policy. . . . Each board employs writers to expound that policy." [10] If reviewers or reporters seek to write independently, to express what they believe, they will find themselves unemployed. Thus, under the guise of presenting facts, newspapers tend simply to reinforce prescribed conclusions. Worse still, through such submission they lose "the power to change and the power to grow." [11] Women, lacking on the whole both money and influence, retain in Woolf's view a better chance of resisting this sacred dance.

First Lucy, then Isa find rapport with outsiders such as the homosexual William Dodge, whose tastes and manner so disgust Giles. The new guest's alluring companion, Mrs. Manresa, elicits, as we shall see, a markedly different response. While Mrs. Manresa longs for "a picture paper, and a bag of sweets," something to do before the performance begins, Lucy and Dodge enjoy the detachment a view of the surrounding fields supplies: "How tempting, how very tempting, to let the view triumph; to reflect its ripple; to let their own minds ripple; to let outlines elongate and pitch over" (66). Words for them do not come so easily as for Manresa, who dominates the scene with her strong preferences.

Escaping her exuberance by retiring indoors, Lucy establishes a largely unspoken intimacy with Dodge while conducting a tour of Pointz Hall. Then, having paused by a window just as a breeze flutters the blind, they find themselves addressing one another.[12] "Mrs. Swithin put her hands to her hair, for the breeze had ruffled it. 'Mr....' she began. 'I'm William,' he interrupted. At that she smiled a ravishing girl's smile, as if the wind had warmed the wintry blue in her eyes to amber" (72–73). For emphasis, Woolf describes this corresponding breeze—"lolloping along the corridors" (73)—with a verb that echoes the festive climax of Clarissa Dalloway's party.

From the window Lucy sees the audience assembling, "streaming along the paths and spreading across the lawn" (74). It is not solely their fluid motion that inspires a desire to join them, however, but the sight of the clergyman "striding through the cars with the air of a person of authority, who is awaited, expected, and now comes. 'Is it time,' said Mrs. Swithin, 'to go and join —' She left the sentence unfinished, as if she were of two minds" (74).

Lucy, schooled by a church whose hierarchical structures radically distort its own origins, celebrates a Christianity that remains comfortably introspective.* Caressing her golden crucifix when indulging private visions of beauty and goodness ("one-making"; 175), she is at such times the unwitting disciple of patriarchy. Here at the window her first impulse is to follow the leader. Ironically, it is Lucy's generosity toward outsiders that moves her prophetically to resist such training.

On the terrace below, the exuberant Manresa feeds a discourse bound by cliché. Offering a stimulating center for the men circling flirtatiously around her, "she made old Bart feel young" (43) and tempts Giles to new thoughts of conquest. For the duration of the afternoon she makes Isa's husband feel "less of an audience, more of an actor" (108). At the culmination of the play, the sight of her calmly reddening her lips before the sea of mirrors crystallizes for Bart all that remains sanely stable in the world. "'Magnificent!' cried old Bartholomew. Alone she preserved unashamed her identity, and faced without blinking herself" (186).

Lucy and Isa identify with those who feel out of place and largely undefined. Manresa is at home in a world she knows from top to bottom.[13] The features of the world she prizes, like the details of Giles's handsomely Aryan face, are typical and familiar: "nose straight, if short; the eyes, of course, with that hair, blue; and finally to make the type complete, there was something fierce, untamed, in the expression which incited her, even at forty-five, to furbish up her ancient batteries" (47).

Such adoration is not foreign to Isa. The controlled ferocity of Giles—the way he comes into the dining room "looking like a cricketer, in flannels, wearing a blue coat with brass buttons; though he was enraged" (46)—excites her as well. As she dwells on the origins of this attraction, she finds that an "old cliché," born of "pride and affection," can still arouse, as

---

*"The founder of Christianity," Woolf suggests, in choosing disciples from outside his own "working class" origins, "believed that neither training nor sex was needed for this profession." *Three Guineas* (New York, 1966), p. 122.

with Clarissa Dalloway in the presence of Peter Walsh, feelings of "pride again in herself, whom he had chosen. It was a shock to find . . . how much she felt when he came in, not a dapper city gent, but a cricketer, of love; and of hate" (48).

Isa fell in love with him when they first met in Scotland while both were fishing for salmon. Her line tangled, she had stopped to watch him casting so expertly into the riffle. At that moment when the salmon leapt on his line, "she had loved him" (48). To "die" for such a man signifies no doubt more than Elizabethan hyperbole. If Woolf never read *Beyond the Pleasure Principle,* she nevertheless appears equally responsive to the idea of a death wish.

Like the "strong and independent" leader Freud describes in a book Woolf had recently read, Giles exists largely at odds with those outside his "libidinal ties." Freud's analysis in *Group Psychology and the Analysis of the Ego* applies readily to her fictional character: "He loved no one but himself, or other people only in so far as they served his needs. To objects his ego gave away no more than was barely necessary."[14]

Only the mechanical repetition of will power—"casting, casting" (48) as the stream rushes between his legs—seems to sustain his interest. Water, a substance to be "read" in expectation of the catch, may well inspire a certain repugnance even in such an accomplished fisherman. Something to be overcome, both between and during strikes, it represents the perpetual threat of an unmastered depth. To survive and triumph, Giles must plant his feet firmly on the ground and stake out his claim much in the manner of Manresa. Despite, or perhaps because of this need, we cannot imagine him singing the praise of water as Isa does so often: "Most consciously she felt—she had drunk sweet wine at luncheon—a desire for water. 'A beaker of cold water, a beaker of cold water,' she repeated, and saw water surrounded by walls of shining glass" (66).

When the megaphone first interrupts the pageant to announce an interval for tea, and the music, washing like a wave, disperses the audience, Giles's resistance is predictable: "*Dispersed are we*, the music wailed; *dispersed are we*. Giles remained like a stake in the tide of the flowing company. 'Follow?' He kicked his chair back. 'Whom? Where?' He stubbed his light tennis shoes on the wood. 'Nowhere. Anywhere.' Stark still he stood" (96). Fixed in mind and body, he will not allow the audience to lead him seaward.* Taking an opposing direction to the Barn—a path the dry summer has made hard as brick—he pursues his own singular game: Centering on "one stone, the same stone," he drives it ever more furiously toward one projected goal. His impulse even to play derives from self-loathing as well as the urging of others: "The gate was a goal; to be reached in ten. The first kick was Manresa (lust). The second, Dodge (perversion). The third, himself (coward). And the fourth and the fifth and all the others were the same" (99).

Reaching the gate "in ten," Giles does not pause but instead shifts his attention to the nearest object at hand. A snake lying on the ground, unable to swallow a toad, reenforces his misanthropy. "The snake was unable to swallow; the toad was unable to die." Reinspired to war against the nature of things, Giles survives the endgame: "It was birth the wrong way round—a monstrous inversion. So, raising his foot, he stamped on them. The mass crushed and slithered. The white canvas on his tennis shoes was bloodstained and sticky. But it was action. Action relieved him" (99).

The gesture of raising his foot recalls Bernard's incapacity to lift his foot in *The Waves*. Bernard cannot move once the illusions that have made him a man and a writer are eclipsed. "A man without a self," he becomes "a heavy body leaning on

---

*Lucy Swithin's crucifix may suggest at one point a similar indisposition toward water. Standing before the lily pond, she is described as "between two fluidities, caressing her cross" (204).

a gate," until moved, like Giles in the riffle, to cast his spear once more.[15]

Without a battleground, Giles's sense of identity diminishes. It seems his nature as well as his duty to fight. Perhaps the failure to choose a military career informs the self-recrimination with which he kicks his stone. The text supplies evidence that he and Isa have fought for some years, that we witness but one in a series of recurring battles. Maturing between two real wars—Giles's politics make Spain a less attractive battleground than for other men of his generation—Giles has found the sole arena at hand to be domestic. Hitler should satisfy his needs more fully.

More than matrimonial incompatibility, the Olivers' combat reflects the contradictions of a culture in which love and hate, like peace and war, coexist. The interlude in which the action of the novel takes place represents an extended interruption of this destructive symbiosis. As *Between the Acts* ends, Isa and Giles by all indications prepare to resume their battle: "Before they slept, they must fight; after they had fought, they would embrace. From that embrace another life might be born. But first they must fight" (219).

Metaphorically, Isa must collaborate for the species to survive. While Dodge offers the women of Pointz Hall a more satisfying basis for human relationship, to entertain such experience would constitute, for the younger generation if not for Lucy's, an evasion of history. The fact that he is homosexual makes him more accessible to women and less real. "They knew at once they had nothing to fear, nothing to hope" (113). If Isa and Dodge think of themselves as "conspirators" while talking intimately together in the greenhouse, their subversion, like Lucy's earlier moment at the window and Isa's daydream with Haines, is largely ineffectual. Aside from the pageant, which is to say the illusions of art, such intentions have, in a manner of speaking, no separate place in which to grow.

It seems clear that for Woolf, Isa's future—allegorically the future of the race—must emerge through some new accommodation with Giles. The old structure of hierarchical attachments no longer suffices. As Isa states prophetically at the end of the play: "It was time someone invented a new plot" (215).

In *Between the Acts* every character, every group, seems tied to a leader. For the audience, we recall, there is the Reverend Streatfield, "their representative spokesman" (190). For the men of Pointz Hall, it is Manresa, the protective earth-mother promising eternal renewal: "She went, like a goddess, buoyant, abundant, with flower-chained captives following in her wake" (202).[16] When, at the end of the pageant, the empty stage threatens everyone, she springs forward to lead Giles and the others back to their familiar world. The novel's penultimate scene finds the family reunited with that most central arbiter, the newspaper—"The circle of the readers, attached to white papers" (216)—just as minutes earlier Giles is described as "attached to Mrs. Manresa" (208).

No lapse of resolve explains the evident failure of Giles and Bartholomew to remain spokesmen for their women. Isa, as we have seen, is ambivalent toward her husband's admonitions. "'Our representative, our spokesman,' she sneered. Yet he was extraordinarily handsome" (215). More than personal grievance, such discontent informs Woolf's critique of those reactionary decorums the Oliver men are committed to defend and perpetuate: prescriptions, under the guise of safeguards, that threaten human freedom as fully under democratic as under totalitarian regimes.

On one occasion Lucy expresses a desire to go backstage and thank Miss La Trobe, only to be reprimanded by old Bart. Citing the rules of the theater, he points out that "one mustn't thank the author" (206). His duty is to ensure that conventions do not change. However benign this may seem in comparison with more flagrant denials of human rights, all such dictatorial investitures, Woolf would emphasize, originate from a competitive impulse to rule and dominate.[17]

The artist is affected no less provocatively by customs that ensure power and control. The theatrical convention Bart respects affords Miss La Trobe the distance she requires to maintain control. The choice some months earlier of a setting for the pageant is made at least in part with this tradition in mind: "There the stage; here the audience; and down there among the bushes a perfect dressing-room for the actors" (57).

The audience takes comfort in these theatrical prescriptions. Wandering aimlessly after tea with nothing to do between the acts, "they kept their distance from the dressing-room" (151). Only Lucy, "ignoring the conventions" (152), strikes out on her own, earning society's as well as her brother's censure: "The villagers winked. 'Batty' was the word for Old Flimsy, breaking through the bushes" (153). In company with the village idiot, whose unannounced intrusions unsettle Mrs. Parker and cause the Reverend Streatfield to lose command of language, Lucy proves only marginally disruptive. Her eccentric behavior barely touches their normative lives. Like the summer pageant, a page in each villager's calendar, her recurring performances even impart a certain sequence.

La Trobe, clearly the professional, knows that to create a successful play she must restrain experimental inclinations. We first see her, script in hand, walking among the birch trees with "the look of a commander pacing his deck" (62). The performance has the semblance of a military engagement. Deciding whether or not to risk the battle out-of-doors, she scans the horizons "in the attitude proper to an Admiral on his quarter-deck" (62). At other moments she becomes the "General," slipping her noose around a hostile army. If the enemy evades her control, the game is lost. Manipulating players as well as viewers, she would direct all toward a single end. Once her design is interrupted and the distance separating art from reality narrows, the effect is instantaneous. "Her power had left her. Beads of perspiration broke on her forehead. Illusion had failed. 'This is death,' she murmured, 'death'" (140). Ordering her "troops" around with masculine aplomb, she is known to them privately as "Bossy." "Her abrupt manner and stocky figure; her thick ankles and sturdy shoes; her rapid decisions barked out in guttural accents—all this 'got their goat'" (63). Like most of us, however, they are imbued in hierarchical assumptions, and accept a fundamental premise: in art as in business, in peace or war, "someone must lead" (63). La Trobe's self-assurance, moreover, inspires confidence.

Ironically, in the course of the afternoon it is precisely the undermining of her sovereignty that brings the play and its audience to life in unanticipated ways. The event is not completely fortuitous. Thrust outside the very continuity her illusion seeks to establish, La Trobe is victimized, more accurately "dispersed," as thoroughly as her audience. Sensing, perhaps, that she must relinquish all pretense of leadership before her design can grow in the minds of others, La Trobe undercuts, as we shall see, her own arrangement. The fact that she is an outsider by inheritance and temperament makes such self-renunciation less problematic.

La Trobe is suspect at once in the village. "With that name she wasn't presumably pure English" (57). Something about her appearance conveys both the foreign and the uncivilized, the two merging in the British mind. Mrs. Bingham suspects she is part Russian: "'Those deep-set eyes; that very square jaw' reminded her—not that she had been to Russia—of the Tartars" (58). Rumor has it that she failed as an actress and shopkeeper, and that she is probably a lesbian.[18] Her use of strong language and her generally inelegant manners suggest to more than one that perhaps "she wasn't altogether a lady" (58).

La Trobe is aware that "she was an outcast," that "nature had somehow set her apart from her kind." This limits her relationships at the same time that it threatens the quality of her art. Written in a margin of the script are the words: "I am the slave of my audience" (211). The notion may partly explain her authoritarian ways. At the close of the play her own anonymous voice, among its many fragmented truths, announces: "*A tyrant remember, is half a slave*" (187). Although the same imperatives seem to bind both playwright and audience, urging them jointly toward foreseeable conclusions, La Trobe's intentions, like Lucy's in the presence of her clergyman, are ambivalent. In the face of her own training, she tolerates conditions that ultimately mar her effort to create an artistic whole.

The choice of an outdoor setting invites difficulties that are appealing from the outset. La Trobe keeps out of the conventional squabbles—"The boys wanted the big parts; the girls wanted the fine clothes" (64). Her attention, when she first settles on the spot, is drawn to swallows darting through the air with a motion of their own: "dancing, like the Russians, only not to music, but to the unheard rhythm of their own wild hearts" (65). As she opens her script to the unplanned intrusion of natural phenomena, the boundaries of her text are expanded by wind, rain, and animals. Beyond this, La Trobe chooses to obfuscate her narrative through the structure of the play itself. In presenting her audience with a series of historical tableaux—a traditional pageant offering—she designs each climax for a moment when the plot is broken, or, in terms of this analysis, when the narrative is interrupted.

Although the first intermission, required by custom, is pressed on her—she has agreed to cut her play and allow the half hour for tea—the subsequent intervals seem inspired by something more than the usual conventions. The next break occurs just as her audience appears to have forgotten the gulf between art and life, at the point when the viewers have begun to enter La Trobe's theatrical illusion. The sight of the various actors—dukes, priests, shepherds—whirling voluptuously around the queen of England brings the audience to life, only to see the spectacle end as abruptly as it started. La Trobe responds to the advent of unexpected events much like Giles: "'Curse! Blast! Damn 'em!' Miss La Trobe in her rage stubbed her toe against a root. Here was her downfall; here was the Interval. . . . Just as she had brewed emotion, she spilt it" (94).

From the beginning, however, the external world has intruded, first through the late-arriving Lucy Swithin: "The play had begun. But there was an interruption. 'O,' Miss La Trobe growled behind her tree, 'the torture of these interruptions!' 'Sorry I'm so late,' said Mrs. Swithin" (79). As other late-comers seat themselves, the rustling of chairs drawn back and the continuing babble of voices commenting on the action complicate the director's task while paradoxically extending the range of her artifact.*

All through the performance the audience appears most involved in the narrative at those points when, for one reason or another, it wavers. The end of the Elizabethan tableau collapses, as we have seen, into a jumble of different evocations. In the general confusion it is hard to distinguish what anyone is saying. Words, merging with the clatter of dancing feet, sound as confusing to Isa as to the others: "That was all she heard. There was such a medley of things going on, what with the beldame's deafness, the bawling of the youths, and the confusion of the plot that she could make nothing of it" (90).

As the actors and actresses circle wildly, hand in hand, the appearance of the village idiot scampering "in and out" among them adds a final note to the general disorder. If La Trobe suffers, the audience is entranced and captivated. Dodge claps till his palms hurt; Manresa cries out, "Bravo! Bravo!"; players and spectators, "intoxicated by the music," come together in this moment when the text of the play seems all but irrelevant. "It didn't matter what the words were; or who sang

---

*Walter Benjamin's remarks regarding Bertolt Brecht seem particularly relevant here: "In short, the play was interrupted. One can go even further and remember that interruption is one of the fundamental devices of all structuring." *Illuminations* (New York, 1969), p. 151.

what" (94). In the midst of failure an unexpected synthesis takes shape. Having "brewed" these emotions, La Trobe welcomes the reaction.

This is one of three instances in which something essentially extrinsic to the text enlarges it. The next tableau, featuring the Restoration play *Where There's a Will There's a Way*, is obscured by gusts of wind rustling the leaves of trees and making language again all but inaudible. As "words died away" and the stage becomes suddenly "empty" of speech, a herd of cows grazing in the background intrudes, bellowing like some "primeval voice sounding loud in the ear of the present moment" (140). The failure of La Trobe's illusion serves again to unite playwright with audience. The third such instance occurs at the beginning of the last act, when a brief rainstorm, like the wind blowing the drapes at Mrs. Dalloway's party, mysteriously precipitates movement.

It should not surprise us to find the last of Woolf's fictional artists first enduring and then celebrating such pauses. In the midst of the Restoration play, hearing a voice complain ("All that fuss about nothing!"), La Trobe glows, as the audience laughs, with a sense of accomplishment: "The voice had seen; the voice had heard" (138).

Stephen Spender assumes that if Woolf had lived longer she might have written in the vein of Samuel Beckett.[19] The theme of nothingness pervades all aspects of *Between the Acts*. As in absurdist theater, Woolf seems intent on driving us to the existential question: "Why something? Why not nothing?" In her mind at least, the rejuvenation of life, artistic and social, depends on such radical interruptions of daily routine.

With the stage emptied, the audience withdraws during the first interval to the Barn, an ancient building reminiscent of a Greek temple. The building, we hear, is as old as the church. Had it rained, the play would have been held there, under its dark rafters. The anonymous narrator, arriving at the great open doors before the others, announces three times that "the noble Barn . . . was empty" (99–101).

An early manuscript of the novel illustrates the time and effort Woolf gave to the idea of empty rooms and to the problem of supplying emptiness with a voice. In one version an empty dining room in Pointz Hall confronts the narrator just after the butler has left it: "But who observed the dining-room? Who noted the silence, the emptiness? What name is to be given to that which notes that a room is empty? This presence certainly requires a name, for without a name what can exist? And how can silence or emptiness be noted by that which has no existence?"[20] In the published version the vacant room cries out as if with a voice of its own: "Empty, empty, empty; silent, silent, silent" (36).

With other existentialists, Woolf concludes that it takes courage to confront anarchic nothingness. The experience seems to force the artist back toward the origins of her own creative impulse: "A shell, singing of what was before time was; a vase stood in the heart of the house, alabaster, smooth, cold, holding the still, distilled essence of emptiness, silence" (36–37).

The absence of voice, as Woolf suggests in an essay on Walter Sickert, tends in its way to reverse the Darwinian basis of human grandeur; we become once again insects in a primeval forest, "all eye."[21] Interrupting summation—"the face of a civilized human being is a summing up"—Sickert's paintings, urging us into their "zone of silence," subvert our instinct for conclusiveness.[22]

Stationed in the empty Barn, we experience with the narrator forms of life that predate and likely will survive our species. Between pauses in the recurring refrain—"the Barn was empty"—mice scurry in and out of holes, swallows build nests in the rafters, and countless beetles and insects of all kinds burrow in the woodwork. The air itself, veined with smells of sweetness, seems enriched by the absence of human intervention: "All these eyes, expanding and narrowing, some adapted to light, others to darkness, looked from different angles and edges" (100).

The image of a large fly settling on a piece of cake appears in this break as inobtrusively right. We revel perhaps more easily with the butterfly warming "itself sensuously on a sunlit yellow plate" (100). Despite the romantic emphasis of these anthropomorphic descriptions, the scene succeeds in conveying Woolf's vision that existence is wider than the sum of human understanding.

The function of the Barn on this afternoon is announced by the long table filled with plates and cups, food and tea urn. Servants, along with guests, conspire to exclude irrelevancy: the servants necessarily through the demands of work, the guests through the subterfuge of play. Mrs. Sands's perceptions from "her station behind the tea urn" are as narrowly bound by convention as those of the guests she serves—"butterflies she never saw"—while the audience, newly arrived and more vulnerable without a role to play, fills the air with nervous chatter.

When "the beauty of the Barn" momentarily touches Manresa and Mrs. Parker, they are tempted to pause. A sense of duty and decorum, however, recalls them to order, first through polite intercourse and then through social action. Mrs. Parker compares the Barn to the one in her village; her companion turns to praise decorations "left over from the Coronation." Then, reverting to the roles that define their class, they lead the masses to tea. "The people looked to them. They led; the rest followed." Sincerity is sacrificed for the larger good: "'What delicious tea!' each exclaimed, disgusting though it was, like rust boiled in water, and the cake fly-blown. But they had a duty to society" (103).

Looking up into the rafters, one person at least sees more than decorative remnants of the regal past. Like La Trobe among the birch trees, Lucy is enthralled by the swallows and those mysterious faculties that for centuries—from the time "when the Barn was a swamp" (103)—had brought them from Africa. The fanciful connections Lucy prizes are irrelevant for those like Manresa, caught up in the business of preserving institutions and keeping things whole. Lucy is alive to the design of nonhuman intercourse. Her thoughts and words, like the narrator's opening response to Mrs. Haines, find room to explore the dark and fertile recesses of this surrounding space. If she is most at home in darkness, it is because there she is herself.[23] In the light of day she must occupy her brother's world. Unfortunately, such unguarded moments, existing in an arena virtually free from interruption, are destined, as we have seen, to remain insular and ineffectual.

La Trobe's play has reached others as well as Lucy. With the first act still running in their heads, Isa and Dodge feel suddenly free to say almost anything. Even Bart, falling under the influence of song, finds poetry softening volition. Having lost his son in the crowd—Giles is with Manresa—he returns home to quote Swinburne (115):

> O sister swallow, O sister swallow,
> How can thy heart be full of the spring?

Throughout this intermission, fragments of music from the gramophone float above the dispersing audience, shifting in tone from compressed rhythms that recall nursery rhymes to the spacious bars of a waltz. As they extend the loose ambience of the first tableau, boundaries of gender, class, and artistic form soften—we recall the Pargiter party—and groups begin to intermingle and overflow.[24] Even "the trees tossing and the birds swirling" outside the window of Pointz Hall seem to Bart and Lucy "called out of their private lives, out of their separate avocations, and made to take part" (117).

The members of the audience, reassembling for the next tableau, appear newly united by the rhythm of this interim. Less solemn and self-centered, their perceptions have widened. "For I hear music, they were saying. Music wakes us. Music makes us see the hidden, join the broken. Look and listen. See the flowers, how they ray their redness, whiteness, silverness and blue. And the trees with their many-tongued much syllabling, their green and yellow leaves hustle us and shuffle us, and bid us, like the starlings, and the rooks, come together" (120).

Isa, above all, is moved by the ambience of intermissions to raise existential questions about the direction of her life: "'Where do I wander?' she mused. 'Down what draughty tunnels? Where the eyeless wind blows? And there grows nothing for the eye. No rose. To issue where?'" (154–55).*

Inspired to "go on" in this interval before the Victorian tableau, she drops the flower that has called up private reveries to consider a more active role. She recalls the fable Bart told earlier of "the donkey who couldn't choose between hay and turnips and so starved." Then, seeing people streaming back to their seats, she is moved, simultaneously, to advocate new resistance: "Rise up, donkey. Go your way till your heels blister and your hoofs crack" (155). As she enters the fable more fully, a sense of trespass begins to transform the narrative of her own existence; she turns to revise conclusions concerning both life and art: "She roused herself. She encouraged herself. 'On, little donkey, patiently stumble. Hear not the frantic cries of the leaders who in that they seek to lead desert us'" (156).

What Isa would have us hear are, rather, the sounds of those in need: a shepherd coughing in the field; "the brawl in the barrack room when they stripped her naked; or the cry which in London when I thrust the window open someone

---

*Mitchell Leaska, linking these lines with Swinburne's "The Garden of Proserpine," suggests the answer by quoting Woolf's early draft: "Where? In some harvestless dim field. Where no evening falls or sun rises. All's equal there. Unblowing, ungrowing are roses there. Change is not." *Pointz Hall* (New York, 1983), p. 444.

cries" (156). As she returns to her seat, however, she moves with the others, like the gramophone announcing the London street scene, "in obedience to Miss La Trobe's command" (157).

It is during the final interlude between Victorian and present times, as La Trobe's contradictory intentions emerge more starkly, that such dispositions to follow a leader dissolve. Against her better judgment she has written a space into her script—"try ten mins. of present time" (179)—allowing the audience to escape her illusion without benefit of a formal intermission.* Deprived of a shepherd, her viewers are exposed instead to the unmediated impact of "present-time reality." Such immediacy, however, proves "too strong" for La Trobe as well as for her audience. Then, as the gramophone ticks nonsensically from the bushes, intensifying the atmosphere of disarray ("They were neither one thing nor the other; neither Victorians nor themselves. They were suspended, without being, in limbo"; 178), La Trobe senses, however uncomfortably, a rapport with her audience: "She felt everything they felt" (180). Relinquishing command, she collaborates in the subversion of her own omniscience. More important, the impact of retaining "nothing," like Isa's feeling of lost possessions after dropping the flower, seems to invite what follows: "This is death, death, death, she noted in the margin of her mind; when illusion fails. Unable to lift her hand, she stood facing the audience. And then the shower fell, sudden, profuse" (180).

Denying her own voice conclusiveness, the act of facing the audience assumes for La Trobe some new connection, just as opening herself to the sky occasions transformation. Lowering her guard as North or Peggy Pargiter could not, La Trobe

---

*Woolf writes in her diary: "The test of a book (to a writer) [is] if it makes a space in which, quite naturally, you can say what you want to say." *The Diary of Virginia Woolf* (New York, 1980), 3: 297.

relinquishes the center. The inundation—"Down it poured like all the people in the world weeping" (180)—unites her further with the audience and more immediately with Isa, whom the text describes presumably at the same instant: "Looking up she received two great blots of rain full in her face. They trickled down her cheeks as if they were her own tears. But they were all people's tears, weeping for all people" (180). Manresa's assumption that Isa wrote the play becomes, in this context, ironically apt; it has become in fact a collaborative venture.

By most criteria La Trobe has failed to produce a work of art. "If we're left asking questions," says one villager as the pageant ends, "isn't it a failure, as a play?" (200). Its author is left with similar doubts: "But what had she given?" (209). Aware that "her gift meant nothing," she expresses in the same breath a less acquisitive alternative: "It was in the giving that the triumph was."

The play ends with a rush of miscellaneous players—children, riffraff, elves, imps, demons—holding mirrors up to the audience. The effect of this uproar, "quite beyond control," is to disrupt every thought of closure. The players' exuberance, breaking all decorum, extends to the nonhuman world as well: "And Lord! the jangle and the din! The very cows joined in. Walloping, tail lashing, the reticence of nature was undone, and the barriers which should divide Man the Master from the Brute were dissolved" (184).

Language in company with theatrical convention collapses and disperses in the general melée as actor and actress cry out fragments of their roles. Assaulting every aspect of wholeness, Woolf's modern vision describes "a suspended derelict irrelevant beauty." These words appear in what was no doubt to be her next book. "There is no sequence," we read in "Anon." "It does not connect; the parts are severed. . . . We are left in the end without an end."[25] Enlarging on the portrait of La Trobe,

"Anon," the first chapter of "a Common History book," was to probe the artist's origins from earliest times.[26]

Like "the voice that broke the silence of the forest,"[27] La Trobe's unacknowledged words from the bushes interrupt the audience's final efforts to sum up. "But before they had come to any common conclusion, a voice asserted itself. Whose voice it was no one knew. It came from the bushes—a megaphonic, anonymous, loud-speaking affirmation" (186).

In the fragment, the artist's greatest attribute, be he dramatist or lyric poet, is love of the natural external world. "He is never tired of celebrating red roses and white breasts."[28] By virtue of remaining nameless, moreover, he maintains a more promising basis for collaboration. We recall Woolf's praise of anonymity, while writing *Mrs. Dalloway*, as the state of someone writing simply in the spirit of love.[29] Concerning the anonymous playwright, "Anon" affirms that "nameless vitality, something drawn from the crowd in the penny seats and not yet dead in ourselves. We can still become anonymous and forget something that we have learnt when we read the plays to which no one has troubled to set a name."[30]

La Trobe's anonymous voice similarly urges her audience to forget their training, to "break the rhythm and forget the rhyme" (187), and come together stripped of old values and distinctions: "Some bony. Some fat. . . . Liars most of us. Thieves too. . . . The poor are as bad as the rich are. Perhaps worse" (187).

Only the avatars of society and culture, retaining their specious dignity, reject La Trobe's invitation to reassemble under the aegis of "scraps, orts and fragments." Colonel Mayhew has envisioned a grand ensemble of "Army; Navy; Union Jack." His wife, no less impatiently, supplies another ending, "what she would have done had it been her pageant—the Church" (179). Giles, longing for the play's conclusion as he longs for the end of all such unproductive interplay, responds gruffly to "Present Time. Ourselves" with the words: "Let's hope to God that's the end" (177). And Bart, back home after the performance, "was damned glad it was over" (204).

It remains for the churchman to bring the pageant to a close, an achievement complicated by the fact that La Trobe remains hidden in the bushes. "It was an awkward moment. How to make an end? Whom to thank?" (194). In her continued absence, disruptive sounds from nature further irritate Streatfield: "Every sound in nature was painfully audible; the swish of the trees; the gulp of a cow; even the skim of the swallows over the grass could be heard" (194–95).

As if in concert with nature, the players, their pageant concluded, continue to celebrate. Not even the gramophone strains of "God Save the King," intended to rescue Streatfield, will recall them to the real world. "Was that the end? The actors were reluctant to go. They lingered; they mingled" (195).

With police and publican off duty—literally still in costume—the journalist, Mr. Page, takes on himself the role of spokesman: "'Home, gentlemen; home ladies; it's time to pack up and be off,' the reporter whistled, snapping the band round his notebook" (196). His review at least is whole and conclusive.

Back in Pointz Hall the family regroup around the same morning newspaper. Slipping back into docile subservience, Lucy turns the pages of her *Outline of History* "quickly, guiltily, like a child who will be told to go to bed before the end of the chapter" (218). Isa alone remains firm in her resistance: "Here, with its sheaf sliced in four, exposing a white cone, Giles offered his wife a banana. She refused it. He stubbed his match on the plate" (213). Aware that it is time for "a new plot," her last act before speaking, as if renouncing the role of primordial weaver, is to "let her sewing drop."[31]

"Anon" offers a final gloss on the concluding line of *Between the Acts*: "Then the curtain rose. They spoke" (219). In both works the image of rising curtains presumes a future. "For the curtain goes on rising incessantly," and as it does we are invited to anticipate and imagine different species of plays as well as of plots.[32]

Framed by a window "all sky without colour," stripped of consolations—"The house had lost its shelter"—Isa and Giles reengage. From the margins of time, from the heart of this impinging darkness—"It was night before roads were made, or houses" (219)—language surfaces once more, for the instant at least free from hierarchical legacies of the past. We are moved to hope, however tentatively, that some more mutual accommodation may emerge from the midst of such ungoverned moments.

Chapter Ten

CONCLUSION

All great art is anarchy.

GERTRUDE STEIN

Virginia Woolf never mentions Pierre-Joseph Proudhon or Peter Kropotkin and discusses William Godwin only in an essay on Mary Wollstonecraft.[1] Her novels, however, abound with anarchist notions.[2] In regard to an aesthetic of interruption, her recurring impulse to break derived sequences of art and politics reveals a growing critique of something more fundamental than either patriarchal hierarchy or the "bourgeois Victorianism" that so inspired Bloomsbury irreverence.[3] Along with the most prominent of anarchist theoreticians, she comes to question the basis of present social structures, which is to say, those hierarchical assumptions that underlie most Western theories of governance.

The intellectual source of such ideas was no doubt the Bloomsbury circle. Their early beliefs, reported in Leonard Woolf's autobiography and elsewhere—a determination to question all authority, an unqualified faith in human reason and the natural goodness of life, a rejection of all versions of original sin—resemble more than a few anarchist paradigms. Challenging the authority of Church, Army, and State in a discussion of the Dreyfus case, Leonard moved closest to attacking the institution of government itself. Perhaps apprehensive of such conclusions, he drew back by quoting George Bernard Shaw on the dangers of "moral chaos and anarchy."[4] Far more circumspect than his wife, Leonard was inclined to treat all signs of unchecked chaos as symptoms of malaise and decline.

I have suggested repeatedly how moments of renewal in Virginia Woolf's life and work follow the breaking of sequence. Given at such chaotic moments to celebrate the diversity of experience, she assumes with anarchists, as well as romantics, that the very basis of Western epistemology deters such openness.[5] Under the guise of learning we seek to master things, much as an army endeavors to surround and dominate the opponent; understanding takes on by intention a military inflection. Like Proudhon, Woolf views such power as inevitably prone to some variety of absolutism.[6] She would no doubt share William Godwin's advice that "human beings should meet together not to enforce but to enquire."[7] As we have seen, to view the rich autonomy of nature and the world free of coercive inclinations calls for radically new structures, for both "a new language" and "a new hierarchy of the passions."

Abhorring interruption, the authority Woolf associates with an entrenched line of order remains the enemy of human discourse. The experimental college of *Three Guineas*, we recall, free of rulers, implies a continuous upheaval of ideas: "Let the pictures and the books be new and always changing."[8] Its teachers will profess theories with less assurance and from less elevated stations. Such egalitarian intentions extend with the novels *The Waves* and *Between the Acts* to include every aspect of omniscient leadership.[9]

Although anarchism affirms the sovereignty of individual

choice, it is more than casually disposed to the idea of collaborative conclusions, inspired (much as "talk" in Bloomsbury was, according to Quentin Bell) by the incentive of truth rather than victory.[10] Dialogue expresses the nature of that cooperative community most anarchists envision, one free of any vestige of the authoritarian state.

I have stressed that natural forces in Woolf's novels impinge on every human formulation. Unable to confront these potentially creative moments of dissolution, Septimus falls prey to the proselytizing order of a society obsessed with designs of wholeness. In moments of anarchic confusion, the sight and sound of an airplane sky-writing advertisements, the small talk of people in the park, the presence of a tree, all take on new life in his mind. Similarly, once left to themselves, the worlds of Woolf's two parties, in Mrs. Dalloway and at the conclusion of The Years, become fluid, overflowing boundaries, plunging all the celebrants into rich confusion.

For anarchists, this quality of flux mirrors nature itself. "A world that changes constantly and never reaches the stillness of perfection because imperfection is a cause and a consequence of its everlasting movement" becomes, in Proudhon, the model for his new society.[11] Anarchists generally find the notion of perfection offensive. What is most real in the motions of nature for Proudhon, namely, its capacity for change, challenges and confounds the prescriptiveness of human culture. Kropotkin, viewing such movement in more scientific terms, makes it the model for denying the hierarchical state: "No government of man by man; no crystallization and immobility, but a continual evolution—such as we see in Nature."[12]

We have seen in Woolf how natural forces like the storm aboard the Euphrosyne, the Amazon forest enveloping Rachel and Hewet, the rain in La Trobe's pageant, interrupt narrative expectations. Such incidents are designed to loosen our hold on the external world and to encourage thereby a radically different basis for describing what is in fact real. A general mis-

233

Conclusion

apprehension regarding anarchism is that in embracing chaos it denies metaphysical order. In theory, as in practice, most anarchists affirm a "universal order," but one predicated more fundamentally on change. Mikhail Bakunin, in a passage that echoes Roger Fry's "the only constant is change," describes natural order as "the infinite variety of phenomena, appearing and repeating themselves according to necessity."[13]

The neoclassical architecture of Pointz Hall, reflecting the Olivers' ancestral resolve "to escape from Nature," represents the legacy of permanence that Old Bart and his male heirs are expected to preserve. From opening to ending, the mingling of art and nature in *Between the Acts* invites anarchy. Isa's swanlike appearance, Lucy's imaginative excursions into primeval forests, La Trobe's outdoor experiment, all resist the patriarchal effort to keep things orderly. Creating a space for transgression, nature in each instance serves as the vehicle for change. If Old Bart has become more benign with age, he still rules "as if he were commanding a regiment." When we first see Lucy looking out the window in the early morning—"The church clock struck eight times"—she seems the captive of time as well as of her brother's house.[14] She was to set up her own house following her husband's death; now house, in collusion as it were with clock time, restricts her sense of flight to fantasy.

For anarchists, no mechanism of human society reflects its captivity so decisively as what George Woodcock aptly terms "the tyranny of the clock." Industrial capitalism, ordering time in a manner known formerly only in monasteries, achieved an unprecedented control over man as well as nature. Woodcock describes the consequences in anarchist terms: "Men actually became like clocks, acting with a repetitive regularity which had no resemblance to the rhythmic life of a natural being. They became, as the Victorian phrase put it, 'as regular as clockwork.'"[15]

Woolf's characters come to life between the reifying beats

234

Conclusion

of clock time in those intervals, I have suggested, when the managers of state and industry are off duty. Those who remain bound to clock time, like Nicholas in the London air raid, fall invariably into static postures portending stasis and death.

The striking of clocks in *Mrs. Dalloway* is linked with death, first on Victoria Street when Clarissa remembers two recent casualties of war, most centrally in regard to Septimus's suicide. Rezia, listening to a clock striking in the confusion just after his leap from the window, finds solace in its deathlike prescriptiveness: "The clock was striking—one, two, three: how sensible the sound was; compared with all this thumping and whispering; like Septimus himself." Clarissa, hearing of it later at her party, reconstitutes the event in explicitly similar terms. "The clock began striking. The young man had killed himself." [16]

At the same moment that Rezia hears the clock ringing, the "high bell" of an ambulance inspires Peter Walsh, in another part of London, to praise "the efficiency, the organization" of Western "civilization." Enjoying, like Jacob Flanders and Giles Oliver, the advantage of sex and station, Peter sings society's praises as Woolf's heroines do not. Rachel Vinrace, who wastes time to good purpose, who is adept at doing nothing, is the first in a succession of heroines who disrupt the time-honored sequence of literary romance. Attempting, however fragilely, to defend her own convictions, she questions her culture's unwavering dogma that, as Mrs. Ramsay puts it, women must marry.

Clarissa Dalloway's distaste for love and religion reflects her resistance to society's overbearing need for proportion and centrality. In a world of diminishing authority, only clocks, striking punctually throughout the city, seem to offer some basis for order. Between acts of proportion and conversion, Woolf's characters find room to be themselves, to collaborate more reasonably as well as more affectionately. In these interims, free of authority, the human mind can be said to revive.

235

Conclusion

If Virginia was less the rationalist than Leonard, she defended reason with no less conviction than he or, for that matter, than an eighteenth-century rationalist like William Godwin. Godwin, too, assumed that reason was "at all times progressive,"[17] the enemy of all established truth—an intellectual position that in my view both Woolfs subscribed to. For Virginia as for the anarchist philosopher, moreover, the reasonable person is moved toward the intrinsic excellence of the thing itself. Being oneself presumes the liberation of thought. It is no mindless excursion she documents through her novels, but the virtue of thinking for oneself. This leads her, as it led Godwin, to a critique of human egotism. Both sought in their different ways to free the human mind from the circularity of self-sustaining dogmatism.*

Three Guineas, calling as it does for an end to all systems that deny movement and reciprocity, offers Woolf's most explicit exposition of the anarchist persuasion. The very notion of circularity becomes the paradigm, as we have heard, for authoritarian closure.[18] At the very beginning of *Mrs. Dalloway,* we find the booming of Big Ben described as a widening circle of lead: "first a warning, musical; then the hour irrevocable." All movement within its boundaries exists against the background of its curtailing presence. Even the woman Clarissa sees moving so mysteriously in the window across the street from her house seems "attached to that sound," Big Ben striking the half hour.[19] Woolf urges us to break this circle as early as the engagement dance in *The Voyage Out,* but in the course

---

*"What magic is there in the pronoun 'my,'" Godwin declares in his well-known fable of the archbishop of Cambrai and his chambermaid, and if in this instance his belief in an "everlasting truth" appears unduly absolutist, we should consider the effect of the age from which he writes. The comparison with Woolf here might employ her faith that there exists "some order, . . . a token of some real thing behind appearances." "A Sketch of the Past," in *Moments of Being* (New York, 1976), p. 72. The quotation from Godwin appears in his *An Enquiry Concerning Political Justice* (New York, 1926), 1: 42.

of her lifetime her view of the enemy becomes increasingly less personal. The "vicious circle" she would have us break in *Three Guineas* is the call of professional life, which demands that we circle like caterpillars around "the sacred tree of property."[20]

Enlarging this focus on patriarchy to include all hierarchical systems, Woolf goes on to challenge the idea of Western "society" itself. Again the image of ringing clocks emerges, but here the anarchist inflection is unmistakable:

The very word "society" sets tolling in memory the dismal bells of a harsh music: shall not, shall not, shall not. . . . Inevitably we ask ourselves, is there not something in the conglomeration of people into societies that releases what is most selfish and violent, least rational and humane in the individuals themselves? . . . Inevitably we look upon societies as conspiracies.[21]

Her picture of the Society of Outsiders is even more descriptive of essential anarchism.[22] With no need of money and consequently of a treasurer, it would be a society "without office, meetings, leaders or any hierarchy."[23] Woolf had noted the advantages to be gained from such libertarian accommodations in writing of Mary Wollstonecraft. Describing her relationship with Godwin as the most fruitful of many experiments, each designed "to make human conventions conform more closely to human needs," Woolf proposed that living outside society's laws allowed "all sorts of powers and emotions [to be] liberated in Mary."[24]

At the close of *Three Guineas* the act of remaining outside society, of absenting oneself from its "systems," is offered as the best remedy for deterring its unending penchant for war. We must presume that in the space of interrupted time Isa and Giles will stand a better chance of reconciliation. In this interval, free of societal restraints, they, like Lily Briscoe, may envision a world where "anything might happen," once "things have been blown apart" and the integrity of human thought has, from an anarchist perspective, been restored.[25]

Conclusion

Woolf's choice of words rather than bombs to unsettle bourgeois faith does not preclude revolutionary intentions. Despite the popular misconception of anarchism as synonymous with nihilism and indiscriminate terrorism, most of its serious thinkers reject violence as an expression of that dictatorial coerciveness they seek to curtail in human behavior. War, associated as it is with ideas of patriotism, conscription, and authoritarian military leadership, represents the antithesis of mutuality.[26] For Woolf, it remains the consequence of a system she is bound never to repeat, of a sequence, as I have emphasized throughout this book, she is committed to disrupt. "We can best help you to prevent war," she concludes in *Three Guineas*, "not by repeating your words and following your methods but by finding new words and creating new methods."[27] The catalyst for such endeavors, as I have argued, is the liberating space of unguarded moments.

Notes

Except for the works by Virginia Woolf listed below, which are routinely cited in short form throughout the Notes, all works are cited in full at the first occurrence in each chapter and in short form thereafter.

Collected Essays. 4 vols. New York, 1967.
The Diary of Virginia Woolf, ed. Anne Olivier Bell. 5 vols. New York, 1977–84.
A Haunted House and Other Short Stories. New York, 1944.
The Letters of Virginia Woolf, ed. Nigel Nicolson and Joanne Trautmann. 6 vols. 1975–80.
Moments of Being: Unpublished Autobiographical Writings, ed. Jeanne Schulkind. New York, 1976.
A Room of One's Own. New York, 1963.
Three Guineas. New York, 1966.

BOOK EPIGRAPHS: Mikhail Bakhtin, *Problems of Dostoevsky's Poetics* (Minneapolis, 1984), p. 236; William Godwin, *The Adventures of Caleb Williams* (New York, 1963), p. 221.

Chapter One

EPIGRAPH: Woolf, *Room of One's Own*, p. 81.

1. *Diary*, 5: 340. Here as elsewhere throughout the book, I retain such idiosyncrasies as Woolf's "its" for the contraction. However, for expository purposes, I have freely changed punctuation and initial capping in omitting sentences or sentence fragments from quoted material. And in order to distinguish such omissions (shown in the conventional way by ellipsis points, with or without a period as needed) from Woolf's own use of ellipses (for interruptions and the like), I have used closed-up dots in the French manner for Woolf.

2. Many critics have discussed the theme of narrative interruption. Listed below are the writers who have contributed most to this study. In regard to Woolf, let me call attention particularly to Reuben Brower's "Something Central Which Permeated," reprinted in Claire Sprague, ed., *Twentieth Century Views: Virginia Woolf* (Englewood Cliffs, N.J.), pp. 51–62. Of a more theoretical nature are J. Paul Hunter, "The Loneliness of the Long Distance Reader," *Genre*, 10.4 (Winter 1979), pp. 455–83; Georges Poulet, *The Interior Distance*, tr. E. Coleman (Baltimore, 1959); Maurice Blanchot, *L'Entretien infini* (Paris, 1969), particularly sec. 1, part 8, "L'Interruption"; and Ernst Bloch, "Diskussionen uber Expressionismus," Paul Raabe, ed., *Expressionismus der Kampf um eine literarische Bewegung* (Munich, 1965), pp. 283–93. Discussing the condemnation of Expressionism as an anti-revolutionary movement, Bloch takes issue with György Lukács's concept of reality as necessarily constituting an "infinitely mediated totality-continuity" (*unendlich vermittelter Totalitatszusammenhang*). Bloch, much like Woolf, raises the question whether "perhaps genuine reality is also discontinuity or interruption [*unterbrechung*]." I am indebted to Gabriele Wittig Davis for this source. Among more recent discussions on the subject is Peggy Kamuf, "Penelope at Work: Interruptions in *A Room of One's Own*," *Novel*, Fall 1982, pp. 5–18.

3. Woolf, "A Sketch of the Past," in *Moments of Being*, p. 114.

4. Woolf, "On Being Ill," in *Collected Essays*, 4: 193–95.

5. Woolf, "Sketch of the Past," p. 83.

6. Ibid., p. 72.

7. Ibid., p. 79.

8. Woolf, "The Mark on the Wall," in *Haunted House*, p. 37.

9. Ibid., pp. 38–40.

10. Woolf, *Room of One's Own*, p. 73.

11. Ibid., p. 95. Woolf's diaries acknowledge an aversion to as well as a fascination with interruption.

12. Woolf, "How Should One Read a Book?," in *Collected Essays*, 2: 2, 5. Ruth Gruber argues that throughout Woolf's fiction the room represents reality, and the view from the window illusion. *Virginia Woolf—A Study* (Leipzig, 1936), p. 78.

13. A similar intention describes Sören Kierkegaard's Knight of Faith lounging by "an open window" in *Fear and Trembling*. Observing the breadth of everything going on, no longer cowed by processes or training, "he does not lack courage to make trial of everything and to venture everything." *Fear and Trembling* (New York, 1954), pp. 51–53.

14. Mikhail Bakhtin, *The Dialogic Imagination*, ed. Michael Holquist (Austin, Tex., 1983), p. 20.

15. Woolf, *Diary*, 5: 340.

16. Woolf, "The Leaning Tower," in *Collected Essays*, 2: 170–81.

17. Herbert Read, *Annals of Innocence and Experience* (London, 1940), p. 82.

18. Bakhtin, *Dialogic Imagination*, p. 16.

19. Lawrence employs the phrase in a letter to Edward Garnett dated June 5, 1914. *The Letters of D. H. Lawrence*, ed. Aldous Huxley (New York, 1932), p. 200.

20. Woolf, "The Leaning Tower," p. 177.

21. Woolf, *Moments of Being*, pp. 64–65.

22. Mark Rothko's familiar rectangles, with their varying horizontal lines so suggestive of uncurtained windows, inspire similarly a bewildering vision of time and space. One critic describes the experience of viewing his paintings as being "drawn . . . into vast spaces that threaten to dissolve both the viewer and his world." Irving Sandler, *The Triumph of American Painting: A History of Abstract Expressionism* (New York, 1970), p. 183.

23. Woolf, *Moments of Being*, p. 83.

24. Bakhtin, *Dialogic Imagination*, pp. 4–5.

25. Woolf, "Robinson Crusoe," in *Collected Essays*, 1: 71. P. K. Joplin's fine analysis of Terence Hewet's recitation of *Comus* and its effect on Woolf's first heroine conveys this appeal: "Milton's words seem to possess poetic authority approaching that of the divine author whose performative utterances transformed 'words' into

'things.'" "The Art of Resistance: Authority and Violence in the Work of Virginia Woolf," Ph.D. dissertation, Stanford University, 1984, p. 66.

26. Woolf, *Moments of Being*, p. 72.
27. Woolf, *Diary*, 3: 52.
28. Woolf, "On Being Ill," p. 196.
29. James Hafley, *The Glass Roof: Virginia Woolf as Novelist* (Berkeley, Calif., 1954), p. 80.
30. Leonard Woolf, *Quack, Quack!* (New York, 1935), p. 14.
31. Woolf, *Haunted House*, p. 44.
32. Hafley, p. 18.
33. Hermione Lee makes this point repeatedly in *The Novels of Virginia Woolf* (New York, 1977), pp. 1–30.
34. Bernard Blackstone, *Virginia Woolf: A Commentary* (New York, 1949), p. 65.
35. See Carolyn G. Heilbrun, *Toward a Recognition of Androgyny* (New York, 1973), pp. 155–63; and Mitchell A. Leaska, *Virginia Woolf's Lighthouse: A Study in Critical Method* (New York, 1970). One of the earliest "negative" treatments of Mrs. Ramsay is Glenn Pederson's "Vision in *To the Lighthouse*," PMLA, 73 (1958), pp. 585–600.
36. Maria DiBattista, *Virginia Woolf's Major Novels: The Fables of Anon* (New Haven, Conn., 1980), p. 76. The first quotation is from Hafley, p. 89. For a similar emphasis, see Alice van Buren Kelley, *The Novels of Virginia Woolf: Fact and Vision* (Chicago, 1973), p. 118.
37. DiBattista, pp. 69, 103–4.
38. Ibid., p. 153.
39. Kelley, p. 199.
40. Woolf, *Room of One's Own*, p. 108.
41. Avrom Fleishman, *Virginia Woolf: A Critical Reading* (Baltimore, 1975), p. 171.
42. Kelley, p. 221.
43. Woolf, "Why?," in *Collected Essays*, 2: 281.

Chapter Two

1. Woolf, *Letters*, 1: 183. The next letter in this volume, no. 223 (p. 186), employs the phrase "on the voyage out."
2. Woolf, *Diary*, 3: 235.
3. Ibid., 2: 72.
4. Quotations are from Virginia Woolf, *The Voyage Out* (New York, 1948).
5. Stressing that Woolf "explicitly avoided the external ('place'

figures very little in her novels)," Harvena Richter offers a somewhat different view. *Virginia Woolf: The Inward Voyage* (Princeton, N.J., 1970), p. 16.

6. Woolf, *Diary*, 2: 321.

7. Woolf, *Moments of Being*, p. 72.

8. Virginia Woolf, *Nurse Lugton's Golden Thimble* (London, 1966).

9. Woolf, *Three Guineas*, p. 74.

10. Woolf, "Mr. Bennett and Mrs. Brown," in *Collected Essays*, 1: 319–37.

11. Woolf, *Collected Essays*, 4: 200.

12. Avrom Fleishman compares Woolf's novel with Conrad's *Heart of Darkness* in *Virginia Woolf: A Critical Reading* (Baltimore, 1975), p. 1.

13. Virginia Woolf, *Mrs. Dalloway* (New York, 1953), pp. 191–92.

14. P. K. Joplin discusses how Rachel's cry in both the published version and an earlier version (now published as *Melymbrosia*, ed. Louise A. DeSalvo; New York, 1982, pp. 197–98) applies first to Rachel's dead mother, Theresa, and then to her present lover, Terence. "The Art of Resistance: Authority and Violence in the Work of Virginia Woolf," Ph.D. dissertation, Stanford University, 1984, pp. 46–48.

15. D. H. Lawrence, *Women in Love* (New York, 1982), p. 53. For a fine comparative analysis of Woolf and Lawrence, see Robert Kiely, *Beyond Egotism: The Fiction of James Joyce, Virginia Woolf, and D. H. Lawrence* (Cambridge, Mass., 1980). More recently, Carol Lashof explores the two authors from a Heideggerian perspective. "World Without Distance: A Study of the Fiction of D. H. Lawrence and Virginia Woolf," Ph.D. dissertation, Stanford University, 1983.

16. Joplin, pp. 32–36.

17. The need is expressed by both Ursula and Birkin in Lawrence's novel.

Chapter Three

1. Woolf, "The Narrow Bridge of Art," in *Collected Essays*, 2: 223.

2. Woolf, *Diary*, 3: 113.

3. Virginia Woolf, *The Voyage Out* (New York, 1948), pp. 374–75.

Notes to Pages 48–84

4. Woolf, *Collected Essays*, 2: 250–51.

5. Woolf, "On Being Ill," in *Collected Essays*, 4: 194; D. H. Lawrence, *Lady Chatterley's Lover* (London: Penguin Books, 1961), p. 104.

6. For a discussion of this presumption, see Quentin Bell, *Virginia Woolf* (New York, 1972), 2: 69.

7. Ibid., p. 42.

8. Woolf, *Letters*, 2: 394.

9. Woolf, "Jane Austen," in *Collected Essays*, 1: 153.

10. Quotations are from Virginia Woolf, *Night and Day* (New York, 1948).

11. Jane Marcus discusses one such comic intention in "Enchanted Organ, Magic Bells: *Night and Day* as Comic Opera," in Ralph Freedman, ed., *Virginia Woolf: Revaluation and Continuity* (Berkeley, Calif., 1980), pp. 97–122.

12. Woolf, "Why?," in *Collected Essays*, 2: 281.

13. Woolf, *Diary*, 1: 259.

14. Woolf, "The Russian Point of View," in *Collected Essays*, 1: 243.

15. Woolf, *Room of One's Own*, p. 100.

16. Woolf, *Collected Essays*, 1: 324.

17. Woolf, *Diary*, 2: 248: entry of June 19, 1923.

Chapter Four

1. Woolf, *Diary*, 2: 13–14.

2. Quotations are from Virginia Woolf, *Jacob's Room* (New York, 1960).

3. Woolf, *Collected Essays*, 1: 336.

4. Robin Majumdar and Allen McLaurin, eds., *Virginia Woolf: The Critical Heritage* (London, 1975), p. 117.

5. Woolf, *Diary*, 2: 263, 265.

6. Ibid., p. 186.

7. See Woolf, *Three Guineas*, p. 36.

8. Strachey's letter and Woolf's defensive acknowledgment appear in Majumdar and McLaurin, pp. 93–94.

9. For a more sympathetic reading of Jacob's response to the Plumers, see Hermione Lee, *The Novels of Virginia Woolf* (New York, 1977), p. 88.

10. James Hafley suggests there are two narrators in *Jacob's Room*: the one who says characters are knowable, the other who claims they are not. *The Glass Roof: Virginia Woolf as Novelist* (Berkeley, Calif., 1954), p. 52.

11. Woolf, *Collected Essays*, 1: 322.

12. Woolf, "An Unwritten Novel," in *Haunted House*, p. 21.

13. For a fine discussion of this theme, see Jaakko Hintikka, "Virginia Woolf and Our Knowledge of the External World," *Journal of Aesthetics and Art Criticism*, 38.1 (Fall 1979), pp. 5–14. Hintikka compares Woolf's ideas with Bertrand Russell's thesis in *Our Knowledge of the External World* (London, 1914), especially pp. 70–105.

14. Woolf, *Diary*, 2: 14.

15. Regarding Cambridge-educated young men, Woolf asks in *Three Guineas* (p. 29): "Do they not prove that education, the finest education in the world, does not teach people to hate force, but to use it?"

16. Wilfred Stone reminds me that this is a central theme in E. M. Forster's *The Longest Journey*.

17. Woolf, *Three Guineas*, p. 8.

18. Hafley, among others, reads this scene more positively. *Glass Roof*, p. 54.

Chapter Five

1. Quotations are from Virginia Woolf, *Mrs. Dalloway* (New York, 1953).

2. Virginia Woolf, *Mrs. Dalloway's Party*, ed. Stella McNichol (London, 1973), p. 21. The sketch entitled "Mrs. Dalloway in Bond Street" was first published in *Dial* in July 1923.

3. Woolf, *Diary*, 2: 248.

4. Alex Zwerdling's "Mrs. Dalloway and the Social System" (*PMLA*, 92, 1977, p. 79) suggests otherwise: "'Mrs. Dalloway in Bond Street' remains a satiric object . . . utterly loyal to her country, her class, and its leaders."

5. Woolf, *Mrs. Dalloway's Party*, p. 27.

6. Ibid., p. 26.

7. Ibid., p. 27.

8. Woolf, "The Russian Point of View," in *Collected Essays*, 1: 241, 244.

9. Woolf, *Mrs. Dalloway's Party*, p. 27.

10. J. Hillis Miller, "Virginia Woolf's All Souls' Day: The Omniscient Narrator in *Mrs. Dalloway*," in Melvin J. Friedman and John B. Vickery, eds., *The Shaken Realist* (Baton Rouge, La., 1970), p. 113.

11. Woolf, *Mrs. Dalloway's Party*, p. 20.

12. Woolf, "The Pastons and Chaucer," in *Collected Essays*, 3: 9.

13. Ibid., p. 6. Note also in this regard *A Room of One's Own*, pp. 38–39.

14. Woolf, "Robinson Crusoe," in *Collected Essays*, 1: 71.
15. From a page in "The Prime Minister," dated Oct. 16, 1922: New York Public Library, Berg Collection, manuscript 2, p. 82.
16. Woolf, "Montaigne," in *Collected Essays*, 3: 23–24.
17. Woolf, "On Being Ill," in ibid., 4: 193, 196.
18. Woolf, "The Narrow Bridge of Art," in ibid., 2: 229. Note also Woolf's discussion of her ideal college in *Three Guineas*, pp. 33–34.
19. Compare Mrs. Swithin's childlike perception in *Between the Acts*.
20. Woolf, "On Being Ill," p. 200. In the same essay (p. 200), Woolf suggests that the words of a Donne or a Mallarmé reveal an even richer meaning, "having come to us sensually first, by way of the palate and the nostrils, like some queer odour."
21. *Nurse Lugton's Golden Thimble*, as we have seen from our discussion in Chap. 2, plays on a similar theme.
22. Woolf, "Montaigne," pp. 19, 24.
23. G. E. Moore, *Principia Ethica* (Cambridge, Eng., 1971), p. 188.

Chapter Six

1. Woolf, "Walter Sickert," in *Collected Essays*, 2: 236. This is a pervasive theme in Georges Poulet, *The Interior Distance*, tr. E. Coleman (Baltimore, 1959).
2. Compare Woolf's description of "a complete lull" on the streets of London in *Room of One's Own*, p. 100.
3. Avrom Fleishman, *Virginia Woolf: A Critical Reading* (Baltimore, 1975), p. 130.
4. Woolf, *Diary*, 3: 18–19.
5. Ibid., p. 62.
6. Woolf, *Moments of Being*, p. 93.
7. Ibid.
8. Ibid., p. 35. For a good discussion of Woolf's painful struggle "to give up the effort of creation in exchange for maternal love and protection," see Phyllis Rose, *Woman of Letters: A Life of Virginia Woolf* (New York, 1978), p. 167.
9. Quotations are from Virginia Woolf, *To the Lighthouse* (New York, 1955).
10. Most published analyses of this scene read it far more affirmatively. Alice van Buren Kelley, for example, perceives the dinner as a "miracle" symbolizing "the eternal possibility of coherence, of vision." *The Novels of Virginia Woolf: Fact and Vision* (Chicago,

1973), pp. 129–30. Michael Rosenthal discusses it as an aspect of Mrs. Ramsay's talent for "creating from the flux and chaos round her, moments of order." *Virginia Woolf* (New York, 1979), p. 108. Maria DiBattista speaks of it as "an expression of the total form of love." *"To the Lighthouse:* Virginia Woolf's Winter's Tale," in Ralph Freedman, ed., *Virginia Woolf: Revaluation and Continuity* (Berkeley, Calif., 1980), p. 177.

11. She resembles, in this context, the wife in the Grimm's fairy tale that she is reading aloud to James. Howard Harper suggests that "like the fisherman's wife, Mrs. Ramsay is utterly dominant." *Between Language and Silence* (Baton Rouge, La., 1982), p. 141.

12. Critics tend to read the Charles Elton quotation rather as a reflection of ideal relationship. Maria DiBattista, for example, calls it "the novel's most moving celebration of marital love, . . . of human community." *Virginia Woolf's Major Novels: The Fables of Anon* (New Haven, Conn., 1980), p. 87.

13. Woolf, *Moments of Being*, p. 79.

14. These details of war do not appear in *The Original Holograph Draft* of the novel. See Susan Dick's edition (Toronto, 1982), p. 202.

15. Woolf seems at this time to be questioning the notion of language as a means of consolation. She notes in her diary: "I am now writing to test my theory that there is consolation in expression." *Diary*, 3: 81. On the same day, May 9, 1926, she writes of those "consolations" that come to Mrs. McNab, a theme she had been pursuing in the preceding holograph pages. *Original Holograph Draft*, p. 215. With the published version of *To the Lighthouse*, these speculations have been deleted.

16. The absence of brackets, employed throughout "Time Passes" to convey historical events occurring outside the narrative, seems to emphasize the narrative centrality of Lily's return. For support of the argument that the American edition better reflects Woolf's final intentions, see J. A. Lavin, "The First Editions of Virginia Woolf's *To the Lighthouse,"* *Proof*, 2 (1972), pp. 185–211. For an opposing view, see Anne Olivier Bell's note 5 in *Diary*, 3: 127–28.

17. Woolf, "How It Strikes a Contemporary," in *Collected Essays*, 2: 158.

Chapter Seven

1. Woolf, *Diary*, 3: 113.   2. Ibid., p. 111.
3. Ibid., p. 111.   4. Ibid., p. 112.
5. Ibid., p. 112.

Notes to Pages 144–56

6. Avrom Fleishman employs the phrase "literary biography" in describing the genre of *Orlando*. *Virginia Woolf: A Critical Reading* (Baltimore, 1975), p. 139.

7. Note Woolf's diary entry for Nov. 7, 1928, where she suggests apropos of *Orlando*: "I did not try to explore." *Diary*, 3: 203.

8. Woolf, *Letters*, 3: 232.

9. Ibid., p. 352.

10. Ibid., p. 241. For a more sanguine rendering of this correspondence, see Louise A. DeSalvo, "Lighting the Cave: The Relationship Between Vita Sackville-West and Virginia Woolf," *Signs*, 8.2 (Winter 1982), pp. 195–214.

11. In a letter dated Jan. 26, 1926, Woolf quotes Vita's charge that she is prone to romanticize reality. *Letters*, 3: 231.

12. Woolf, *Diary*, 3: 209.

13. Ibid.

14. Ibid., p. 243.

15. See Woolf, *Letters*, 3: 372, note 2.

16. Woolf, *Diary*, 3: 139.

17. Virginia Woolf, *The Waves: The Two Holograph Drafts*, ed. J. W. Graham (Toronto, 1976), Draft I, p. 2. The image recalls an earlier story, "The Death of the Moth," written shortly after Vanessa's letter, where life and death appear as mysterious counterparts of a common ground.

18. Woolf, *Diary*, 3: 229.   19. Ibid., p. 233.

20. Ibid., p. 235.   21. Ibid., pp. 259–60.

22. Woolf, "The Mark on the Wall," in *Haunted House*, p. 44.

23. Woolf, *Diary*, 3: 209.

24. Woolf, *Two Holograph Drafts*, Draft I, p. 2.

25. Woolf, *Diary*, 3: 236.

26. Quotations are from Virginia Woolf, *The Waves* (New York, 1978).

27. Woolf, *Moments of Being*, p. 78.

28. Woolf, "The Death of the Moth," in *Collected Essays*, 1: 361.

29. Freud's discussion of Jesus in *Civilization and Its Discontents*, published by Hogarth Press in translation a year before *The Waves*, may have been a source for this notion.

30. Jessie L. Weston, *From Ritual to Romance* (New York, 1957), pp. 141, 146.

31. See Weston's discussion of Finn McCumhail, p. 130.

32. Woolf, *Diary*, 3: 210.

33. In *A Room of One's Own* she describes their "rage for acquisition" (p. 38).

248

34. Woolf, "Impressions at Bayreuth," in *Books & Portraits*, ed. Mary Lyon (New York, 1978), p. 19.

35. The term "mysterious hieroglyph" is from Woolf, *Two Holograph Drafts*, Draft I, p. 2.

36. Most critics see Bernard as Woolf's spokesman. Alice van Buren Kelley, for example, suggests that "Bernard in his summary and in his life has displayed the artist's ability to create unity. And Virginia Woolf, in *The Waves*, has done the same." *The Novels of Virginia Woolf: Fact and Vision* (Chicago, 1973), pp. 198–99.

37. Jean Guiguet asks: "Does this mean nothingness sanctioning the victory of time and space, our enemies and our defeat, or does it mean eternity sanctioning our victory over their vain and illusory opposition?" *Virginia Woolf and Her Works* (New York, 1965), p. 397. James Naremore proposes that "it suggests both." *The World Without Self* (New Haven, Conn., 1973), p. 188.

38. Naremore, Kelley, and Fleishman discuss, in the words of Fleishman, "the ultimate assimilaton by Bernard of the point-of-view of the italicized passages." *Virginia Woolf: A Critical Reading*, p. 159n.

39. Virginia Woolf, *Jacob's Room* (New York, 1960), pp. 31, 154.

40. Bernard's identification with Percival at the close of the novel is in no small part a literary one.

41. Woolf, "The Narrow Bridge of Art," in *Collected Essays*, 2: 223.

42. Woolf, *Two Holograph Drafts*, Draft I, pp. 343, 397; Draft II, p. 656.

43. Ibid., Draft II, pp. 736–37.

44. Ibid., p. 737.

45. Woolf, *Moments of Being*, p. 72.

46. Woolf, *Two Holograph Drafts*, Draft I, p. 398 verso.

47. See also the opening of "The Mark on the Wall," in *Haunted House*, p. 37.

Chapter Eight

1. Quotations are from Virginia Woolf, *The Years* (New York, 1965).

2. She drew these lines from Canto XV of *Purgatorio*, in *La Divina Commedia*, ed. H. Oelsner, tr. Thomas Okey (London, 1933). Her diary entry for March 27, 1935, indicates her struggle: "I cannot make the transition from Pargiters to Dante without some bridge." *Diary*, 4: 291.

3. Ibid., 5: 135.

4. See Mitchell A. Leaska, "Virginia Woolf, The Pargiter," *Bulletin of the New York Public Library*, Winter 1977, pp. 172–210.

5. Compare Woolf's own response to what Leonard Woolf termed the "ramshackle informality" of Monk's House when she first saw it. Leonard Woolf, *Downhill All the Way* (London, 1970), p. 112.

6. "He was talking. She listened. He seemed too big for the quiet, English dining-room; his voice boomed out. He wanted an audience" (201).

7. In a lecture Ludwig Wittgenstein delivered to "The Heretics" in Cambridge sometime between September 1929 and December 1930, he discussed the irrational "experience of feeling *absolutely* safe. I mean the state of mind in which one is inclined to say 'I am safe, nothing can injure me whatever happens.'" *The Philosophical Review*, 74 (Jan. 1965), p. 8. Virginia Woolf, who delivered "Mr. Bennett and Mrs. Brown" to "The Heretics" on May 18, 1924, spent some time with Wittgenstein while he stayed with Maynard Keynes at Tilton. This information was supplied to me in a letter from Leonard Woolf dated July 28, 1965.

8. Woolf, "The Mark on the Wall," in *Haunted House*, p. 37.

9. Paraphrasing Dante's *Purgatorio*, Woolf notes, possibly at this time: "A thousand years are a shorter space to eternity than the twinkling of an eye...Purgatorio, Canto XI. (p. 133)." *Diary*, 4: 278.

10. By suspending decorums, "the telephone," Woolf writes, "which interrupts the most serious conversations and cuts short the most weighty observations, has a romance of its own." "How It Strikes a Contemporary," in *Collected Essays*, 2: 157.

11. "I must buy the Old Testament," Woolf recorded in her diary on Jan. 1, 1935, as she contemplated finishing *The Years*, or *Ordinary People* as she then called the novel. *Diary*, 4: 271.

12. Woolf, *Three Guineas*, p. 74.

13. Ibid., p. 80.

14. "Isaiah" is one of the two Old Testament books in which a "prophetess" appears. (There is a feminine form in Hebrew for "prophet.") It is also a book that can be described as moving poetically to the rhythm of contradiction. In the world the prophet envisions, the wolf (appropriately) will live with the lamb, the leopard with the kid, the calf with the lion. No less applicably, Isaiah disavows an idolatry that shortsightedly ignores social and political oppression, and that calls his nation to self-righteous patriotism. Urg-

ing his people to change their behavior radically, he points them, as Woolf points her reader at the conclusion of *The Years*, toward a world where children will lead their parents.

15. Virginia Woolf, *Freshwater*, ed. Lucio P. Ruotolo (New York, 1976).

16. Woolf, *Moments of Being*, p. 72.

17. Woolf, *Collected Essays*, 2: 281.

18. Ibid., 1: 244.

19. Affirming this act of enclosure, Alice van Buren Kelley suggests alternatively that Woolf thereby sustains a poetic "pattern linking past to present in an unchanging rhythm. Now all that remains is to suggest the continuation of this rhythm into the future." *The Novels of Virginia Woolf: Fact and Vision* (Chicago, 1973), p. 221.

Chapter Nine

1. Woolf, *Diary*, 5: 252.

2. Lucy's Christianity is repeatedly pictured as a self-supporting enterprise. See footnote, p. 214.

3. The incident is reported by Leonard Woolf in *The Journey Not the Arrival Matters* (London, 1973), p. 46.

4. The idea appears most centrally in Jean-Paul Sartre's *Anti-Semite and Jew*, tr. George J. Becker (New York, 1965). Emphasizing the nonpolitical aspect of *Between the Acts*, Phyllis Rose argues that "the neutrality of Woolf's art is nowhere more exquisitely observed than in this novel, which wholly abstains from prescription." *Woman of Letters: A Life of Virginia Woolf* (New York, 1978), p. 236. I agree that the novel is free of any proselytizing tone, but the basis for another ideology reemerges, I would argue, throughout the text.

5. Woolf, "Craftsmanship," in *Collected Essays*, 2: 251.

6. Quotations are from Virginia Woolf, *Between the Acts* (New York, 1969).

7. In the recently published manuscript "Anon" (ed. Brenda Silver, *Twentieth Century Literature, Virginia Woolf Issue*, 25.3–4 [Fall–Winter 1979], ed. Lucio P. Ruotolo), we find Anon at the beginning "lying under the hawthorn to *listen* to the nightingale" (my emphasis), p. 382.

8. This line from *Préface de "Cromwell"* appears in Lilian Furst, ed., *European Romanticism: Self-Definition* (London, 1980), p. 104.

9. Woolf, "Craftsmanship," p. 250.

10. Woolf, *Three Guineas*, p. 95.

11. Ibid., p. 114.
12. The scene anticipates the closing line of the novel.
13. She recalls in this respect Ida Arnold in Graham Greene's *Brighton Rock.*
14. Sigmund Freud, *Group Psychology and the Analysis of the Ego,* ed. and tr. James Strachey (New York, 1959), p. 55.
15. Dante's "lagging foot" at the outset of the *Commedia* also seems relevant. For a discussion of this passage, see John Freccero, "Dante's Firm Foot and the Journey Without a Guide," *The Harvard Theological Review,* 52.3 (Oct. 1959).
16. Mitchell A. Leaska, in his edition of *Pointz Hall: The Earlier and Later Transcripts of 'Between the Acts'* (New York, 1983), suggests how closely such lines recall Vita Sackville-West. Stressing the "Vita-Manresa equation," he finds the latter "lovable" (pp. 11–12). In contrast to my perspective, most critics view Mrs. Manresa more positively. Rose, for example, comparing her with Miss La Trobe, suggests that she "represents movement and energy, however vulgar." *Woman of Letters,* p. 234. Alice van Buren Kelley writes that Mrs. Manresa "is the woman who brings Giles back into the ebb and flow of things." *The Novels of Virginia Woolf: Fact and Vision* (Chicago, 1973), p. 234.
17. Among her other Bloomsbury friends, E. M. Forster voiced similar concerns at the time. See P. N. Furbank, *E. M. Forster: A Life* (New York, 1978), 2: 193.
18. Woolf's earlier typescripts, now published in Leaska's edition of *Pointz Hall,* make this more explicit. George W. Bahlke first pointed out the earlier emphasis to me.
19. Viviane Forrester, *Virginia Woolf* (Paris, 1973), p. 85.
20. Leaska, ed., *Pointz Hall,* p. 61.
21. Woolf, "Walter Sickert," in *Collected Essays,* 2: 235.
22. Ibid., p. 236.
23. Compare Maurice in D. H. Lawrence's short story "The Blind Man."
24. Again we recall "The Russian Point of View," in *Collected Essays,* 1: 244.
25. Woolf, "Anon," in *Twentieth Century Literature,* p. 398.
26. Woolf, *Diary,* 5: 318.   27. Woolf, "Anon," p. 382.
28. Ibid., p. 398.   29. Woolf, *Diary,* 2: 248.
30. Woolf, "Anon," p. 398.
31. "Anon" foresees a time when playwright and audience will be "more closely related and less at the mercy of the plot" (p. 398).

32. Ibid., p. 424. As Brenda Silver indicates, this is one of a number of different endings Woolf contemplated at this early stage of her manuscript.

Chapter Ten

EPIGRAPH: Quoted in Marianne DeKoven, *A Different Language: Gertrude Stein's Experimental Writing* (Madison, Wis., 1983), p. 17.

1. Godwin is mentioned briefly in Woolf's "Not One of Us," in *Collected Essays*, 4: 22, 23.

2. It should be noted that Woolf was a reader of Leo Tolstoy and collaborated in the translation of *Tolstoy's Love Letters* and *Talks with Tolstoy*. *What Is Art?* appears on the list of books taken from Monk's House. She also reviewed a book by Gorky on Tolstoy. I find no reference, however, to the anarchism he came to affirm particularly toward the end of his career. Her father, Leslie Stephen, it may be pointed out, signed a petition in 1883 urging the French Minister of Justice to release Peter Kropotkin from prison. The petition, presented by Victor Hugo, stressed the importance of Kropotkin's scientific contributions.

3. Leonard Woolf, *Sowing: An Autobiography of the Years 1880–1904* (London, 1962), p. 130.

4. Ibid., p. 142. Shaw, a critic of the movement, had written a Fabian tract in 1891 entitled "The Impossibility of Anarchism."

5. Much in this manner, Roland Barthes, in *The Pleasure of the Text* (tr. Richard Miller; New York, 1975), celebrates what Marianne DeKoven aptly terms "the anarchic plenitude of language." DeKoven describes Barthes' "la jouissance de la texte" in terms of the "liberation of meaning from the strictures of hierarchical, sensible, monologistic order." *Different Language*, p. 16.

6. George Woodcock, *Anarchism: A History of Libertarian Ideas and Movements* (Cleveland, 1962), p. 18.

7. Quoted in ibid., p. 80.

8. Woolf, *Three Guineas*, pp. 33–34.

9. Proudhon writes, in "The Birth of Anarchy": "The more ignorant man is, the more obedient he is, and the more absolute in his confidence in his guide." George Woodcock, ed., *The Anarchist Reader* (Atlantic Highlands, N.J. 1977), p. 65. Robert Horn, a professor of constitutional law, expresses the hierarchical rejoinder: "A society if it is to survive must have leadership and must be willing to acknowledge the authority of its leaders. Indeed we should venerate the authority of good leaders. This is but to recognize that society is

at bottom hierarchical and . . . all egalitarian impulses must make their peace with that hard fact." Senior Class Day address, Stanford University, June 16, 1979.

10. Quentin Bell, *Bloomsbury* (London, 1974), p. 33. There are, it should be pointed out, a number of more individualistic anarchists, such as Max Stirner, who envision a community of egoists.

11. Quoted in Woodcock, *Anarchism*, p. 30.

12. Quoted in ibid., p. 23.

13. Bakunin, "Church and State," in Woodcock, ed., *Anarchist Reader*, p. 85. Roger Fry in 1925 described his politics as "individualistic anarchist." Virginia Woolf, *Roger Fry: A Biography* (New York, 1940), p. 232.

14. Virginia Woolf, *Between the Acts* (New York, 1969), pp. 7, 12.

15. George Woodcock, "The Tyranny of the Clock," in Woodcock, ed., *Anarchist Reader*, p. 135.

16. Virginia Woolf, *Mrs. Dalloway* (New York, 1953), pp. 227, 283.

17. William Godwin, *An Enquiry Concerning Political Justice*, ed. R. A. Preston (New York, 1926), 2: 48. Brenda Silver, in *Virginia Woolf's Reading Notebooks* (Princeton, N.J., 1983), refers to six pages of Woolf's reading notes on Kegan Paul's biography of Godwin. Leonard Woolf's library included the Preston two-volume edition of *Political Justice*.

18. Woodcock, ed., *Anarchist Reader*, p. 273: "The boy that is anticipated and led by the hand in all his acquirements is not active. I do not call a wheel that turns around fifty times a minute active."

19. Woolf, *Mrs. Dalloway*, pp. 5, 192.

20. Woolf, *Three Guineas*, pp. 74, 99.

21. Ibid., p. 105.

22. See Jean Guiguet, *Virginia Woolf and Her Works*, tr. Jean Stewart (New York, 1962), p. 187.

23. Woolf, *Three Guineas*, p. 115.

24. Virginia Woolf, *The Second Common Reader* (New York, 1960), pp. 146–48.

25. Woolf, *Between the Acts*, p. 219; Virginia Woolf, *To the Lighthouse* (New York, 1955), p. 147.

26. Kropotkin's support of the Allies' war against Germany in 1914 contradicted, in the opinion of friends and enemies alike, everything he had taught for the preceding fifty years. It should be

emphasized that the mass of the world anarchist movement, foreseeing various forms of non-cooperation as the basis of popular uprising, opposed Kropotkin's defense of the war. For an analysis of Kropotkin's shift, see George Woodcock, *The Anarchist Prince* (New York, 1971), pp. 373–87.

27. Woolf, *Three Guineas,* p. 143.

Index

Index

Index

Index

Index

Index

Library of Congress Cataloging-in-Publication Data

Ruotolo, Lucio P.
  The interrupted moment.

  Bibliography: p.
  Includes index.
    1. Woolf, Virginia, 1882–1941—Criticism and
interpretation.   I. Title.
  PR6045.072Z8676   1986   823'.912   86-6002
  ISBN 0-8047-1342-1 (cl)
  ISBN 0-8047-1523-8 (pb)